Baudrillard and the Media

Baudrillard and the Media

A Critical Introduction

William Merrin

polity

First published in 2005 by Polity Press

Polity Press
65 Bridge Street
Cambridge CB2 1UR, UK

Polity Press
350 Main Street
Malden, MA 02148, USA

ISBN: 0-7456-3072-3
ISBN: 0-7456-3073-1 (pb)

A catalogue record for this book is available from the British Library.

Typeset in 10.5/12pt Bembo
by Servis Filmsetting Ltd, Manchester
Printed and bound in Great Britain by MPG Books Ltd, Bodmin, Cornwall.

The publisher has used its best endeavours to ensure that the URLs for external websites referred to in this book are correct at the time of going to press. However, the publisher has no responsibility for the websites and can make no guarantee that a site will remain live or that the content is or will remain appropriate.

Every effort has been made to trace all copyright holders, but if any have been inadvertently overlooked the publishers will be pleased to include any necessary credits in any subsequent reprint or edition.

For further information on Polity, visit our website: www.polity.co.uk

Contents

Acknowledgements   vi

Introduction: 'There is no theory of the media': Baudrillard and
media studies   1

1   Television is killing the art of symbolic exchange: Baudrillard's
    theory of communication   10

2   To play with phantoms: the evil demon of the simulacrum   28

3   Are friends electric? Baudrillard's critique of McLuhan   45

4   The delirious spectacle of the non-event   63

5   Shreds of war rotting in the desert   81

6   'Total screen': 9/11 and *The Gulf War: Reloaded*   98

7   'The matrix has you': virtuality and social control   115

8   'The saving power': the 'reflex miracle' of photography   133

Conclusion: 'Speculation to the death': Baudrillard's theoretical
violence   150

Notes   160

References   165

Index   183

Acknowledgements

I would like to thank a number of people for their help and support in this project. Scholars whose contact I have valued include Nick Gane, William Pawlett, Gary Genosko, Marcus Doel, Richard Smith, Nicholas Zurbrugg, Paul Taylor, Gerry Coulter and Binoy Kampmark. I would also like to thank my colleagues Andy Hoskins and Kevin Williams, my former colleagues Paul Blackledge and Kristyn Gorton, my old friends Phil Banyard, Leslie Phair and Eric Rutherford, and many former students, including Alison Pierse and Emma Bell. I am also grateful to the editorial boards and referees of *Economy and Society*, *Theory, Culture and Society*, *Mortality* and *Scope – an Online Journal of Film Studies*, where versions of these chapters have been previously published. I would like to thank the Arts and Humanities Research Board for their generous research leave award (ref no. AN9959/APN15912) and the University of Wales, Swansea, for accepting this. I am also indebted to John Thompson and Andrea Drugan of Polity for their interest in and help towards this project. My greatest academic debts are to Mike Gane, whose work first inspired me to read Baudrillard and whose advice, assistance and friendship have been invaluable, and to Jean Baudrillard, though he will have no recollection at all of our brief meetings in 1992 and 1998. Finally I would like to thank my wife, Heather, for her love and support, my children, Henry and Alice, for their love and lack of support, and Barbara and Karen Merrin and Evelyn Merrin (1911–1996) and Philip Tempest for making me what I am.

Well I saw a lot of trees today and they were all made of wood.
They were wooden trees and they were all made entirely of wood.
Laurie Anderson, 'Walk the dog'

INTRODUCTION

'There is no theory of the media': Baudrillard and media studies

In his typically provocative way, Jean Baudrillard opens his 1971 essay 'Requiem for the media' (RM) with the sweeping assertion that 'there is no theory of the media' (p. 164). Despite the apparent simplicity of the statement it remains an ambiguous claim allowing several possible interpretations. Baudrillard's initial and most explicit meaning is simply that there is, as yet, no adequate theory of the media, as he criticizes existing theories for remaining 'empirical and mystical' (p. 165), singling out especially McLuhan's 'delirious tribal optimism' (p. 172), Enzensberger's dreams of a 'democratic' and 'socialist' media, and Jacobsen's rational, abstract 'communication theory' (pp. 178–9). This leads into a second possible and related position: that there is no theory of the media, but *he* will now provide one; hence, as I show, his own development of a theory of communication founded on a theory of symbolic exchange. More radically, however, Baudrillard's claim could be taken to mean that no theory of the media is possible, given his critique of their 'anti-mediatory and intransitive' form and their fabrication of 'non-communication' (RM, 169). But a fourth meaning might also be mined here as we take from him the implicit criticism that there is no accepted theory of the media within the discipline itself, with fundamental disagreements over its approaches and their history, method and content. It is this last idea that interests me most here.

Baudrillard's claim is, of course, merely strategic, enabling him to place himself in relation to competing theories within the field of media theory, and it is easy to counter him with the obvious fact of this field's existence. But what then does this field consist of? Kevin Williams has provided one of the most recent attempts to map out its history and development, from its birth in nineteenth-century debates through its formulation in the US in the 1930s based on mass society theory, theories of propaganda and public opinion and the work of the Chicago School. The new quantitative, empirical research which superseded it in the 1940s was itself displaced by the critical turn of the 1960s and the popularity of Marxist ideological and structuralist analyses, as well as new feminist and McLuhanist perspectives. Poststructuralist and post-modernist theory began to make an impact from the 1980s, as did neo-Marxist debates on the public sphere, though the 1990s were dominated by audience reception theory and effects research. More recently, debates around 'new media' have introduced new theories and revived interest in earlier techno-logical perspectives (K. Williams, 2003).

This sketch is accurate but it is also misleading. In practice, the discipline of media and communication studies is less aware of and agreed on this history than this account suggests. Whereas related disciplines such as sociology regularly offer introductory modules tracing the history of their own agreed canon, these are rare in media and communication studies, and the interpretation of what even constitutes 'media theory', let alone its actual content, varies between individuals and institutions. The explanation for this may be found in the origins of the discipline, which stems from three main sources: American communication studies, the sociology of the media and British cultural studies. Each of these strands and their combination have produced different media studies – different conceptions of acceptable knowledge, different methodologies, different empirical and theoretical biases and different interpretative models. These have given rise in turn to differing emphases, subject matter and syllabuses and research objectives and critical conclusions, in addition to the expected internal divisions between competing methodologies, theoretical perspectives and older and newer research paradigms.

As a result 'media and communication studies' has become a broad discipline, encompassing a wide range of possible courses on the ground, a situation aided by the explosion of interest in the subject through the 1990s and into the new millennium. With the ongoing revolution in digital technology and the ubiquity of media and popular culture, student numbers have boomed, courses have expanded and proliferated, and publications serving this new market have mushroomed. Though some have responded to this with a retrenchment of divisions in the field, overall the effect has been positive in opening the subject up to new ideas and knowledges, increasing the 'cultural' emphasis within the discipline, and demonstrating the value of a wider, multidisciplinary approach. Today, therefore, even more than in 1971, we can recognize that there *is* no agreed theory of the media.

To give one example of how divisions in the field have affected media theory, consider the case of 'postmodernism'. Williams is correct that this movement has been influential in media and communication studies, in the widespread integration of structuralist and poststructuralist thought (2003:63), but this claim overlooks the hostility to these movements and the continuing resistance within the field to many newer ideas and thinkers. With its background in more empirical research and more politically engaged cultural theory, media studies has been slower to incorporate newer continental ideas and cyber-theory than related disciplines, often doing so only under simplistic – and now dated – labels such as 'postmodernism'. The result is that many of the most important contemporary theorists of technology, media and communication such as Baudrillard, Virilio, Deleuze and Guattari, Žižek, Lyotard, Kittler, Castells, Haraway, Moravec, Kurzweil, Negroponte, Kelly, etc., are covered, if at all, only within debates on new media, being almost unknown within certain fields of media and communication studies. This has lead to the anomalous situation whereby disciplines such as sociology and cultural studies often display a more open and advanced conception of media theory than the field itself. If, with the contemporary expansion of the subject, such 'cultural theory' is becoming more acceptable, progress in media theory and media studies still feels slow and uneven.[1]

With this background in mind we can understand the positioning of Baudrillard within media studies to date.\His work has been largely ignored by the mainstream discipline, due to the latter's differing origins, interests, methodologies and theory.\ The limited availability of his work, his debt to unfashionable traditions (such as McLuhanism) and debates (such as 'the masses'), his association with postmodernism and problems of understanding, integrating or even reading and dealing seriously with his work have also played a part within Anglo-American media studies. Those parts of the discipline most open to his inclusion have been those most influenced by or receptive to cultural studies and cultural theory. As these courses have been the primary beneficiaries of the contemporary expansion in the discipline, we are beginning to see an increasing recognition of Baudrillard within the field and his acceptance as one of the key contemporary thinkers. This new interest, however, has not necessarily led to a greater understanding of his work. Media studies has merely followed other disciplines in positioning Baudrillard as a 'postmodernist', an attribution of limited value that misses his true place within and value for the discipline.

Evidence of Baudrillard's place within the discipline is easily found in the literature. Many further and higher education introductory textbooks in media studies make no mention of him whatsoever (see Branston and Stafford, 1996; Straubhaar and La Rose, 1997; Wilson and Wilson, 1998; Downes and Miller, 1998; Price, 1998; O'Sullivan, Dutton and Rayner, 1998; Turow, 1999; Lull, 2000; Burton, 2000; McQuail, 2000; Briggs and Cobley, 2002; Hartley, 2002). Moreover, despite his undeniable contribution to the subjects, he is also absent from many texts in communication studies on signs, semiology, structuralism, and linguistic and visual meaning (Hodge and Kress, 1988; Fiske, 1990; Corner and Hawthorn, 1993; Messaris, 1994; Cobley, 1996; Lacey, 1998). Many mainstream media studies texts also fail to consider his work (for example, Barrat, 1986; Herman and McChesney, 1997; Potter, 1998; Geraghty and Lusted, 1998), while, with only a few exceptions (Marris and Thornham, 1996; Durham and Kellner, 2001), his essays are also excluded from most 'readers' in the discipline (Boyd-Barrett and Newbold, 1995; O'Sullivan and Jewkes, 1997; Berkowitz, 1997; Mackay and O'Sullivan, 1999).

\When Baudrillard is mentioned, it is almost without exception as a 'post-modernist'\ (see Fiske, 1987; O'Sullivan et al., 1994; Boyd-Barrett and Newbold, 1995; Grossberg, Wartella and Whitney, 1998; Mackay and

O'Sullivan, 1999; Croteau and Hoynes, 2000; Tulloch, 2000; Moores, 2000; Newbold, Boyd-Barrett and Van Den Bulck, 2002; McCullagh, 2002). He may also be described as a semiotician or McLuhanist, but his primary positioning is as 'a leading light in the so-termed postmodern movement' (Watson, 2003). Such inclusion, however, does not connote acceptance, as his treatment in these texts is rarely sympathetic: his work isn't discussed in detail, his critical position is overlooked, his ideas are oversimplified and often misinterpreted and, as a postmodernist, he is regularly assumed to be celebrating the nihilistic world he describes (Jay, 1994; Bruhn Jensen, 1995). Though some commentators are open to more nuanced readings and recognize his possible significance (for example, Silverstone, 1994; Stevenson, 1995), limited and hostile readings remain the norm. Watson and Hill's adoption of Sarup's simplistic denunciation (Watson and Hill, 1997:175; Sarup, 1993) is representative of this, while Price's student commentary is unsurpassed for both its errors and its hostility (1996:448–51).

The consensus in the literature appears to be, therefore, that if Baudrillard has a place within media studies it is as a postmodernist/McLuhanist (Kellner, 1989; Stevenson, 1995; K. Williams, 2003), although so far there has been no attempt within the discipline to consider his work in detail, how it might be applied to contemporary phenomena, or the exact meaning and critical value of his key concepts. Baudrillard's discussion of media has attracted more attention within his own secondary literature (Chen, 1987; Kellner, 1989; Genosko, 1994b, 1997, 1999; Huyssen, 1995; Zurbrugg, 1997; R. Butler, 1999), but even here there has been no comprehensive study of his media theory and its contribution to the field. This book aims to provide that study, challenging especially his positioning within the discipline as a postmodernist in order to consider his own critical position and its value. This positioning, however, is not the discipline's own: the association of Baudrillard with postmodernism is long standing and we need to understand why his work became linked to the concept.

Baudrillard first came to prominence in the English speaking world in the early 1980s as a number of left-leaning scholars in Australia, Canada, America and, later, Britain, attempting to understand the new movement of 'postmodernism', began to publish selections of his work[2] and his 'postmodern' texts (*In the Shadow of the Silent Majorities* (*SSM*); *Simulations* (*Sim.*); *Forget Foucault* (*FF*)). With little regard for the history of his work or his own rejection of the concept, Baudrillard was soon identified as 'the high priest of postmodernism' (Baudrillard, 1989d). As such he soon became the target of the left's critique, Kroker's early sympathetic reading (Kroker, 1985; Kroker and Cook, 1988) provoking Kellner's critical ire, developed across a series of articles, introductions and the first book on Baudrillard (Kellner, 1987, 1988, 1989; Best and Kellner, 1991; Kellner, 1994), as well as responses from Callinicos (1989) and Norris (1990; 1992). For them Baudrillard's work was reactionary, in its rejection of Marxism; nihilistic, in its rejection of truth and reality; and charlatanistic in its style and method. This is a reading that, though seriously flawed, has proved inexplicably popular, especially among textbook writers looking for an easy take on a difficult author.

The contemporary Baudrillard literature, however, is derived from another perspective and tradition. Mike Gane was the first to challenge Kellner's errors, refuting the simplistic association with postmodernism and emphasizing productive influences on Baudrillard's work such as the Durkheimian tradition (Gane 1991a, 1991b, 1995, 2000a). This rereading inspired new work on Baudrillard and, with the waning of the postmodern controversy, a better understanding of his career and project began to emerge. Through the 1990s and into the present there has been a growing list of published articles and books dealing seriously with his work (Stearns and Chaloupka, 1992; Rojek and Turner, 1993; Kellner, 1994; Genosko, 1994a, 1999; Levin, 1996; Zurbrugg, 1997; R. Butler, 1999; Grace, 2000; Gane, 2000b; Hegarty, 2004). Nearly all of Baudrillard's work is available in translation, with new texts appearing promptly; his work is globally disseminated and discussed on the internet, and in January 2004 the online *International Journal of Baudrillard Studies* made its welcome appearance (Coulter, 2004). Today, therefore, Baudrillard has become intellectually unavoidable, his ideas penetrating and reshaping disciplines as diverse as sociology, cultural studies, visual culture, design studies, geography, photography, art theory and history, social and cultural history, philosophy, and architecture – as well as media and communication studies. Established as one of the most important contemporary thinkers, his original analyses have become standard reference points for any understanding of our cultural processes.

For all that, Baudrillard has retained his controversial status, his work still arousing passionate responses. While many academics retain a deep suspicion towards his beyond-the-pale, postmodern excesses, for a wider public and media he has been elevated to ubercool icon – to a media and pop-cult sign, name-dropped by journalists taking the temperature of the cultural zeitgeist to signal their own cutting-edge, clued-up cachet. He has become required reading for the aspirant avant-garde and intellectual cognoscenti who liberally misquote and misinterpret his work, an essential sign of good taste for the Ikea pine-effect coffee tables of the culturally literate, and a ready-made quotation or reference point for any knowing cultural production, article or argument. In the metaphorical epitome of semiotic commodification, with the Philosophy Football range of intellectually inspired football shirts in the 1990s, Baudrillard also became a T-shirt. Today his public lectures sell out; his international photographic exhibitions attract widespread attention; his visits to Britain are reported in the broadsheet press, accompanied by articles, photographs and interviews – one even labelling him 'the David Bowie of philosophy' (Poole, 2000a) – while conferences, personal appearances and book signings draw minor crowds. When Neo opened his copy of *Simulacra and Simulation* in the 1999 film *The Matrix*, Baudrillard also became one of the few cultural thinkers to inspire a big-budget Hollywood film, attracting en route (and to his chagrin) many new fans. For his critics this popularity has only reinforced all their suspicions of his superficiality and confirmed his unholy spell. For them, Baudrillard retains his hint of sulphur as the evil genie of postmodern appearances.

The popular association of Baudrillard with postmodernism has survived, due largely to the term's usefulness in allowing a simple positioning in the field and in textbooks and to the failure of commentators and casual readers to follow developments in both Baudrillard's own work and in the secondary literature as assiduously as they followed earlier debates around postmodernity. This may be understandable, however, as today anyone wanting to understand Baudrillard properly has a huge body of original work to grapple with; coming to a corpus that has always been difficult and multilayered, drawing on and radicalizing a range of influences, and resisting easy interpretation and understanding while simultaneously encouraging simplistic errors in hasty readers and predisposed critics. His later works especially complicate interpretation in continuously returning to, developing and reworking his earlier themes to produce a spiral of ideas that still refuses to settle into a simple framework of analysis.

Baudrillard's work, therefore, has provoked a variety of critical readings and responses. Many of these, such as Kellner's and Norris's, are merely negative. They seek only to inoculate readers against him, to filter out dangerous ideas and present an ideologically correct bank balance of what is acceptable in his work and thus contain and reduce it before the law-court of their own correct moral and political perspectives. Other readings of Baudrillard are far more productive because, rather than beginning from an established critical position that anticipates and forecloses Baudrillard, they instead allow one to develop in the course of exploring and understanding his work. To employ a Baudrillardian metaphor, whereas the negative approach begins with such a predictable hostility that the analysis itself need not have happened – and sometimes can be considered *not* to have happened – more productive readings allow the *event* of his thought to occur, developing a critique of it as it unfolds that allows for his contradictions and deficiencies but ends with the openness that a recognition of his positive critical value brings.

My own work attempts to follow the latter path, building on the work of Gane, Pawlett (1997) and Hegarty (2004) and their emphasis on the importance of the radical Durkheimian tradition, encompassing the work of Durkheim, Mauss and Hubert, Caillois, Bataille and the College of Sociology (see below), to Baudrillard's project. While this tradition provides only one way to read Baudrillard, it does have the merit of following his own critical position. Although he extends and develops his employment of this tradition and its ideas, his debt to these continues throughout his work, up to the present. Baudrillard, of course, also employs other theories and methodologies, most notably semiology and poststructuralism,[3] and his work has obvious affinities with other perspectives such as McLuhanism and Situationism, but these attributions all divert attention away from his central critical position, which deserves the strongest emphasis. Although Baudrillard draws on many influences to help *describe* our world, he employs a coherent radical Durkheimianism for his career-long *critique* of its mode of relations, meaning, experience and communication.

Hence my rejection of Baudrillard's positioning as a postmodernist. The term adds nothing to related theoretical movements such as poststructuralism, its ideas are now dated and overly simplistic, and its popular success and take-up has come at the price of declining academic interest in its debates. This, together with Baudrillard's limited use of or approval for the term and the erroneous perception of his critical sympathies its attribution brings,[4] is sufficient, I believe, to discount its use. Instead I propose that we take the opportunities offered by the increasing interest in his work in media and communication studies and its own contemporary multidisciplinary expansion to jettison this association and develop new, more productive readings of his work for the discipline. This book offers one such reading, presenting a critical exploration of Baudrillard's radical Durkheimian media theory. Identifying him as working within a specific, established tradition drawn from social theory, social anthropology and philosophy, it argues that he provides its first systematic application to the contemporary electronic mass media, linking its central argument – the loss of the sacred and its replacement by safe, secular, simulated forms of its communion – to the latter's processes. While a functionalist Durkheimianism has proved popular in media studies the critical possibilities of this opposing radical tradition have to date been overlooked by the discipline.

In following this radical Durkheimian reading, and in emphasizing the key division in Baudrillard's work between the symbolic and semiotic, I am not attempting to impose a reductive framework on his theory. The division is clearly Baudrillard's own and is easily recognized in his work, remaining at the heart of its transformations through to the present. Moreover, these two processes do not have one single form or simple relationship: the concepts are reworked continuously as Baudrillard radicalizes his interpretations of their forms and effects. In particular his work traces their spiralling interrelationship and their merging, and my own reading follows this, being concerned not only with the appearance and meaning of these processes but also with the complexity of their relationship and the problems this produces for his critical project. Nor am I attempting here to reduce Baudrillard to a normalized, academic sociology. Though I emphasize his debts to the Durkheimian tradition it should be remembered that this is a *radical* tradition: one that, in the almost unassimilable thought of Caillois, Bataille and Klossowski, explodes beyond and radically questions the conventions, methodologies, knowledge and practices of that science of society. If Baudrillard thus moves beyond academic sociology at the level of content he does so even more at the level of form, in his methodology. It is here that symbolic and semiotic merge most fruitfully, the meeting of his belief in the potlatch and in simulation unleashing the avant-garde elements of and influences on his work. This is how I want to read Baudrillard here: as offering, at the level of content, a radical

Durkheimian critique of the semiotic and simulation – in a critique of electronic media that itself becomes susceptible to an internal ungrounding – and, at the level of form, a radical and avant-garde response to both the world of simulation and his own attempts to understand it.

Given the growing interest in media and communication studies in questions that are central to his work – questions of mediation, experience, communicative relationships, images, reality, media events, and real-time communications and their effects – the lack of a detailed critical introduction to Baudrillard in the discipline is a significant omission. This book, therefore, has five aims. Firstly it aims to develop the first full-length critical survey of Baudrillard's media theory. Secondly it aims to promote a more detailed understanding of his work within the discipline. Thirdly, it aims to reposition him as a critical thinker working in the radical Durkheimian tradition; and fourthly, it aims to demonstrate how his ideas are applicable to contemporary media events and processes. Finally, it aims to develop a more informed critique of his work and its possible contribution. The book develops the existing literature on Baudrillard in offering a wider and more detailed context for understanding his work, challenging many common assumptions concerning his intellectual debts and lineage and foregrounding especially the question of methodology that, I argue, animates all of his work. Its structure is organized to lead readers through the main themes and issues of Baudrillard's media theory. The first three chapters position Baudrillard theoretically and discuss the influences on his media theory; the next three chapters discuss his theory of the non-event and its operation in practice in his own examples; and the last two chapters discuss his treatment and theorization of specific media, in particular new media, digital cinema, and photography. The conclusion offers a final critical evaluation of his place within and contribution to media and communication studies.

Chapter 1, therefore, introduces Baudrillard's theory of 'communication', establishing the distinction of symbolic and semiotic which runs throughout his work, the Durkheimian sources of the symbolic and his use of this as the basis of his critical position on the media. The chapter introduces his claim that a specific mode of meaning and relations – 'symbolic exchange' – is reduced and replaced by the semiotic media, which, in simulating its processes, fabricate instead a 'non-communication'. Chapter 2 builds on this discussion of the symbolic by exploring its opposite, the semiotic and the related concepts of 'simulation' and the 'simulacrum', contextualizing these concepts within debates in anthropological, theological, philosophical and social and cultural and media theory. It argues that Baudrillard repeats the western attempt to demonize and domesticate the simulacral image, implicitly employing the symbolic as a referential ground and 'real' against it, considering also the problems this raises for his critical project. The chapter also introduces and explores the relationship of the symbolic and semiotic at the level of form, exploring how Baudrillard balances these in his radical theoretical methodology. Chapter 3 considers Baudrillard's relationship with Marshall

McLuhan, the media theorist with whom his work is most closely associated. It argues that Baudrillard employs McLuhan's work but subjugates it to his own Durkheimian theory, leading him to develop an opposing critical position that is closer to another, to date overlooked, influence on his work: the 1960s media theorist Daniel J. Boorstin. The chapter concludes by looking again at Baudrillard's methodology, exploring its affinities with both McLuhan's and Boorstin's approaches.

Chapter 4 sets out a key element of Baudrillard's practical media theory – his discussion of the 'non-event', unpacking this complex and counter-intuitive concept and its development through his work. It also considers its value in relation to other approaches within the discipline, offering a defence of Baudrillard's radical Durkheimian position. Chapter 5 considers Baudrillard's most famous example of a non-event, his claim that 'the Gulf War did not take place'. It considers in detail the sources and meaning of his argument, and his analysis of the western model of 'non-war' deployed in the Gulf deserts and the role of electronic media on the battlefield and in mediating the experience of the war for the domestic audience. Chapter 6 explores his later, revised theory of the event: his discussion of the event's 'double game' and the spiralling within it of both semiotic and symbolic elements. It considers his analysis of the 9/11 attacks on the World Trade Center and of the resulting American response, the 2001 Afghan War, extending this analysis to the 2003 Iraq War and its aftermath. Rejecting claims of Baudrillard's nihilistic celebration of contemporary processes, it argues instead that his work defends resistant internal and external forces against the global semiotic system and the simulation it employs as a means of social control, integration and pacification.

Chapter 7 develops a reading of Baudrillard's appearance in *The Matrix*, using this as an opportunity to discuss his comments on cinema, special effects, and the idea and functioning of the virtual, demonstrating again the latter's practical role as a means of social control. Finally, chapter 8 returns to the central relationship of symbolic and semiotic. It evaluates their later development in Baudrillard's work, considering them in relation to his own contemporary theory and personal practice of photography, and the apparent reversal in his long-standing opposition to mediating technology in his claim that the medium contains a 'saving power' in its path to the symbolic. The conclusion offers a critical evaluation of Baudrillard's work and its place within media and communication studies, identifying those parts of his work which make a significant contribution to its field and asserting the value of his radical Durkheimian media theory. The book concludes with a defence of his methodological challenge to the discipline: of his 'theoretical violence' and 'speculation to the death'.

1 Television is killing the art of symbolic exchange: Baudrillard's theory of communication

There are great advantages in for once removing ourselves distinctly from our time and letting ourselves be driven far from its shore back into the ocean of former world views. Looking at the coast from that perspective, we survey for the first time its entire shape, and when we near it again we have the advantage of understanding it better on the whole than do those who have never left it.

Nietzsche, *Human, All Too Human*

From one perspective, Baudrillard's work has always been about media. His first book, *The System of Objects (SO)*, published in 1968, describes the existence and operation of the immense signifying system that constitutes our contemporary western cultural experience. This is a system in which all objects, messages, and products, and all history, culture, meaning, relations and experience, become transformed into signs that replace and mediate experience, communicating, in their structural interrelationships, a variety of meanings and messages. Thus Baudrillard expands the realm of media to encompass our entire experiential, communicational environment, with our everyday life itself comprising a saturated media sphere. If Baudrillard's work has always been about media, it has also, therefore, always been about communication, and it is his specific formulation and use of this concept that I want to explore here as an introduction to his media theory. In Baudrillard we find a theory of human communication that serves as the basis for an original critical philosophy of the media. Although his earlier work contains important discussions of the media, he most clearly articulates the basis of this theory in his 1971 essay 'Requiem for the media'.

Baudrillard's starting point there is the absurd claim that 'the mass media are anti-mediatory and intransitive. They fabricate non-communication – this is what characterizes them' (p. 169). Clearly this contradicts all received wisdom concerning the media. Instead of having been communicating with us all this time Baudrillard claims that they have been doing the opposite and that their very essence is 'non-communication'. To understand this we need to understand what Baudrillard means here by 'communication' and how he applies this to contemporary society and media. We need to understand an aspect of his work that is often overlooked in discussions of his media theory but which is the basis of his analysis of and critical position on media phenomena. We need to return to his theory of 'symbolic exchange', the sources from which he derives it, and its role as the positive, organizing principle of his career.

Even today, misinterpretations of Baudrillard's project are common, typically due to overlooking his critical position, the symbolic, and its derivation. Readings which focus on his description of the contemporary world often overlook or underplay his opposition to it and fail to seriously consider his critical concept of the symbolic which serves as the basis of this opposition. Hence the prevalence in the textbooks of claims that Baudrillard celebrates or promotes the processes he describes and that his work is nihilistic, postmodern or an uncritical apology for capitalism, offering no alternative or solution. One reason why the symbolic is not adequately dealt with is that the concept has a very different history in the English-speaking world, where it is usually treated as synonymous with the sign. Despite its decisive influence on generations of French thought, including Dumézil, Lévi-Strauss, Lacan, Bourdieu, Foucault, Derrida, Kristeva, Lefebvre, Debord and Vaneigem, the tradition from which Baudrillard derives the concept – the French Durkheimian tradition of philosophical social anthropology in its radical line of descent through Durkheim to Mauss and Hubert and Bataille and Caillois – is still comparatively unknown in the English-speaking world.

Without understanding this tradition, however, we cannot understand Baudrillard's work. What he takes from it is a conception of an order of relations and meaning, and a mode of human communication – 'symbolic exchange' – and the belief in both the reduction and replacement of this mode by contemporary media processes and its survival as a radical site of critique and reversal. Although the concept is later rethought as 'seduction', 'the fatal', 'evil', 'reversibility', 'radical alterity', 'radical illusion' and 'singularity', etc., these reformulations retain a conceptual unity and thus the same underlying symbolic force can be identified as running throughout his career as the basis of his critical project and position. Perhaps the best way to begin to understand the symbolic is from Baudrillard's description of it as 'an act of exchange and a social relation' (*Symbolic Exchange and Death* (*SED*), 133). Mauss and Bataille are widely recognized as the sources of this description, though few discussions provide a sufficient context for them, or Baudrillard himself, within the wider Durkheimian tradition.

'CONVULSIVE COMMUNICATION'

The Durkheimian tradition of social anthropology developed from *Année Sociologique*'s study of 'primitive' societies, and especially from Hubert and Mauss's *Sacrifice: Its Nature and Function* of 1899 (1964), Durkheim and Mauss's *Primitive Classification* of 1903 (1963), Mauss and Hubert's *A General Theory of Magic* of 1904 (1972) and Mauss and Beuchat's *Seasonal Variations of the Eskimo* of 1904–5 (1979). The school's classic statement is found in Émile Durkheim's own 1912 study of tribal religion, *The Elementary Forms of the Religious Life*

(Durkheim, 1915), but Marcel Mauss's own later lectures on Durkheim and 1925 study *The Gift: Forms and Functions of Exchange in Primitive Societies* (Mauss and Hubert, 1966) were also influential in this tradition. In particular they inspired the 'College of Sociology', a short-lived grouping from 1937 to 1939, whose members included Georges Bataille, Roger Caillois, Michel Leiris, Alexandre Kojève, Pierre Klossowski, Anatole Lewitzky, Hans Mayer, Jean Paulhan, Jean Wahl, René M. Guastalla, Georges Ambrosino, Pierre Libra, and Jules Monnerot (Hollier, 1988). The College radically developed Mauss's Durkheimianism, producing numerous texts of social and philosophical anthropology, including Caillois's *Man and the Sacred* of 1939 (1980), and Bataille's early essays (Bataille, 1985) and his later books such as *The Accursed Share* of 1949 (1991), *Eroticism* of 1957 (1962), and *Theory of Religion* of 1973 (1992). Baudrillard is perhaps best understood as taking his place here, as coming out of this tradition and standing as its foremost contemporary representative, reviving their ideas and radically updating and extending their critique. His concept of 'symbolic exchange' is directly derived from this tradition's identification and privileging of an immediately actualized, collective mode of relations and its transformative experience and communication.

Durkheim's concept of 'the sacred' is the exemplar of this mode of relations. Durkheim identified a fundamental division in the tribal world between two opposed and irreconcilable categories: the 'sacred', the contagious state and experience of the divine, and the 'profane', the realm of the non-sacred and of the everyday, routine and productive labours of life. The sacred is attained, he says, in the effusive and violent, organized congregations of the festival where, in the energy unleashed, the individual undergoes a genuine transformation, feeling 'a new life flowing within him whose intensity surprises him' (1915:225). 'This exaltation is real,' Durkheim says, 'and it is really the product of forces exterior to the individual' (1915:225), though the forces are social not spiritual, being the product of the group and their collective union. Durkheim's work goes on to discuss the operation of religion and its symbolism as a means of binding and renewing the group and its ideals (Gane, 1992:61–84), but what is important for us here is the idea of a higher mode of collective experience and meaning that transforms everyday individual life.

For Durkheim, therefore, the communion and confrontation of the group realizes and releases energies that are amplified by each member to produce the experience of a full and profoundly different reality. The individual does not know their cause, but only that 'he is raised above himself and that he sees a different life from the one he ordinarily leads' (1915:220). Durkheim's description of this 'state of effervescence' is powerful:

When arrived at this state of excitation, a man does not recognise himself any longer. Feeling himself dominated and carried away by some sort of an external power which makes him think and act differently than in normal times, he naturally has the impression of being himself no longer. It seems to him that he has become a new being . . . and as at the same time all his companions feel themselves transformed in the same way and express this sentiment by their cries, their gestures, and their general attitude, everything is just as though he really were transported into a special world, entirely different from the one where he ordinarily lives, and into an environment filled with exceptionally intense forces that take hold of him and metamorphose him.

(1915:218)

The collective force penetrates, elevates and magnifies the individual's being, Durkheim argues (1915:209), producing a 'real communion' (1915:230) that stands in stark opposition to the separation and closed consciousness of everyday individual life and the boredom of its productive grind. Religion operates, therefore, 'to raise man above himself and make him lead a life superior to that which he would lead if he followed his own individual whims' (1915:414). Thus our highest experience is attained collectively and socially through a communion with others.

Durkheim's work was disseminated after his death by Mauss, who also developed it again with *The Gift*, a study of anthropological evidence from Polynesia, Melanesia, and North American Indian societies and a range of early literature. He discovered in these sources the existence in 'primitive' and non-western societies of a system of exchange based on 'the gift' (*don*), on the divestment not the accumulation of property. The implications of this for him were obvious: capitalist political economy was neither natural nor inevitable, being predated by an opposing system of practices, based on the group, the cycle, obligation, and loss, rather than the individual, the market, the contract, and private profit. Extending beyond a limited 'economic' sphere, the gift encompassed and drew together the entire social, cultural and religious life in a 'system of total prestations' (Mauss and Hubert, 1966:3) that was the primary determinant of the society.

The gift had three rules: one had to give, receive and, after a suitable interval, return a counter-gift of greater value (1966:10–11, 37–41). The aim was not profit but there was a three-fold gain, subject to reversal on repayment. Giving brought social rank, with the capacity and willingness to give bringing honour and respect; it created strong social relations, as a positive act of communication forming affective ties and alliances between families or tribes; and it brought social power, creating a power relation of indebtedness, obligation and loss of face, with honour only being regained through a counter-gift. Closely associated with festivals, the gift could also take the form of a sumptuous display, extravagant expenditure, or even the destruction of wealth to humble and eclipse the other.

We find in Mauss, therefore, a remarkable image of a system of interconnecting and escalating gifts – of 'potlatches' – between individuals and groups all vying for prestige, relationships and power. It is an image of an intense, competitive and dramatic scene of exchange contrasting with the later individualized, utilitarian, formal, impersonal and contractual relations of economic exchange. The gift is explicitly personal, as epitomised by the Maori 'hau' – the 'spirit' of the thing given and personification of the giver that has to find its way home through the system of gifts (Mauss and Hubert, 1966:8–10). At its heart, however, the gift retains its dual character as both positive communication and agonistic confrontation. It is based on a challenge to the other that necessitates a personal response, staking one's own human- ity in a cyclical struggle for recognition, supremacy and face. Like the Durkheimian sacred, therefore, the scene of the gift is a social, collective one, raising the participants in a moment of meaning and communication, pro- ducing a higher life in its contagious transformation and risking it in the rivalry of the challenge.

Mauss saw the gift as having been historically swept aside by the victory of rationalism and mercantilism. In raising the principles of individual profit, utility and formal contractual relations these had turned humanity from a col- lective being into an 'economic animal': a *Homo oeconomicus* that was little more than 'a calculating machine' (1966:74). However, in arguing that the 'ancient principles' of the gift had not been completely superseded and in seeing them as reappearing in our society 'like the resurrection of a dominant motif long forgotten' (1966:66), Mauss develops a genealogy, adopted by the Durkheimian tradition and found again in Baudrillard. This genealogy sees a mode of relations destroyed by the modern west which replaces it with an inferior, individualized mode, while retaining a belief in the continued pres- ence and possibility of this collective mode as a radical principle opposed to and capable of transforming the contemporary world. If ultimately Mauss's hopes for a limited reform of capitalism through the gift are unconvincing (1966:69), his desire to return to its principles and to another, deeper mode of existence carries more weight.

It did for the College of Sociology, whose 1937 founding document com- mitted them to a 'sacred sociology', defined as 'the study of all manifestations of social existence where the active presence of the sacred is clear' (Hollier, 1988:5). They followed a Durkheimian interpretation of the sacred as a heightened mode of collective experience and communication with others: as what Bataille describes as 'a privileged moment of communal unity, a moment of the convulsive communication of what is ordinarily stifled' (1985:242). But the College also saw themselves as part of this process, describing themselves as a 'moral community', one 'bound precisely to the virulent character of the realm studied' and accepting the 'contagious and *activist*' implications of the subject matter (Hollier, 1988:5). Thus in their interest in the sacred as an experience, their belief in its communication with Being itself and emphasis on its essential violent, excessive and confrontational elements, the College moved beyond the detached academic stance, secular interpretation and emphasis on the positive communication created of the Durkheimian tradition.

Caillois's *Man and the Sacred*, for example, takes an obvious pleasure in describing the effervescent celebrations of the festival which opposes, he says, 'an intermittent explosion to a dull continuity' (1980:99). The festivals are 'a time of intense emotion and a metamorphosis of . . . being' (1980:99), he argues, and thus constitute both 'the paroxysm of society, purifying and renewing it simultaneously' and 'a summation, manifesting the glory of the collectivity, which imbues its very being' (1980:125–6). He sees later societies as fearing any interruption of the profane and its accumulation for individual profit, replacing the sacred with simulated, controlled and safe forms. Thus the festival makes way for the 'vacation', whose individualized retreat from others represents, Caillois argues, 'not the flow but the ebb of communal life' (1980:127).

This sense of loss pervades the Durkheimian school, which sees the evolution of western society as a movement away from this collective communion and historical decline of the sacred. Thus Caillois sees the sacred as becoming 'abstract, internalized and subjective' with the liberation and 'intellectual and moral autonomy' of the 'individual' whose detached, rational, scientific consciousness henceforth sees the world as an object of knowledge and thus as profane (1980:134). Bataille charts a similar process, seeing Judeo-Christianity, scientific rationalism, Protestantism, industrialism and capitalism all contributing towards the reduction of the sacred and emergence of an 'economic mankind' (1991:127) living a 'thing-like' rather than 'sovereign' existence (1991:131). As it touches on the experience of being most fully human and of a genuine spiritual reality, the issue of the survival of the sacred is, therefore, the central one for the College, who accordingly saw their own activities as essentially 'religious' (Hollier, 1988:387).

Bataille extended the Durkheimian concept of the sacred as 'communication between beings' in the College's final lecture in 1939, as he moved towards a wider, spiritually oriented Nietzscheanism. Following Nietzsche's description in *The Will to Power* of the world as 'a monster of energy' (1968a:550), he develops a philosophy of the interconnectedness and flow of the energy of life, of 'a vaster reality' glimpsed only through the mediation of violence and the community it creates (Hollier, 1988:327). Thus, Bataille argues, the 'sacred communication' of religious rites allows us to overcome the separation of the profane world and experience the continuous world of 'intimacy' with Being (1991:57–8). Having first sketched these ideas in 1933 (1985:116–29), Bataille returns to them in *The Accursed Share,* where he allies them with Mauss's anti-economism to contrast the 'restricted economy' of capitalism with the 'general economy' of life: a holistic flow of energies and their exchange that encompasses all material existence (1991:19–41). If Bataille's work increasingly becomes a manifesto for an experience he is seeking, his continuing belief in a convulsive communication discovered through religious rites, his critique of political economy, genealogy of the loss of the sacred and critique of contemporary relations all highlight his debt to Durkheimianism. In his work, however, the festival, sacrifice, the gift and the communion of beings are intimately attuned to the economy of life and to Being itself.

It is this Durkheimian mode of relations that Baudrillard takes as the basis for his concept of the 'symbolic'. In 'symbolic exchange' he unifies the festival, the gift and sacrifice around their central theme: their creation of a mode of relations and communication. This is a strong, active, full, present, dual or collective, human relationship, founded on or created through these customs, rituals and exchanges, whose meaning is actualized in the moment and which exists as both a mode of communication and confrontation. Following the Durkheimian school, Baudrillard sees the 'primitive' world as exemplifying this symbolic mode, develops his own related genealogy of its transformation and holds out a similar hope for its radical survival and recovery. It is his original depiction of this contemporary order, therefore, that I next want to consider.

'EVERYTHING IS SIGN, PURE SIGN'

The symbolic already appears as the key critical site in Baudrillard's first book, *The System of Objects*, though references to it there are eclipsed by his primary goal of describing the operation of the semiotic in contemporary consumer society. Postwar France had seen a series of modernizing socioeconomic and technological changes creating a new consumer society foregrounding consumer goods, the media, advertising and fashion. As the structures of 'everyday life' were being transformed this became an important new area for theorization and a vibrant intellectual milieu developed that would be influential on Baudrillard's project. His early sympathies were with existentialist and humanist Marxist thought, especially Sartre's analysis of concrete, situated existence, Lefebvre's discussion of alienated everyday life and critique of 'the bureaucratic society of controlled consumption', and the later critique of the alienations of 'one dimensional society' by Marcuse and of the 'society of the spectacle' by Debord and the Situationists. But Baudrillard also became interested in the opposing structuralist movement associated with Barthes's semiology, the work of Lévi-Strauss, Althusser and Lacan, and the emerging poststructuralism of Derrida and the Tel Quel group, as well as the discussion of technology and media in the work of Ellul, Simondon, Boorstin and McLuhan. He was drawn both to the Marxist critique of consumer society as representing not an increase in individual freedom but the penetration of control, constraint and alienation throughout everyday life, and to structural and technical analyses of the operation of this society and its production of the individual: themes which figure strongly in his own work.

The main influence on *The System of Objects* is Roland Barthes's application in *Mythologies* of 1957 of Saussurean linguistics (Saussure, 1986) to the new postwar world of goods, objects and messages, and ideological critique of the sign's mythological operation (Barthes, 1973a). Baudrillard's analysis, however, is less systematic than Barthes's and, in emphasizing human relationships (*SO*, 40), develops a very different, Durkheimian critique of the sign. For Baudrillard consumption is a contemporary phenomenon in its semiotic organization and governance by a code of signification. Consumption, therefore, is not the physical act of buying or using an object but the idealist act of appropriating a signifier: the idea and meaning of the object or message. It is '*an activity consisting of the systematic manipulation of signs*'.

Against this, Baudrillard contrasts 'traditional symbolic objects' which are bound to and actualized in human activity, mediating 'a real relationship or a directly experienced situation' and bearing its 'clear imprint' (*SO*, 200). For Baudrillard the sign is born when this relationship is broken, a process of the transformation of all relations and meaning into signs to be combined, appropriated and consumed that has become, he says, 'a defining mode of our industrial civilization' (*SO*, 199).

The System of Objects, therefore, already presents us with a Durkheimian analysis: the distinction of symbolic and semiotic modes of relations, the origins of the semiotic in the destruction of the symbolic, the characterization of contemporary society as defined by this semioticization and a critical sympathy with the symbolic and its continuing power against the western semiotic processes. In describing how the processed, produced, profane meaning of the semiotic and its unilateral consumption replaces the immediately actualized and exchanged meaning of the symbolic, Baudrillard reframes and extends the Durkheimian analysis of the loss of the sacred through an original analysis of the contemporary dominance of the semiotic and its impact on human relations. His early works, *The System of Objects* of 1968 and *The Consumer Society* (*CS*) of 1970, are filled with examples of this process, all describing a world where it is signs and objects – and even doors (*SO*, 21) – that communicate, rather than people, and where the individual is integrated into a totalitarian code (*SO*, 18) unable to do anything other than engineer and manipulate a cybernetic communicational environment whose goal is 'the perfect circulation of messages' (*SO*, 29).

Despite employing the symbolic from the beginning, Baudrillard doesn't finally separate it from the processes of the semiotic until the second half of *For a Critique of the Political Economy of the Sign* (*CPES*) in 1972. His early texts, however, do make its Durkheimian derivation clear, especially in his discussion of gift exchange and the passage 'from symbolic exchange to sign exchange' (*CPES*, 30–1, 65). In the symbolic exchange of the gift, for example, the object 'is inseparable from the concrete relation in which it is exchanged' and the 'transferential pact' it seals. Once given it is an 'absolutely singular' phenomenon, actualizing the 'unique moment' of the relationship (p. 64) and becoming 'the concrete manifestation of a total relationship' (p. 65). The sign originates with the breaking of this bond, no longer gathering its meaning from it (p. 66), but taking on a relationship to all other signs in the semiotic system in its precoded difference, being unilaterally, individually appropriated for that meaning (p. 65). Baudrillard's example, highlighting the survival of the gift, is the wedding ring, which, once exchanged, becomes a unique and irreplaceable incarnation of the relationship (p. 66). Contemporary examples of semioticization are perhaps easier to find, from city centre theme pubs with original farming tools and equipment anachronistically nailed to the walls and original oak barrels decorated with plastic barley on the shelves behind the seats, to America-themed diners and pizza restaurants with antique typewriters, Chevy fenders and baseball gear fixed to the walls, all semiotically organized and combining to signify what they might once have actualized and lived.

The wedding ring serves as a good example of the symbolic, emphasizing the emotional element of the relationship. Baudrillard's symbolic is best understood as a dramatic and engaged scene: an immediate, active, reciprocal relationship with its own transformative mood and charge. This is neither a nostalgic nor an idealized conception, however, as Baudrillard and the Durkheimian school emphasize both the survival and possibility of irruption of its forces and its agonistic and threatening character. If its experience is one of fullness, it is also dangerous, hostile and even lethal, risking not only the face but also the life of the participant. It is not simply an ideal communality, it is also a struggle for power, rank, recognition and humanity. Hence Baudrillard's description of the gift as 'ambivalent' as 'a medium of relation and distance' and of 'love and aggression' (*CPES*, 65). As the dramaturgical scene of an escalating challenge, pitting the humanity of each in an act that may involve violence, frenzy and passion and that results not only in communion but also in power, prestige and transformation or humiliation and abasement, the symbolic is both confrontation and communication.

Baudrillard's original contribution to the Durkheimian tradition is this synthesizing analysis of the form of the symbolic and his revised genealogy tracing its semiotic transformation and simulation. As part of this he inherits and extends the Durkheimian critique of political economy and its possessive individualism in his critique of our 'general political economy' – an expanded sphere encompassing the commodity and the sign. He begins his critique by targeting the central assumption of political economy of an individual in nature with natural needs that production develops to provide for and ensure their survival (*CS*, 69). Whereas Marcuse accepted this model, criticizing only the 'false' needs later produced by capitalism (1986:4–5), Baudrillard rejects the very concept of essential human needs, based on their social determination (*CPES*, 74; *CS*, 73) and the Durkheimian argument that survivalist economies do not exist as tribal societies produce excesses for their rites and festivities (*CPES*, 74, 76, 81). He argues instead that this survivalist anthropology is the creation of political economy itself, which creates a 'human essence grounded in nature' in order to naturalize and ideologically legitimate its own economic system and individualistic values (*CPES*, 72, 80) and mobilize us as consumers responding to natural needs (*CS*, 74–5). Hence Baudrillard's claim that consumption has nothing to do with physical satisfaction or happiness. Instead, following Barthes, Veblen and Marcuse, he sees it respectively as a system of meaning and communication, of social hierarchy and distinction, and a means of social integration and control (*CS*, 60–1, 94). Instead of a realm of individual freedom and expression, it represents, he argues, our training into a totalitarian semiotic code and its 'total organization of everyday life' (*CS*, 29).

Baudrillard develops this critique by arguing that today the object of political economy has moved beyond those logics of use and exchange value that defined the commodity, as, in becoming a sign, 'sign value' also develops and becomes dominant (*CPES*, 123–9). Just as, he argues, political economy employs use value and 'human needs' as a secondary content and as an external referent to support its dominant logic, exchange value, and thus ground the entire system, so the sign system supports itself and the dominant sign value of the signifier by employing a secondary content, the signified, and an external referent that appears to give it a natural basis in reality. What results is a poststructuralist extension of the Durkheimian critique of political economy. Just as political economy replaced tribal symbolic relations with its own individualistic relations and supporting ideology, so the semiotic system operates today by imposing its own legitimating metaphysics on the now transformed symbolic reality (*CPES*, 143–63). Thus Baudrillard's most apparently postmodern claim – that our entire reality is a semiotic production and simulation, one already '*designated*, abstracted and rationalized' to appear as 'real' (*CPES*, 155) – is actually based on a Durkheimian critique of the prior reduction and processing of the symbolic and its relations and meaning. In seeing our entire western 'reality principle' as a western production built on the destruction of symbolic relationships, however, Baudrillard presents us with a picture of the systematic desacralization of the world and unlimited extension of the impoverished profane that goes far beyond that ever envisaged by Mauss, Bataille or Caillois.

Nevertheless even for Baudrillard the symbolic still survives. Only *its* processes are outside of political economy, transgressing and destroying the logics of use value, exchange value and sign value in removing the object from the profane for the realm of the sacred. Thus, he argues, only the symbolic is external to and 'beyond' the semiotic (*CPES*, 159). In retaining the possibility of a 'radical rupture' of its system of value (*CPES*, 125), it becomes Baudrillard's radical Durkheimian hope against general political economy: today, he says, 'signs must burn' (*CPES*, 163). Ultimately consumption is an inadequate replacement for the symbolic: the paroxysm of communal life cannot be found in the lonely embrace of the semiotic or, Baudrillard argues, in the unilateral operation of the electronic mass media.

THE GIFT OF SPEECH

With this background we can identify the existence in Baudrillard of a Durkheimian theory of human relations and communication. Formulated as the symbolic, this serves as the basis for his critique not only of our semiotic society but also of our electronic media which, for him, constitute one of the primary sites for the production and dissemination of the sign. The emphasis on the form of media and its effects immediately highlights the influence of Marshall McLuhan and his claim that 'the medium is the message' (1994:7), that the real message or significance of a medium is the technology itself and its psychic and social consequences (1994:4). Baudrillard employs this insight in his own critical project to argue that the most important effect of the electronic media is the transformation of the symbolic into the semiotic. 'In their very form and very operation', he argues, 'the media induce a social relation': one that involves 'the abstraction, separation and abolition of exchange itself' (RM, 169). Thus, if we understand communication from this Durkheimian perspective as 'an exchange . . . a reciprocal space of a speech and a response' (RM, 169), then it is this communication that is explicitly lost in our contemporary media. As Baudrillard argues, their form is one of 'non-communication', being based on the abolition of the symbolic relationship and its communication.

Baudrillard's critique of communication also operates as a critique of established positions within media theory. His arguments were directly aimed at Hans Magnus Enzensberger's essay, 'Constituents of a theory of the media' (1970), which attempted to recover communication for Marxism, opposing its reduction to a superstructural effect and rethinking it as a productive force which could be liberated for democratic use (RM, 166–9). In contrast, Baudrillard rejects such hopes for a mediated communality, arguing that they abolish rather than promote human relations. 'Media ideology operates at the level of form', he argues, in the 'separation' of humanity it produces (RM, 169).

Alongside a critique of Enzensberger, Baudrillard also targets the 'communication theory' formalized by Jacobsen and its picture of isolated poles of 'transmitter' and 'receiver', artificially reunited by a 'message' (RM, 178). This is 'a simulation model of communication', he says, excluding the scene of the symbolic: 'the reciprocity and antagonism of interlocutors, and the ambivalence of their exchange' (RM, 179). Real communication, Baudrillard says, involves more than 'the simple transmission-reception of a message' (RM, 169). Our media, however, follow this model, constituting a 'speech without response' (RM, 170), locking us into a unilateral power relation. Thus no liberation of the media is possible. For Baudrillard the only revolution 'lies in restoring the possibility of a response', allowing speech to 'be able to exchange, give and repay itself', though this would require 'an upheaval in the entire existing structure of media' (RM, 170).

Baudrillard finds this model of 'non-response' reproduced throughout our society (RM, 170), in the unilaterality of the media, of semiotic consumption, of the hyperrealized image that leaves no room for investment, phantasy or response (Seduction (*Sed.*), 30), and in the west's 'non-wars' that employ overwhelming technological force to exclude all opposition and realize their perfected model of warfare (*The Gulf War Did Not Take Place* (*GW*)). Everywhere, unilaterality and the exclusion of the symbolic reign. The media no more create a community, Baudrillard says, than 'the possession of a refrigerator or a toaster' (RM, 171). As we silently gather round it at night, we can see his point: television is killing the art of symbolic exchange. We find in Baudrillard, therefore, a counter-intuitive image of a mediatized society of non-communication in which 'people are no longer speaking to each other', being 'definitively isolated in the face of a speech without response' (RM, 172). Only controlled, preprogrammed feedback is acceptable, in phone-ins, polls and letters that are a simulacrum of a response, reinforcing the media's operation and functioning to censor anything that challenges their power (RM, 181).

May 1968 provides proof of this process for Baudrillard (RM, 172–7). Far from spreading the revolutionary uprisings, he argues, the media transformed a living movement, with its own rhythm and time, into a media object and event, short-circuiting its occurrence. 'Mass mediatization' functions through the 'imposition of models', Baudrillard says, so the media administered 'a mortal dose of publicity' to the events (RM, 174), imposing the media's own models of meaning, development and resolution, resulting in the revolution's 'decompression', 'asphyxiation by extension' and 'defeat' (RM, 176). If, therefore, the revolution will be televised, is any symbolic co-option of the media possible? Baudrillard finds it in the streets: the real revolutionary media during May were the walls and their speech, the silkscreen posters and the hand-painted notices, as it was only there, in that immediate, reciprocal and external space, that 'speech began and was exchanged' (RM, 176). Transgressive, ephemeral, dualistic, both inviting and producing a response, these graffiti breach 'the fundamental rule of non-response enunciated by all the media' (RM, 183). In it, Baudrillard says, 'an immediate communication process is rediscovered' (RM, 182).

This defence of May 1968 and of its graffiti highlights the Situationist influence on Baudrillard's work. His involvement with the pro-Situ journal *Utopie* is well known (see *The Uncollected Baudrillard* (*UB*)), as is the influence of Debord's *Society of the Spectacle,* of 1967 where a similar critique of the media's unilaterality, spectacular replacement of the real and production of 'separation' is seen (1983: paras 1, 12, 18, 24, 36). It is common then to assume, as Plant does, that Baudrillard is merely a reactionary plagiarist of the Situationists (1992:35–7, 134–9, 153–70), but this assumption should actually be reversed. Baudrillard is better understood as the sympathetic inheritor of a radical Durkheimian tradition that the Lettrists, Lefebvre and the Situationists themselves plagiarized. The latter all took up the ideas of the potlatch, the gift, the festival, sacrifice and reversibility while stripping them of their agonistic form to present them as models of idealized, post-revolutionary relations, reverting to a nostalgia and idealism absent in the Durkheimian tradition and in Baudrillard (Lefebvre, 1971:36; Knabb, 1981:337; Debord, 1983: paras 125–46; Vaneigem, 1994:75–82, 256–60; and Vienet, 1992:71–90).

Baudrillard reformulates his conception of the symbolic throughout his career, also later becoming uneasy with the formal, contractual implications of the term 'communication' (*Baudrillard Live* (*BL*), 57). However, a continuity of concerns is visible in his work and he explicitly returns to the ideas of 'Requiem for the media' in his 1992 lecture, 'The vanishing point of communication' (1992d). There, he distinguishes human relations and 'communication', arguing that the latter is 'a modern invention' as 'a new mode of production and circulation of speech, connected to the media and to the technology of the media' (p. 3). Previously, he says, 'neither the word nor the concept' existed. 'People don't need to communicate, because they just speak to each other. Why communicate when it is so easy to speak to each other?' (p. 3). The term 'communication' is now reserved, therefore, for modern societies of non-communication which respond to the symbolic demand for communication by developing electronic technologies to rejoin their own isolated populations and circulate and promote its simulation (p. 4).

'When facing the structure of communication' we must never forget, Baudrillard says, that 'its very essence is non-communication' and that this 'has consequences for the future of all human relations' (p. 4). Today the 'act' of speech has become the 'operation' of communication, the dramaturgical scene of exchange passing over into an operationality without contradiction, tension, intensity, contact or disruption. 'We have invented structures of relationship where humans can communicate without crossing each other', passing like 'commuters', he concludes (p. 5), replacing 'the singularity of the self and of the other' with an aseptic, formal connectedness and circulation and 'the superficial fluidity of the electronic screen of communication' (p. 5). As he argues, this connectedness reduces us to an overexposed 'schizophrenic' state, unable to separate ourselves from the world, existing as 'a pure screen, a pure absorption and resorption surface of the influent networks' (*The Ecstasy of Communication (EC)*, 27). In an electronic fulfilment of Caillois's 'psychasthenic' 'depersonalization by assimilation to space' (Caillois, 1984:30), our electronic environment absorbs and incorporates us.

Baudrillard's arguments end, therefore, in an extreme picture of human relations. The problems of this position, however, are clear, not the least being a blanket rejection of all forms of mediation, and of electronic media in particular, that is inherently limiting. In particular, Baudrillard's claims of media 'non-communication' are interesting but ignore the myriad forms of human relations created by electronic media, from the empathetic relations produced by a global awareness of the lives of others to relations either produced, maintained or rediscovered electronically. Today, for example, stories of electronic contact leading to friendships, relationships or marriage or of reunited families and friends are common and Baudrillard's arguments place him in direct opposition to the entire thriving literature on electronic communities and contact (see Bell and Kennedy, 2000), as well as to our own common sense and everyday experience.

In addition, Baudrillard's emphasis on unilaterality appears to suggest a passive, receiving audience that is rejected by the dominant contemporary paradigms of media and communication studies and their focus on the 'active audience' (Ang, 1985; Fiske, 1987; Abercrombie and Longhurst, 1998). This theory traces its origins in part to the 1970s 'Culturalist' approach of Hall (1980) and Morley (Morley and Brunsdon, 1978; Morley, 1980), whose discovery of audience reception was itself influenced by Williams's rejection of McLuhan's emphasis on form and perceived technological determinism (R. Williams, 1977, 1983, 1990). Thus, in emerging out of this McLuhanist tradition, Baudrillard's work becomes susceptible to the same criticisms.

In contrast, active audience theory rejects the dominance of form and empha-sizes the range of individual responses to the media and the possible oppos-itional readings and practices that may be developed. Finally, the contemporary rise of 'interactive' digital media such as the internet and cable and satellite TV also make Baudrillard's claims for media unilaterality obsolete.

These are all important arguments, but arguably they leave much of Baudrillard's argument intact. Though his position is extreme it does have the merit of making the question of the form and effects of media visible again in an original and provocative way. He makes us question whether electronic media necessarily *add* to human communication or whether they merely replace it as quicker and more convenient, simplifying our effort and invest-ment. He also makes us question the value of its content: whether it actually constitutes *communication* or just a reduction and simplification of human expression and meaning. Even when our media appear to exponentially increase communication, this is predicated, as Baudrillard suggests, on a sep-aration from one's proximate environment and finds fulfilment only in so far as it simulates or promises that symbolic relationship they claim to promote but which their use actually replaces. Phone calls, for example, act not just as a means of communication but also as a means to *avoid* communication. 'Keeping in touch' by phone allows us to forestall physical contact while retaining a nominal friendship, and now even the physical time and effort of the phone call can be conjured away with email or a continuous flow of brief and meaningless texts. Hence the paradox Baudrillard presents us with: a world whose proliferating digital technologies simultaneously represent a much vaunted and almost epochal increase in communication and the simul-taneous systematic destruction, reduction, simplification and replacement of human relations. Our refusal to even see this paradox indicates the extent to which the technologies have penetrated our lives, placing themselves and their effects beyond question.

The mobile phone provides one example of this. Its popular take-up through the late 1990s transformed it from a much ridiculed and even pub-licly despised elite gadget to an essential component of individual life and communication. In the process it also moved beyond criticism such that all critical analysis of its use and its transformation of social relations appears reactionary and old-fashioned. It does, however, provide an excellent Baudrillardian example of a form that only appears to increase communica-tion, the streets full of oblivious, down-turned individuals thumbing their abbreviated and almost meaningless messages back and forth representing a dystopic realization of that world of non-communication he described in 1971. In his *Cool Memories 4* (*CM4*) of 2000, Baudrillard suggests exactly this. For him the man in the street 'talking away to no one' represents 'a new urban figure', one imposing on everyone else 'the virtual presence of the network'. Emphasizing the priority of symbolic relations against such a sociality and public imposition, Baudrillard describes him as 'a living insult to the passers by' (p. 24).

Baudrillard, therefore, rejects the McLuhanist assumption that 'organic' electronic technology offers a more human experience (McLuhan, 1994:248). Whereas at least mechanical technology 'knows it is a machine', the interface of interactive screens and smart technologies leads, he says, to a 'biological confusion' between 'man and his prostheses'. Thus instead of a McLuhanist extension of man, they reverse themselves to implode into, penetrate and assimilate man and end their relations (*CM4*, 82). The mobile phone – 'that incrustation of the network in your head' – leads, he argues, to a state of living death: to the half-life of public 'zombies' (*CM4*, 24), like that figure he reports walking unseeing around an exhibition, 'looking at someone he is not speaking to . . . talking to someone he cannot see' (*CM4*, 81). 'Simultaneously elsewhere', their behaviour doesn't represent an increased sociability, Baudrillard says, but a retreat from the world into 'the mobile confinement of the network' and 'a further phase in the electronic colonisation of the senses' (*CM4*, 24, 103) and thus in our psychasthenic absorption.

If Baudrillard's position is unfashionable within the mainstream discipline his McLuhanist emphasis on form is a valid, opposing perspective; one that is being rediscovered especially in debates around new media. Just as McLuhan argues that the more environmental a medium becomes the harder it is even to recognize its form and effects, and the more urgent this task becomes, so Baudrillard's work takes the same position, allying this to a specific critical project. Thus, in contrast to active audience theories which are often uninterested in the issue (K. Williams, 2003:206), Baudrillard explicitly presents a theory and analysis of media power and its operation. Influenced by the western Marxist critique of consumer society and media in the work of Lefebvre (1971), Marcuse (1986) and Debord (1983), extended through McLuhanism, Barthes' semiology and a Durkheimian critical position, it is one that sees media power as lying in form: in its destruction of the symbolic and its replacement with a semiotic simulation that functions not only as a mode of communication but also as a mode of social control and integration.

Baudrillard's argument has its merits. Our relationship to media *is* limited by their form, by their technical nature, operation and capacities, and this does have corresponding epistemological and relational effects. His McLuhanism demonstrates how individual use and choices are irrelevant in considering the media's operation, while his claims regarding their precessionary, semiotically processed output alerts us to how many of our responses are produced and coded in advance. Active audience theories, therefore, valorize behaviour that is of limited significance in comparison to the effects of the form and structure and operation of the media. Indeed, Baudrillard's work reveals that much of this behaviour – our individual reception and pleasurable use of the media – forms part of that process of 'personalization' that he sees as operating within contemporary consumption and, as such, as representing not an expression of individuality and freedom but only of our precoded production and integration in a system of social control. Thus we can reverse the common assumption in the discipline that Baudrillard is a postmodernist, uninterested in questions of media power, to see instead that the Marxist-Culturalist project of Hall ends in the postmodernism of active audience theories, whose naive individualism is exposed by Baudrillard's critical emphasis on form, effects and power.

Even the new forms of 'interactivity' found in contemporary digital media offer support for Baudrillard's critical position. Most of these, such as internet browsing, email and chat-rooms, allow a greater response and even a private, bilateral relationship, but this again represents only an improvement in the electronic simulation of the symbolic, rather than its discovery, offering no challenge to their mediation and replacement of their relations. Other modes of interactivity, such as that pioneered by digital television, involve only a choice of screens or services or merely update the readers' letters, phone-ins and polls of print and radios and their limited and controlled response. If digital sports channels now offer a more individually tailored, attractive and leisurely experience than actual attendance, with a choice of views making more reality available in the home than for those in the stands, arguably this increase in interactivity only serves as an even greater cover for the fundamental absence of the symbolic and its experience.

The limitations of this interaction are most clearly seen in the common invitation by news channels for email feedback on their stories and viewer voting on issues of the day. In practice limited time is devoted to these emails. Few are read out and those that are, are carefully selected, make only the briefest and simplest of points and are negated by the immediate presentation of a balancing opposing view to forestall any suggestion of bias, to simulate debate, to represent the assumed range of opinions and to signify the unresolved complexities of each issue. This remains, therefore, a tightly controlled simulation of communication. Nothing is changed about the content of the story or the structure of the media; the personal emphasis and subjectivity of the contributors contrasts with the fact-based approach of the bulletins to reinforce belief in the latter's objective truth, and any critical points made instantly vanish into the media's black hole, being immediately forgotten and having no effect or significance.[1] As in that 'referendum' mode Baudrillard identifies as operating today ('The order of simulacra' (OS), 67–9), these reactions do not constitute a bilateral communication but only its simulation. The media do not reflect and represent the reality of the public but instead *produce* it, employing this simulation to justify their own continuing existence. Thus news feedback functions to confirm to itself, and to convince us, that someone is watching, that the news is important, and that the public are politically interested and mobilized. Desperately needing this confirmation, news programmes tailor questions, debates and features to provoke it, encouraging viewers to follow and contribute towards the arguments or the fluctuating percentage results of the selected vote of the day. Instead of an interaction this process constitutes an operational simulation in which precoded and integrated responses primarily function to support the system and its semiotic processing of everyday life.

If, however, Baudrillard's media theory pushes us towards a pessimism regarding the processes of contemporary media, it is a pessimism that is never complete. The Durkheimian school believed in the continuing existence and efficacy of the sacred and the felt need for its relations and meaning, searching for its surviving forms – whether those corrupted forms serving as a safety valve for profane society or the radical forms which might still threaten it. For Baudrillard, similarly, the symbolic is 'inevitable' (*SED* 2), due to both the need felt for its energies and their release, and in its 'reversibility' – its ability to challenge all fixed, unilateral power relations (*FF*), unsettling their single pole to reinstitute a cycle of relations and a speech and response. This power is always present and radically realizable, for, Baudrillard says, 'nothing, not even the system, can avoid the symbolic obligation' (*SED*, 37). Like 'a dominant motif long forgotten', the symbolic haunts us. In *The Mirror of Production* (*MP*) Baudrillard suggests that this is where the contemporary west is weak. It is vulnerable not at the level of the economic 'but at the level of the production of social relations', surviving only by creating the illusion of those symbolic relations it abolishes (p. 143). Thus it responded to the crisis of 1929 by mobilizing its population as consumers rather than just producers, allowing people to discover in semiotic consumption and its 'simulation' of the symbolic 'the illusion of symbolic participation' (p. 144). But Baudrillard suggests that this tension is never resolved, with every society facing the potential 'perdition' of its abolition of the symbolic and the potential counter-gift of those who refuse its simulation. For Baudrillard this perdition may take many forms, including the internal reversal of the semiotic processes themselves, the global response of external symbolic forces to the west, or the internal irruption of symbolic forces within the semiotic.

THE COMMUNION OF THE EXCOMMUNICATED

'A day will come', Durkheim wrote, 'when our societies will know again those hours of creative effervescence' (1915:427–8). As Bataille argues, however, contemporary societies cannot countenance such disruption, the unifying sacred appearing as a subversive force in societies built on its expulsion and 'destruction' (1994:107). Thus our media operates today to simulate in a safe form that lost sociality and shared meaning functioning, along with consumption, as a means of social control. For the festivals and violence of tribal society it substitutes today permanent football, the national lottery game show, morning television and its best-friend presenters, premier-plus 'event' movies, rolling news coverage, voyeuristic makeover programmes, sensationalist, tabloid-hyped soaps and the public pain, humiliation and hate figures of reality TV. The whole serves to expurgate expressive energies and social forces that might otherwise demand another, more immediate release. The hatch, match and dispatch of celebrity culture and the spectacle of a good royal funeral and sports final become essential purgatives, providing a simulated collective meaning for a profanized, individualized society, all instantly available without even having to leave our homes or have any social contact.

For Baudrillard this system remains haunted by the possible failure of this simulation and by the violence the symbolic demand might unleash. David Fincher's film *Fight Club* (Fincher, 1999) provides one fanciful depiction of a rejection of an Ikea lifestyle and a turn to the symbolic – to physical violence and personal risk – to rediscover a meaning lost in the participants' lives. But more generally we can see the same processes operating in public criminality and violence and in the periodic festivals of urban rioting. Writing in 1986 about Reagan's America and its policies of disenfranchisement and desocialization, Baudrillard identified a process of 'excommunication' which attains a particular significance in our 'communications based societies'. Today's threat, therefore, comes from those abandoned in their 'new deserts' (*America* (*Am.*), 113), from the desocialized rejecting even the simulated communication of television in favour of the violent communion of the excommunicated: the paroxysm of the riot and of destruction. As Baudrillard says, 'something in all men profoundly rejoices in seeing a car burn' (*MP*, 141). Thus, for Baudrillard, a counter-gift is always possible to a system which tries to replace, ignore or drown out with images and messages and consumer technologies that which is inevitable:

Against the triumphant abstraction, against the irreversible monopolization, the demand arises that nothing can be given without being returned, nothing is ever won without something being lost, nothing is ever produced without something being destroyed, nothing is ever spoken without something being answered. In short, what haunts the system is the symbolic demand.

(*MP*, 147)

It is this relationship between the processes of simulation and this symbolic demand that will form the key theme of this book, being returned to and explored throughout the later chapters. However, having now defined and defended the symbolic, I next want to turn to and consider the opposing force of the semiotic and its own reciprocal simulacral ungrounding of the symbolic.

2 To play with phantoms: the evil demon of the simulacrum

> But what becomes of the divinity when it reveals itself in icons, when it is multiplied in simulacra? Does it remain the supreme power that is simply incarnated in images as a visible theology? Or does it volatize itself in the simulacra that, alone, deploy their power and pomp of fascination – the visible machinery of icons substituted for the pure and intelligible Idea of God? This was precisely what was feared by Iconoclasts, whose millennial quarrel is still with us today.
>
> Baudrillard, 'The precession of simulacra'

> They that make them are like unto them: so is everyone who trusteth in them.
>
> Psalms, 115:8 (on idols)

In the previous chapter I introduced the central organizing principles of Baudrillard's work: the distinction of symbolic and semiotic, the origins of the semiotic in the abolition of the symbolic, the characterization of our society as defined by this transformation, and his critical sympathy with the symbolic as a surviving force against the semiotic. In this chapter I want to consider Baudrillard's theory of the semiotic and, in particular, its operation as a 'simulation' or 'simulacrum'. These are significant ideas in his work with his media theory resting on a critique of their processes. His discussion of media simulations and non-events will occupy the later chapters, but we first need to understand the concepts themselves, their origins, development and specific employment in Baudrillard's work. In this chapter, therefore, I provide an explanation of Baudrillard's development of the simulacrum, a historical contextualization for the idea and the force it names, and a discussion of his later reformulation of the concepts and the problems it poses for his work. This will enable me to introduce the basis of a critique of Baudrillard that must be borne in mind through the later chapters and that I will return to again at the end.

Before I can do this, however, we first have to clear the critical ground. The simulacrum is one of Baudrillard's most famous and controversial concepts and certain problems with its reception and interpretation must be dealt with before we can approach it anew (see also R. Butler, 1999:23–6; Grace, 2000:105–8). The first of these is its association with postmodernism. As a result of Baudrillard's subsumption within this movement the simulacrum becomes the defining and iconic postmodern concept. With the popularity of postmodernism the concept attracted much critical attention, becoming both widely used in cultural and media and communication studies and a fashionable trope for broadsheet journalism to be applied to any manifestation of our imagic society. It also became the focus of opprobrium for the critics of postmodernism, being perceived as the most blatant example of that movement's rejection of truth and certainty, political and ethical bankruptcy and pseudo-intellectual mystifications. For these critics, the concept itself was unacceptable, to be met with and rejected by a moral appeal to reality, and any attempt to seriously consider its meaning or application was seen as sufficient to disqualify one's work from consideration. This denial of the simulacrum and its force, however, displayed a remarkable historical ignorance, running contrary to the entire western tradition which has recognized and opposed its existence from the beginning. As I shall argue, the simulacrum is not a postmodern concept as many seem to believe (Best, in Kellner, 1994:42), but a far older, stranger and more fundamental phenomenon. This history has been obscured by its continued contextualization within postmodernism and by its standardized and repeated, poorly explained and by now almost meaningless definition in these textbooks as 'a copy without an original'.

This association with postmodernism is largely responsible for another error dominating the popular understanding of the simulacrum: its misidentification by its critics as an idealist or sceptical category implying the denial of physical reality and the claim that ours is a 'fictive', artificial or virtual reality, an unreality or mass media 'illusion'. This view is found especially in the work of Kellner and Norris, who employ a simplistic Marxist materialism in which any questioning of the concept and experience of the real constitutes a 'semiological idealism' and a denial 'that reality exists' (Best and Kellner, 1991:139). Such basic errors stem again from the failure to consider the historical context of the concept, but this is an omission shared by many sympathetic interpreters of Baudrillard too. With the exception of Butler's deeper philosophical analysis (1999) and Rajan's recent discussion (2004), most commentators have been content to limit themselves to a discussion of Baudrillard's most famous essays, 'The order of simulacra' (OS), and 'The precession of simulacra' (PS).[1] Such a focus comes at the expense of earlier and later analyses of the concept by Baudrillard that would both deepen and complicate this picture and, in explaining the simulacrum only through a summary of his own language and formulation, adds little to our understanding of it. Even when critics attempt to draw links to other figures such as Plato, Nietzsche, Foucault, Marx, Kracauer, Benjamin and Debord,[2] the approach is non-systematic and misses the wider implications and trajectories. The acceptance of an agreed line of intellectual descent for Baudrillard's work and a fixed framework for its interpretation has prevented the broader historical, philosophical and theological significance of the concept from being recognized.

In order to grasp and appreciate the nature and force of the simulacrum, therefore, we need to contextualize it within these histories. The simulacrum is an ancient concept but its force appears or is discoverable within the philosophical, theological and aesthetic traditions of every culture, centring on the concept of the image and its efficacy. The image has always been conceived of as powerful, as possessing a remarkable hold on our hearts and minds and as having the power to assume for us, in that moment, the force of that which it represents, to become the reality and erase therein the distinction of original and image. In the west this power has long been interpreted as a moral threat to the real and as a demonic force, with every effort being made to domesticate the image again as a copy and banish its evil demon. The image, however, is not so easily reduced, retaining its power to unground all foundations for truth and overturn those ontological and epistemological traditions the west has built itself on. Baudrillard's work recognizes this nihilistic power of the image, seeing it as reappearing in contemporary simulacra, though the 'violent phantasm' of nihilism has now given way, he says, to a new, cool, communicational, operational and transparent form: that of the world of simulation and hyperreality (*Simulacra and Simulation* (*SS*), 159).

While Baudrillard describes these processes, it must be remembered that in his commitment to the symbolic against the semiotic he also opposes them. Thus the nihilism he identifies is not *his*, as critics naively assert (Kellner, 1989:117–21; 1994:11–12; Best and Kellner, 1991:126–8), but that of the image itself, which Baudrillard also targets. Baudrillard's critics, however, have paid too little attention to his critical position, seeing him in some way as positively advancing the idea and the cause of simulacra, and thus opposing him with the real. As I will argue, this opposition is misplaced as Baudrillard himself appeals to the real as a critical force against the simulacrum. If, therefore, we want to destabilize his work we must oppose him not with the real but with the simulacrum, not rejecting but accepting, employing and escalating its force to challenge his work and his critical privileging of the symbolic. This is, after all, a strategy he recommends. As he argues in *Symbolic Exchange and Death*, 'we must . . . turn Mauss against Mauss, Saussure against Saussure, and Freud against Freud' (p. 1). So too, therefore, we must turn Baudrillard against Baudrillard.

'SO WE LIVE, SHELTERED BY SIGNS'

The main themes of the simulacrum are already present in Baudrillard's earliest work. His first book, *The System of Objects*, follows Barthes's *The Fashion System* in seeing a transformation of the object into a sign for consumption and 'a simulacrum of the real object' (Barthes, 1990a:xii). Unlike in Barthes, however, the sign originates for Baudrillard in the transformation of the 'traditional symbolic objects' into a sign of the lost relation (*SO*, 200): a Durkheimian theme of the transformation of the symbolic into its semiotic simulacrum that dominates his early work.

Baudrillard's first major discussion of electronic media in *The Consumer Society* makes this clear. For him, the electronic mass media function by translating the symbolic into the semiotic, transforming 'the lived, eventual, character of the world' into signs of itself (pp. 122–3). 'So we live,' he says, 'sheltered by signs, in the denial of the real', consuming reality as a sign, with all events, meaning and history no longer being produced from 'shifting, contradictory, real experience', but 'produced as artifacts' by the media (p. 125). In this 'vast *process of simulation*', coded significatory elements are combined to create a 'neo-reality' which 'assumes the force of reality', abolishing it 'in favour of this *neo-reality of the model*' (p. 126). Baudrillard, however, is clear: this is not an unreal process but one with 'material force', occurring 'over the whole span of daily life' (p. 126). In these early texts, therefore, Baudrillard advances a simple critique of the transformation of the lived, symbolic reality into signs which are combined to create a culturally constructed 'neo-reality': a process of 'simulation' in which the real is eclipsed and replaced for us by its simulacrum.

This synonymity of the symbolic and the real is reconsidered in *For a Critique of the Political Economy of the Sign*, where Baudrillard not only finally separates the symbolic and semiotic but also, as part of his poststructuralist critique of the political economy of the sign, develops an important, and to date overlooked, critique of the 'real' as a semiotic category. As we have seen, this critique involves the identification in both commodity and sign of a secondary content that appears to be natural and external (use value and needs, and the signified and the referent), that is actually internal to and produced by the dominant form to support and promote its operation (exchange and sign value). This content serves as an 'effect of concrete reality and objective purpose' (p. 148), grounding the form and acting as the absolute guarantor for it such that this content – human needs and referential reality - become unquestionable categories.

This referent - the 'reality' the sign points to – is not, however, external but is a product of the sign and its prior reduction of the complex, experiential symbolic relationship. Thus what we call 'reality', Baudrillard argues, is only 'the simulacrum of the symbolic' (p. 162), the 'phantasm' of the symbolic meaning it reduces to semiotic difference (p. 149). The referent, therefore, 'is only an extrapolation of the excision established by the logic of the sign onto the world of things' (p. 155). It is only ever 'the world as it is seen and interpreted through the sign': 'The "real" table does not exist. If it can be registered in its identity (if it exists), this is because it has already been *designated*, abstracted and rationalized by the separation which establishes it in this equivalence to itself' (p. 155).

Our 'real', therefore, is only a semiotic 'reality effect' (p. 160): the world as it is filtered and processed through the linguistic and imagic sign. For Baudrillard the symbolic remains outside of these processes as a lived, though unnamable and unsignifiable, reality standing in opposition to the dominant semiotic processes. The fundamental 'bar' of separation is not that structural line holding the logics of the commodity and sign together, but 'a line of radical exclusion' - 'the bar that separates all these terms from symbolic exchange' (p. 128). As the external threat of a 'radical rupture' of value (p. 125), and as that which 'tears all signifiers and signifieds to pieces' (p. 162), the symbolic becomes, therefore, Baudrillard's Durkheimian hope against the simulacrum.

Baudrillard escalates this description in *The Mirror of Production*, theorizing an acceleration of semiotic processes absorbing the referent, 'to the sole profit of the play of signifiers' (p. 127). This is the 'structural revolution in value' with which he opens *Symbolic Exchange and Death* (first published in 1976), and which he sees as inaugurating the current era of 'simulation' (*SED*, 6–9). Here, in a well-known genealogical sketch echoing Foucault's *The Order of Things* of 1966 (1970), Baudrillard traces the changing reference of the sign since its emancipation from the symbolic feudal world in the Renaissance with the 'counterfeit' sign's simulation of nature (OS, 50–3), through the serially produced simulacra of the industrial commodity (OS, 55–7), to contemporary forms '*conceived* according to their reproducibility', and reproduced from their model (OS, 56). In this present phase, 'signs are exchanged against each other rather than against the real', the combination of their signifiers resulting in 'a total relativity, general commutation and simulation' (*SED*, 7). In his later work Baudrillard adds a fourth 'fractal' order of simulacra to this (1992c:15–16; *The Transparency of Evil* (*TE*), 5–6) in which 'there is no longer a referent at all' as value 'radiates in all directions' (1992c:15), but the real remains again the product of a semiurgical combination.

In his early work, therefore, Baudrillard develops a semiotic conception of the 'simulacrum' as the transformation of the lived symbolic into the semiotic image, tracing a historical path for its emergence and demonstrating how our experiential reality has become a modelled, precessionary, semiotic production. These ideas are among the most important contemporary contributions to social and cultural theory, but there are tensions in Baudrillard's account that need to be addressed. Despite the brilliance of his genealogy of the sign, the examples he uses and his analysis of our semiotic production of the real and its referentiality, certain objections are possible. In particular the historical schema presented in 'The order of simulacra' suggests an abrupt division between the semiotic and symbolic orders in the Renaissance that is historically suspect and encourages claims of a 'nostalgia' in his work (Kellner, 1989:42–5). Baudrillard's 1978 essay 'The precession of simulacra' also complicates this schema by offering another historical genealogy for the simulacrum, this time moving back beyond the Renaissance to consider Christian debates on icons ('simulacra') (pp. 4–7).

Discussing the fate of divinity in its reproduction, Baudrillard argues that it was the iconoclasts, the breakers of images, who actually recognized the image's 'true value' and power. They saw that, incarnated and multiplied, God did not remain God but was volatized in images which henceforth 'alone, deploy their pomp and power of fascination'. They realized 'the omnipotence of simulacra', their faculty 'of erasing God from the conscience of man', and the 'destructive, annihilating truth' they reveal that only the simulacrum of God ever existed (pp. 4–5). While they could have lived with a distorted or hidden truth, their 'metaphysical despair' came from the idea that nothing was concealed and that these images were not images reflecting an original model, 'but perfect simulacra, forever radiant with their own fascination' (p. 5). Perhaps the idolaters realized the same thing, Baudrillard suggests, and so 'in the guise of having God become apparent in the mirror of images' enacted his death and disappearance 'in the epiphany of his representations' (p. 5).

At stake, Baudrillard says, is 'the murderous power of images': their power to murder the 'real' by murdering 'their own model' in favour of their own full reality (p. 5). The west has historically relied, he argues, on the 'wager of representation' (p. 5), on a simulation model of meaning (*CPES*, 161) that posits a 'divine referential' to ground the system, a strategy founded on the belief 'that the sign could be exchanged for meaning and that something could guarantee this exchange' (PS, 5). However, just as God's volatization in simulacra led to the 'annihilating truth' of his emptiness that threatened to make the whole system 'weightless' (PS, 5–6), and just as Nietzsche saw the death of the same divine referential in modernity as removing any transcendent guarantor of values and significance and precipitating us into an era of nihilism (Nietzsche, 1968a, 1974), so for Baudrillard these ungrounding forces reappear in our contemporary third and fourth order simulacra. Baudrillard names the same process, seeing the loss of fixed and guaranteed significatory value as cutting us adrift in a cool, weightless, nihilistic universe of simulacra (PS, 5; *SS*, 159).

Out of this discussion of icons Baudrillard develops another genealogy of simulation, tracing 'the successive phases of the image' from a reflection of reality, to masking reality, to masking its absence, and finally to having no relation to reality whatsoever as 'its own pure simulacrum' (PS, 6). He also explains this as the passage from the 'good', reflective image of the 'sacramental order', to the 'evil' image of the 'maleficent' order, to the image playing at appearance that partakes of the order of 'sorcery', to the image moving beyond appearances to enter simulation (PS, 6). But Baudrillard immediately simplifies this genealogy to emphasize 'the transition from signs that dissimulate something to signs that dissimulate that there is nothing', a passage from 'a theology of truth and secrecy' to that simulation marking our own contemporary era (PS, 6–7). These orders, however, do not directly map onto those in *Symbolic Exchange and Death*, and although they trace the same process of the emergence of the simulacrum they are not strictly historical or located historically. Moreover, in being directly inspired by the work of Perniola (1980), whose work appeared in *Traverses* in 1978, after the publication of *Symbolic Exchange and Death*, they simultaneously develop and contradict his earlier discussion of simulacra. They do suggest, however, that if we want to fully understand Baudrillard's use of the concept we need to consider, as Perniola does, the history of the concept and its transformations. Though this history can be sketched here only briefly we can nevertheless identify a consistent western response to the problem of the image in the attempts to demonize and domesticate its simulacral power.

'THOSE THINGS NOT OF GOD'

> Those things which are not of God, must be of his rival.
>
> Tertullian (on the 'idolatry' of women's cosmetics)

The history of the simulacrum is the history of the image and its power. Anthropological evidence suggests that a different attitude to images exists in 'primitive', tribal, traditional and many non-western societies, where images and imitation are commonly seen as *efficacious*: as powerful forms affecting the original from afar (Frazer, 1995:11). Taussig has refined this idea, arguing that the image does not affect the original 'sympathetically' but instead 'shares in or acquires the properties of the represented' (1993:47–8). As Freedberg says, the image becomes the real, 'however temporarily or fleetingly' (1989:277), possessing a power of transformation that implicitly erases the distinction of original and image. The rejection of this power of imagic transformation stands at the heart of the western culture. Hence in Judeo-Christianity the sacred was purified and placed outside of a now desacralized and deficient world. This world now became the mere image of the true reality, being reduced to and approved of as its powerless reflection and mediation, in a process of domestication that would recur throughout the western tradition.

Platonism developed a similar conception of the image and of this world as a mere reflection of a higher, originary reality, the world of forms. For Plato, in *The Republic*, this imagic realm is a deceptive one, tempting our bodies and minds away from the intellectual ascension to the intelligible world (Plato, 1955). Hence his hostility to art, to man-made images compounding our errors in standing 'at third remove from the throne of truth' (1955:425) and containing 'a terrible power to corrupt the best of characters' (1955:436). Plato moderates this condemnation in *The Sophist*, in praising the 'eikastic' image which participates in its form, reserving his hostility now for the 'phantastic' image which is only its 'appearance', 'apparition' and 'simulacrum' (1986:26–7, 66–8).[3] As Deleuze notes, Plato establishes a hierarchy running from the original model to the 'good' copy and to the phantastic image whose '*effect* of resemblance' simulates the real (Deleuze, 1983:49). But the simulacrum refuses this secondary position, Deleuze argues, containing 'a positive power which negates *both* original and copy, both model and reproduction' (1983:53). As 'the act by which the very idea of a model or privileged position is challenged or overturned' (Deleuze, 1994:69), the simulacrum represents for Plato a 'demonic' force in its threat to the real (1983:49; 1994:127). His entire project conspires, Deleuze says, to banish the simulacra, 'keeping them chained in the depths' (1983:48), to prevent their 'universal *ungrounding*' of the conditions of truth and certainty (1994:67).

This Platonic debate is paralleled in the earlier Judaic and later Judeo-Christian traditions and their controversies (see Barasch, 1992; Freedberg, 1989; Ries, 1987). Judaism saw the world as 'good' as a reflection of the divine (Genesis, 1: 1–31), but retained a suspicion of its power to captivate men's minds and senses, hence Judaism's prohibition of 'graven images' (Exodus, 20: 4), and images of the divine in particular (Barasch, 1992:13–22). As we have seen, such 'eidolon' – translated as 'idol' or 'simulacrum'[4] – were believed to contain the power to replace the divine for worshippers. Their apparent life and efficacy were explained as the result of demonic possession (see Deuteronomy, 32: 16–17), an attribution surviving in the Greek Apocrypha and New Testament and becoming a major theme in early Geek and Latin thought (Barasch, 1992). Despite the acceptance of images by the Second Council of Nicea in 787 as allowing a 'relative veneration', the question mark over their status as good copies or evil simulacra remained, occasionally fuelling iconoclastic outbursts and crises in the Christian church (Candea, 1987a, 1987b; Freedberg, 1989:378–428).

|The west responded to the threat of the image by its simultaneous demonization and domestication|as a powerless copy by the establishment of an absolute referential ground for truth and certainty. As Deleuze suggests, however, the image is not so easily dealt with, retaining a simulacral power against all foundations raised against it.|The problem it poses explicitly reappears at the heart of the epistemological debates of the seventeenth to eighteenth centuries. The Cartesian cogito, for example, helpless before the 'evil demon' which surrounds it with images whose resemblance to any external original is unproven (Descartes, 1968:100, 118), requires a God to ground the apparitions produced by this simulacral deity – before, as Foucault observes, God's 'marvellous twin' (Klossowski, 1998a:xxiii). Given, however, that this God is only proved by the ungrounded ground of the same cogito,[5] the subject finds itself once more delivered back to the evil demon of images.

Empiricism's quest for epistemological certainty, founded in the subject's sensations, their repeated experience and external correspondence, faced the same problem of the simulacrum. It is no coincidence that when Bacon spells out his hopes in his *Novum Organum* of an inductive training 'to open and establish a new course for the mind from the first and actual perceptions of the senses themselves' (1952:105), it is the 'idols' – the phantoms of the mind men bow down to – which turn us from truth (1952:109–16). This empiricism faced other problems. Not only does the mind depart from experience in its ideas (Deleuze, 1990:266–79), but, as Berkeley's criticism of Locke made clear, these ideas are ultimately all we know. Only the sensation, not its external cause, is experienced, so, for Berkeley, God is again needed to ground and guarantee appearances. Hume saw no such guarantor, and his entire empiricism demonstrates a remarkable sensitivity to the problem of the simulacrum – those resemblant, ungrounded impressions whose cause and original remain unknown and unprovable and whose reality effect passes away to leave only copies in the memory that simulate their force (1969:132, 142, 155, 157, 8–9). Though Hume later found it prudent to reject this force (1966:17), his work still exposes the internal collapse of empiricism through the simulacrum. Or it would, were not the same simulacra powerful enough to convince us all of their reality. Thus, Hume admits, he only has to immerse himself back in the world to find his own arguments 'cold, strain'd and ridiculous' (1969:316). The same simulacra that remove the possibility of truth also cover up its absence.

For Nietzsche, Hume represents the end of the 'history of an error': the error by which the material world was reduced to a reflection of a transcendent 'real world' (1968b:40–1). Finally exposed by empiricism, we should finally abolish this 'myth', he says, but once we do, 'what world is left?', for '*with the real world we have abolished the apparent world*' (1968b:41). Both original and image give way to a purely simulacral realm of appearances, a world dominated by 'the will to power' whose energetic forces have no guarantee but its own effect (see 1968a). Thus the 'twilight of the idols', of 'the old truth' (1979:116), is itself accomplished by idols.[6] Thus, Nietzsche makes us aware, western epistemology has been marked by the repeated attempt to found a certain ground to guarantee knowledge and truth and its repeated destabilization by simulacral forces that assert their own reality, making these certain distinctions impossible.

It is these same simulacral productions that Baudrillard is concerned with in *Symbolic Exchange and Death*. Contrary to readings that discover in it a passage from the Renaissance to modernity and postmodernity, he does not describe a series of socioeconomic formations but a series of eras definable in terms of their dominant simulacral productions and their epistemological effects. Despite the problems of his account, Baudrillard succeeds in simultaneously tracing a genealogy of these signs, emphasizing their discontinuities and transformations, while, in employing the philosophical and theological concept of the simulacrum, linking these to a longer tradition demonstrating the continued appearance of this simulacral force.

This explains why, of all the contemporary thinkers who have drawn on the simulacrum, it is Baudrillard's use that has come to dominate. Though influenced by Klossowski and Deleuze he moves beyond their use of the concept, unifying Benjaminian and McLuhanist discussions of reproductive technology, Foucaultian genealogy and Marxist and semiological analyses of our media culture, drawing out and historically contextualizing the simulacral processes they describe and relating their operation to contemporary media society. Like Perniola, he demonstrates the continuing appearance and operation of the simulacrum at the heart of our productions, recognizing that the processes of our media can only be understood in the context of the simulacral efficacy of the image. As he says, the iconoclast's 'millennial quarrel is still with us today' (PS, 4). The 'virtual and irreversible confusion' of the sphere of images and of a reality 'whose nature we are less and less able to grasp' are testimony to the continued existence of 'the evil demon of images' and its 'diabolical seduction' (*The Evil Demon of Images* (*EDI*), 13, 28). Given that texts in media and communication studies rarely offer any contextualization for the image beyond contemporary theories and examples, Baudrillard's value lies in restoring a historical and philosophical dimension that the contemporary field clearly lacks.

It is no coincidence that those thinkers whose work has been most influential on Baudrillard are those who have, implicitly or explicitly, recognized this simulacral process. As his references to McLuhan suggest, the latter's concern with the power of our own extended images to remake our psychic and sensory lives after themselves (McLuhan, 1994:41) describes exactly this, then serial and simulacral book form, for example, giving rise to 'typographic man' (McLuhan, 1962). Marx also emphasized the imagic power of the serial commodity form, his idea of 'fetishism' – derived from Christian anthropology's description of the demonically possessed idol's 'bewitchment' of its worshippers (*CPES*, 88; Ries, 1987:80) – directly linking the commodity's processes to the simulacrum. Like Christianity, Marx explains its power as due to an evil possession and animation, its 'wooden brain' forming 'grotesque ideas' as soon as it 'steps forward as a commodity' (1954:76). The commodity, therefore, is phantasmagoric – a spirit in the marketplace, a phantasma and phantom, a fusion of ghostly and imagic life and sensory reality eclipsing the lives of the proletariat and mystifying the real in its simulacral usurpation of its position.

This imagic inversion of the real would become a major theme in twentieth-century Marxism, especially once the impact of developments in mass media and popular culture came to be recognized, being foregrounded in the work of Lukács (1971), Benjamin (1997a, 1999), Kracauer (1995), Adorno and Horkheimer (1997), Marcuse (1986) and Debord (1983), all of which, of course, provides one lineage for Baudrillard's work. For all the prescience of these analyses, however, Marxist proscriptions merely repeat the traditional western response to the image, opposing it with the hope of its demystification and an appeal to a recoverable real. As the later Debord was forced to concede, however, the simulacral process could not be so simply contained (1990:9).

Baudrillard finds a more insightful analysis of simulacral effects in the work of Benjamin and Boorstin. Benjamin's 1936 'artwork' essay obviously charts the same simulacral processes Baudrillard describes, emphasizing in particular the impact on the auratic relationship of the reproductive technologies of photography[7] and film (Benjamin, 1973:211–44), while Boorstin's 1961 book *The Image* repeats these ideas in its description of the twentieth century's 'graphic revolution' and the creation of a world 'where fantasy is more real than reality, where the image has more dignity than the original' (Boorstin, 1992:205). The results for Boorstin are 'new categories of experience . . . no longer classifiable by the old common sense tests of true or false' and thus a 'reshaping of our very concept of truth' (1992:211, 205). If he too hoped for a recovery of the real, his comment that today 'the Grand Canyon has become a disappointing reproduction of the Kodachrome original' (1992:14) suggests again that the simulacral process is too far advanced.

Ironically, therefore, those critics of Baudrillard who reject the concept of the simulacrum and deny its force can only do so by ignoring its historical appearance and its *reality*. But Baudrillard's aim is not just to identify its force but also to oppose its contemporary semiotic manifestation. As we have seen, his critique of the sign is based on an appeal to the Durkheimian symbolic; however its deployment as a critical ground against the simulacrum is problematic. Firstly, Baudrillard's absolute distinction of symbolic and semiotic ties him into a simplistic opposition to the realm of appearances. Secondly, this distinction is compromised by the use of simulation in the primitive festivals and rituals as a means of opening the sacred and creating symbolic relations. Thus Durkheim places an emphasis on the role of mimesis in the tribal reproduction of the totem (1995:335–6), Caillois discusses the simulation of the ancestor-Gods in the festival (1980:97–127) and Klossowski describes the use of simulacra – statuary – in Roman rites (1998b:123–5). If therefore, simulation is commonly used in producing the symbolic, on what basis can Baudrillard distinguish these phenomena from the later simulations he criticizes? Thus the same historical background that allows us to recognize the reality of Baudrillard's concept of the simulacrum also provides us with the means to question the coherence of his use of it.

More importantly this discussion also allows us to historically contextualize the symbolic, not, as Baudrillard believes, as a pre- and anti-western phenomenon that opposes the symbolic, but within the western tradition as another attempt to raise a critical ground against the simulacrum. Thus the symbolic plays the role within Baudrillard's work of that 'real' that he had earlier rejected as a referential category, operating for him as an immediately actualized relationship and mode of experience and meaning serving as a ground against the processes of simulation. Despite his claims that it cannot be named or privileged, it is repeatedly given an explicit Durkheimian lineage and formulation. Thus Baudrillard repeats the western response to the simulacrum in domesticating it before a guaranteed real, the symbolic. He becomes precisely that iconoclast his reputation suggests, sharing, in his desire to break the image, the same recognition of its 'true value' and the same 'metaphysical despair' before its power.

THE 'PORNOGRAPHY' OF THE REAL

> Lying is not only saying what isn't true. It is also, in fact especially, saying more than is true.
>
> Camus, *The Outsider*

Perhaps in response to these problems Baudrillard began to reformulate his position. As Levin argues, between *Symbolic Exchange and Death* in 1976 and *Seduction* in 1979, 'the significance of the sign suddenly reverses in Baudrillard's thought' (Levin, 1996:128). Formerly opposed to the symbolic it now becomes 'the best available medium for the irruption of the symbolic in the smooth functioning of the "cool" universe of tertiary simulation' (1996:128). From *Forget Foucault* in 1977, Baudrillard's key opposition is that between 'seduction' and 'production'. The latter term, meaning 'to render visible, to cause to appear and be made to appear: *producere'* (*FF*, 21), designates the processes of the semiotic order devoted to the forced materialization of the real. Against this Baudrillard describes the order of seduction, which involves 'a mastering of the realm of appearances' (*EC*, 62), and the process of their withdrawal, in a game of signs creating a symbolic relationship, to other participants, to the order of appearances, or to the world itself.

Thus the sign is no longer antithetical to the symbolic but, as the Durkheimian tradition suggests, instrumental in its actualization. Its 'enchanted simulation' turns the 'evil forces' of appearances against truth, he argues, to create a 'charmed universe' of seduction (*EC*, 75; *Sed.*, 144). Against this Baudrillard describes again the realm of the 'disenchanted' simulacrum whose 'hyperreality'[8] eclipses experience in its technical perfection and absolute semio-realization of the real. The simulacrum, therefore, is marked not by an unreality but instead by its *excess* of reality and truth, by a 'diabolical' conformity (*EDI*, 13–15) that makes it 'more real than the real' (*Fatal Strategies* (*FS*), 11). Pornography is exemplary here, Baudrillard says, as its motivating phantasy is reality, believing that the truth of sexuality can be discovered through the production of more reality, by a 'forcing of signs' and hypervisibility (*Sed.*, 28). This is our modern form of 'obscenity', Baudrillard says: a mode devoted to the overexposed, the 'all-too-visible' (*EC*, 22), the 'absolute proximity of the thing seen' and a 'hypervision in close-up' (*FS*, 59–60). Its representation is dominated by a 'vertiginous phantasy of exactitude' (*Sed.*, 30) requiring everything to 'pass over into the absolute evidence of the real' (*Sed.*, 29). This 'orgy of realism', summoning everything before 'the jurisdiction of signs', constitutes, Baudrillard says, the 'devastation of the real' (*Sed.*, 31–2).

The obscene is founded, therefore, on the abolition of the symbolic 'scene' and its relationship. It involves no reciprocity but only a transparent hypervisible image, a 'pure and simple exhibition' in which everything is immediately realized for us in advance in a single hyperreal dimension (*OS*, 72) such that 'we have nothing to add, that is to say nothing to give in exchange' (*Sed.*, 30). Faced with 'this cadaver-like hypersimilitude', our only option, like the visitors to the exhibition of hyperreal sculpture Baudrillard describes, is to stare 'fascinated and . . . dumbfounded' at the obviousness and banality of the real, to 'verify to the point of vertigo the useless objectivity of things' (*SSM*, 43). When the 'hot' symbolic scene is replaced by the 'cold' obscene we face the real, therefore, not as something living but as something 'dead' (*FS*, 51), with the 'nihilistic passion' of 'fascination' (*SS*, 160), a claim echoing Barthes's description of scrutinizing the sleeping body of his lover like a corpse, a detached fascination broken only by his sudden stirring (Barthes, 1990b:71–2).

If the Durkheimian tradition is one source for this conception of symbolic experience, we can also recognize debts to other thinkers. In particular Heidegger's analysis of the transformation of the mode of appearance of Being – from a presencing to and from unconcealment to a forced materialization of the real abolishing all distance but bringing no 'nearness' (Heidegger, 1971a:165; 1977:3–35) – finds an echo in Baudrillard's comments on the 'oscillation' of Being and its fate in our productive, semiotic society (*EC*, 32). The most obvious association, however, is with Benjamin's description of the reciprocal, experiential auratic relationship and its contemporary elimination through reproduction and the masses' desire to get 'closer' to the world and grasp it as a 'picture' or 'copy' (1973:217). Indeed, Benjamin's contrast between the distant and seductive weaving of images and illusions of the painter and magician and the surgeon and cameraman's penetration into the viscera of the real (1973:226–7) could reappear in Baudrillard's work without comment.

Thus, Baudrillard concludes, 'Ours is a pornographic culture *par excellence*' (*Sed.*, 34), and it is exactly this culture that his works of the 1980s to 1990s are devoted to describing. His analysis of obscenity reaches new heights in his latest books, in particular in *The Perfect Crime* (*PC*) of 1995, *Impossible Exchange* (*IE*) of 1999, and *The Vital Illusion*, where he develops a critique of contemporary real-time technologies which aim at 'a generalized virtuality which puts an end to the real by its promotion of every single instant' (*PC*, 29). This desire for a 'saturation by absolute reality' (*PC*, 62) has achieved an unparalleled success, Baudrillard says: today 'the world has become real beyond our wildest expectations' (*PC*, 64). Despite this, Baudrillard has always emphasized the possibility of a resistance to these processes. In his early work he suggests that the simulacrum's hyperreality might undermine itself in making us sensitive to 'a hidden truth, a secret dimension of everything' lost in hyperfidelity (*SS*, 107). Something is lost, therefore, in the accretion of the real. Truth raised to its highest level becomes banal in its obviousness, reducing us to a stupefied acceptance that destroys our relationship to it and thus its 'ring of truth' (*Cool Memories* (*CM*), 118). Just as, for Nietzsche, truth does not remain true 'once the veil has been lifted', so, Baudrillard argues, stripped bare and hypervisible, its appeal fails for us (*Sed.*, 59).

This idea of resistance is developed in Baudrillard's later work, where he argues that, in contrast to the disenchanted simulacrum which works towards 'the perfection of reproduction' and the 'extermination of the real by its double' (1997h:9), the enchanted form employs simulation to expose and reverse this process. Hence his curious claim that there is an 'authentic' as well as an 'inauthentic' form of simulation, an example of which he finds in Warhol's soup cans, in simulacra that 'attacked the concept of originality in an original way' (1997h:11). In *Fatal Strategies* he had also discovered this evil genie in objects – whether the objects of study which reverse the subject's drive for truth, or the objects which surround us in the world (*FS*, 71–110). His example there was Baudelaire's theorization of the 'absolute commodity', of the artwork raising itself 'to shine resplendent in the pure obscenity of the commodity' as a man-made simulacrum acting as a counterforce to the drive for reality (*FS*, 118). Ultimately Baudrillard would find the best example of this reversal in photography, seeing its simulacral, reproductive technology operating as 'an instrument of magic and illusion' (1997e:40). If, therefore, in the drive for its realization the world has 'swallowed its double' the latter still breaks through to disrupt its perfection (1997h:13). From within the heart of the technological simulation of the real, Baudrillard discovers and defends an opposing, reversive symbolic force.

This reversal in Baudrillard's attitude to the sign and to simulation after 1976 enables him to make his peace with and even conscript the evil demon of appearances, leading to a more sophisticated conception of the symbolic that no longer ties him to a simplistic opposition to the image. This strategy, however, is still problematic. Baudrillard's reconceptualization of his critique in terms of seduction–production and enchanted and disenchanted simulacra clearly retains the symbolic–semiotic distinction and the privileging of the former term as a site of opposition. These terms implicitly function as a 'true' realm of experience and relations, serving as a guaranteed 'real' to be raised against their disenchanted forms. Thus Baudrillard's defence of radical illusion and systematic opposition to the contemporary semiotic project of the per-fected reproduction of the real becomes deceptive, as he himself can be seen as offering a defence of the real.[9]

This reconceptualization also leaves unanswered the problem of how we should distinguish 'good' symbolic and 'bad' semiotic simulacra. If the sym-bolic is now admitted to be the product of the play of appearances, what crit-ical force can it still have against simulacra? Perhaps there is an answer to this. Caillois suggested a history of simulation in which its radical force is repressed, eliminated or tamed by the west (1961:97), an idea picked up by Baudrillard in his claims for a disenchantment of the simulacrum. His genealogy of the 'double' in *Symbolic Exchange and Death* already explores this process, tracing the movement from the 'non-alienated dual relation' the primitive has with their double – with the Gods, spirits and shadows which are their partner – to the alienated double of western society – that modern subject split into mind and body, into matter and soul (*SED*, 140–4). Even that latter figure is radicalized by Baudrillard, however, in his description of the implosive absorption of all ontological splits, of original and image and real and imagin-ary, that characterizes our contemporary society (*CS*, 191). Baudrillard's description of this as a passage from the black magic of the double to the 'pro-phylactic', 'white magic' of our saturated, hyperreal world explicitly presents this as a disenchantment, as a reduction in the symbolic power of the enchanted simulacrum and its integration into the semiotic system as a mode of social control (*CS*, 196).

The problem remains, however, of the appeal to an authentic mode of simulation and its relationships against an alienated or inauthentic mode. Though Baudrillard's position allows a critique of inauthentic simulation, it is not clear how valid the distinction itself is. Once Baudrillard admits the role of simulation in the production of the symbolic, the latter's specific character, origins, operation and critical value are lost. Though the simulacrum ends here by absorbing the symbolic, we could also argue that the symbolic was itself only ever a simulacrum. The Durkheimian tradition's emphasis on the use of simulation in producing the sacred certainly suggests that this was only a simulacral, albeit efficacious, transformation. Moreover the simulacral nature of the symbolic is obvious once we realize that Mauss's analysis of the gift was entirely derived from the fieldwork of others and their own representation of the societies they studied. What Baudrillard takes as the symbolic, therefore, is only an image, serving his own critical project. As Lyotard says, 'this society of the gift and counter-gift plays, in Baudrillard's thought, the role of a reference (lost, of course), of an alibi (which cannot be found), in his critique of capital' (1993:106). This reference, Lyotard argues, is only a western racist ideal of a 'good savage' (1993:106): a 'good' savage, we might note, who might be used to oppose the 'evil' simulacrum. If, therefore, the symbolic is itself a simulacrum, on what basis can its critique of the simulacrum proceed?

Baudrillard's 'nostalgia', therefore, does not lie in an ideal of human relations but instead in his hope for a critical foundation against the simulacrum: a nostalgia his critics also share. Thus Baudrillard is most vulnerable to a critique based not on the real, as that is precisely what he himself defends, but instead on the simulacrum. If his strength lies in recovering this historical concept and demonstrating its continued operation in our contemporary media and consumer culture, his attempt to domesticate it once more beneath his own critical ground, the symbolic, is where his work is weak. The simulacrum is more powerful than he supposes, containing the power to unground his critique and expose the limitations of the symbolic as an opposing force.

Thus we are now in a position to understand the key elements of Baudrillard's media theory. We can see that his critique of the media rests on a Durkheimian, symbolic critique of their semiotic, simulacral processes and the transformative hope of either the symbolic's irruption within the semiotic or the latter's own internal reversal and collapse. As we have seen, however, this position is complicated by the simulacrum's own irruption within and reversal of the symbolic, exposing its foundation, erasing its distinction and nullifying its critical challenge. This reciprocal critique of each category must be borne in mind throughout the following chapters as I consider the development of Baudrillard's project and the critical significance of the symbolic, but so too should the consequences of its failure, for if the category falls then what foundation can we turn to and defend in its place? Perhaps the complexity of these issues explains why Baudrillard's critics have found it simpler to deny the simulacrum or admit only its partial success, allowing an appeal to a surviving real that obviates the need to reconsider their own critical position. As the history of the west demonstrates, however, the simulacrum cannot be forever 'chained in the depths'.

TO PLAY WITH PHANTOMS . . .

Baudrillard himself has come to recognize the problems of discovering and defending a ground against a system which absorbs all negativities raised against it (*Paroxysm: Interviews with Philippe Petit* (*Par.*), 23). His response has been to move away from his early active resistance to the semiotic towards new strategies, particularly in philosophical methodology. Thus, if the symbolic has become compromised in the content of his work, he has reasserted its value at the level of form: in his theoretical practice and method of analysis. Here again, however, the symbolic becomes indistinguishable from the simulacrum – the same spiral of symbolic and simulation that defines the content of Baudrillard's work reappearing in its form and methodology. This question of method, therefore, is central to understanding Baudrillard's work, its critical status and its aims.

Given his use of the concept of the simulacrum, Baudrillard must reject any simple, empirical methodology. Instead his theory explicitly proceeds in opposition to its assumptions and project of materializing the real. His aim is not for theory to be true, as, in passively reflecting the real, it would thereby be reduced to banality and obviousness, but rather, he says, theory should *not* be true (*BL*, 56). Like the Maussian gift it should constitute a symbolic challenge, provoking an agonistic opposition, defying the world to escalate to its own position (*EC*, 100; *BL*, 122–3). Hence, he says, 'you posit the idea of the simulacrum, and yet, secretly, not believe in it, hoping the real will avenge itself' (1994c:4; *PC*, 94–105). The simulacrum, therefore, was 'a conceptual weapon against reality', one which reality responds to with its own counter-gift, 'paradoxically proving that you are right' and thus reducing the theory back to a reflection of the real (1994c:4). As Baudrillard says, 'when reality merges completely with the idea, it's the end. The game is over' (*BL*, 205). The truth of a theory, therefore, constitutes its end.

This is Baudrillard's situation: 'simulacra have become reality' (1994c:4) and the challenge of the concept has been nullified. Baudrillard recalls asking a Japanese interviewer why he no longer heard of his work in Japan: 'and he told me, "But it is very simple, very simple you know. Simulation and the simulacrum have been realized. You were quite right: the world has become yours . . . and so we no longer have any need of you. You have disappeared"' (*PC*, 7). Only another gift can respond to this, hence Baudrillard's strategy of continually returning to, revising, radicalizing and escalating his own ideas in a potlatch with the world. However, if the simulacrum was only ever a symbolic challenge it was also a simulacrum of a theory, one exerting, perhaps, its simulacral power to become true, unless, as Baudrillard suggests, the world responds by itself simulating the theory (*PC*, 101) to divert and disarm it (*EC*, 100).

This double spiral of symbolic and simulacrum cannot be disentangled: Baudrillard admits, 'theory is . . . both simulation and challenge' (*BL*, 126). As Butler argues so well, this is Baudrillard's strategy of 'doubling' the world (R. Butler, 1999:119–59), of creating a representation which, in its realization, helps push the logic of the system to the point of its reversal (1999:122). Hence Baudrillard's comment that he has no doctrines to defend, 'I have one strategy, that's all' (*BL*, 82). This is his strategy of 'theoretical violence', of a 'speculation to the death, whose only method is the radicalization of hypotheses' (*SED*, 5), a process constituting both the critique of a phenomenon and its hoped-for point of transformation in helping to push for its reversal and collapse.

But the simulacral efficacy of this representation is not only its own, but also Baudrillard's downfall. In a candid interview of 1984–5 he reveals his courtship of its evil demon had became unbearable: 'I stopped working on simulation. I felt I was going totally nuts' (*BL*, 105). The simulacrum, however, could not be so easily disposed of. Despite his desire to 'cast off its yoke' (*BL*, 184), the idea survived, becoming irrevocably identified with Baudrillard as his real philosophy, eclipsing his critique and all other aspects of his work. Cheap journalism enjoyed the joke, one reporter turning the problems of finding his flat for an interview into the banal hook of whether 'Baudrillard himself . . . might be a simulacrum' (Leith, 1998:14)

If the theory of simulation Baudrillard did not believe in has now been realized then this is the concept's defeat. The simulacrum, therefore, has become a commonplace – 'our absolute banality, our everyday obscenity' (1997h:11). Robbed of its capacity to arouse the world's denial it loses its critical force. Unless, as Baudrillard hopes, it can be reversed again to operate against simulation then the game is over. Hence opposing Baudrillard with the simulacrum is the most effective critique: his work ends not by being wrong but by being *too true*, and with his success he disappears. Only the hyper-defence of Baudrillard, therefore, finds a way to leave him behind. Ironically, it is Kellner's and Norris's tired condemnation of Baudrillard as a nihilistic proponent of simulacra and the theoretical pantomime of their outraged, vituperic moral appeal to reality that has done most to keep his work alive as the evil demon of postmodernism.

Baudrillard, of all people, should have anticipated this disappearance. From the warning in Psalms' to the makers and worshippers of idols: 'they that make them are like unto them: so is everyone who trusteth in them' (Barasch, 1992:20), through Aristotle's recognition in *Poetics* of the instinctive pleasures of imitation in man (1997), to Nietzsche's description of 'the delight in simulation' which explodes to push aside and extinguish 'one's so-called "character"' (1974: para. 361), the power of the simulacrum is well recorded. Perhaps the best warning of simulation, however, is found in Caillois's discussion of animal mimicry and in particular in the story of phylia who 'browse among themselves, taking each other for real leaves' (1984:27). So simulation absorbs the simulator, leading to their mimetic, thanatophilic 'assimilation to the surroundings' and loss of the signs of life itself (1984:28, 30). Caillois's opening epigram announces, 'take care; when you play with phantoms, you may become one' (1984:17), and Baudrillard's game may finally have the same result. If the simulacrum has become our everyday banality, then Baudrillard is condemned to a lifeless disappearance as a sorcerer caught in his own spell; absorbed by his own simulation. His game with phantoms ends, as Caillois warns, with his own phantasmatic transformation and apparitional disappearance, but this is only fitting, for in the pact with the devil it is always your soul that is the stake.

3 Are friends electric?
Baudrillard's critique of McLuhan

They say planetary communications abolish distance. But the impact of cata-
strophes remains inversely proportional to distance: 5000 dead in China are not
the equivalent of ten western lives. In this regard, things are even worse than
they once were, since in the past the indifference could be put down to a lack
of communications. With that obstacle removed, we can confirm that, beneath
the formal solidarity, the discrimination is absolute.

Baudrillard, *Cool Memories 4*

If in the past two chapters we have considered the origins and significance of
Baudrillard's central concepts, the symbolic and the semiotic, it is notable that
the main sources for these are not found in media and communication studies.
Indeed, when Baudrillard does mention these disciplines in 'Requiem for the
media' it is only to position himself against their theoretical models and to
reject the existence of any media theory. To a large extent this positioning is
accurate: Baudrillard has almost no relation to the mainstream British and
American communication studies, sociology of the media or cultural studies
that have historically formed the core of the field. Instead his starting point is
French: in the broader critique of 'technique' offered by Ellul and Simondon,
in Barthes's semiology and the critique of everyday life and consumer culture
found in Lefebvre, Marcuse and Debord. Despite this there is one media
thinker who is generally accepted as Baudrillard's most important influence
within the field: Marshall McLuhan.

The association of McLuhan and Baudrillard is well established in the critical literature, with Baudrillard being widely perceived as both heir and postmodern reincarnation of the Toronto sage. The identification was promoted
by Baudrillard commentators, with Kellner being one of the first to suggest
that he should be read as 'a "new McLuhan" who has repackaged McLuhan
into new postmodern cultural capital' (1989:73). Suitably purged of hostility
and its 'postmodern' label, the title of 'the French McLuhan' was accepted by
Gane (1991b:3–4), being developed by Huyssen (1995), and explored in detail
by Genosko (1994b, 1997, 1999). It is this relationship that I want to return
to here to argue that the close association of the two authors has obscured
fundamental differences in their work, and that Baudrillard actually advances
one of the most important critiques of McLuhan. My aim in this chapter,

therefore, is to reconsider Baudrillard's McLuhanism, exploring how his development and application of the concepts of the symbolic and semiotic to the processes of our contemporary media lead him to an anti-McLuhanist position; one that owes more to another, hitherto neglected influence on his work, Daniel J. Boorstin.

McLuhan's rise and fall is by now well known. His public career was based in part on the popular success of *The Gutenberg Galaxy* (1962) and *Understanding Media* of 1964 (1994) and his extension of the work of Mumford's *Technics and Civilisation* of 1934 (1963), Innis's *Empire and Communications* of 1950 (1986) and *The Bias of Communication* of 1951 (1995), and Havelock's *Preface to Plato* (1963) on technology and media to analyse the contemporary electronic revolution. In part, too, it was based on his personal, media-savvy, soundbite-friendly style which transformed him into both a high profile celebrity on demand on the business circuit, and a counter-cultural guru whose epigrams could be dropped like acid to open the doors of perception into the electronic world. Overexposure, simplification, misquotation and a series of poorly received, mainly collaborative books later, by the time of his death in 1980 McLuhan's star had waned and his work, always under suspicion by the academic community, was relegated to its era. By 1991, when Mike Gane described Baudrillard as 'the McLuhan of today', he immediately had to ask 'but who reads McLuhan now?' (1991b:4).

Today, it seems, we all do. As Genosko says, a 'McLuhan renaissance' is in full swing (1999:1). Today his books are reappearing in print, references to his work are increasing, biographies chart his life (Marchand, 1998; Gordon, 1997a), he is considered a key cultural icon for popular simplification (Gordon, 1997b; Horrocks, 1999), student textbooks are compiled (E. McLuhan and Zingrone, 1995; Moos, 1997) and a video archive is released, together with a CD-Rom and accompanying picture book (Benedetti and Dehart, 1997). Meanwhile, a UK telecommunications company advertises its services with the tag line: 'It's a global village. Don't be the idiot.' McLuhan is *cool* again.

One reason for this revival is the revolution in electronic media since his death, their development and popular dissemination and proliferation leading to a resurgence of interest in McLuhan's work. For Levinson, McLuhan's ideas were not fully appreciated in 'the early mass electronic milieu' of television: it is only in the new 'digital age' that the prescience of his work can finally be recognized (1999:3–4, 18–19). As Benedetti and Dehart explain, 'to some extent time has caught up with McLuhan . . . many of his ideas are more understandable today than they were three decades ago' (1997:35). His utterances have now become essential intellectual signposts for this emerging cyberworld, with McLuhan himself being adopted by *Wired* magazine as its 'patron saint' (Gordon, 1997a:7; Wolf, 1996).

But McLuhan's return also owes much to changes in the academy reflecting these transformations. Subjects he roamed across decades earlier have since attained an academic respectability. His discussion of electronic media and culture, of the global village of instant access, contact, participation, empathy and nomadic exploration, his view of the implosive, live collective experience of global events, and tracing of the multiple transformation of our society and culture by electronic media – all anticipate key debates in postindustrialism, postmodernism, globalization, the information society, new media and cyber-culture. If he is sometimes relegated to footnote status in these texts, this cannot obscure the fact that McLuhan's concerns are now explicitly centre stage in contemporary media, communication and cultural studies. His own image of himself as surfing the electronic maelstrom was surprisingly prophetic (McLuhan and Fiore, 1997a:150–1).

Although a vibrant North American neo-McLuhanism has kept his work alive (see E. McLuhan, 1998; Postman, 1987, 1993; De Kerckhove, 1995; Meyrowitz, 1985; Lanham, 1995; Powe, 1995; Levinson, 1997, 1999; Theall, 2001), with few exceptions (Kroker and Cook, 1988; Kroker, 1992; Genosko, 1999), this tradition has emphasized the technological developments respon-sible for McLuhan's revival, paying less attention to the changing theoretical milieu that he inspired and that has been instrumental in his revival. McLuhan's French inheritance goes unnoticed by these commentators despite the fact that interest in Baudrillard and Virilio has played an important part in leading many back to his work. As Genosko says, McLuhan's contemporary reappearance has 'a distinctly Baudrillardian glow about it' (1999:117).

McLuhan's return might be taken as the occasion for a return of the criti-cisms of his work codified through the 1960s and 1970s – such as his claimed technological determinism, optimism, absent or inadequate economic or political analysis, and his exasperating methodological procedures (see Miller, 1971; R. Williams, 1990; Stearn, 1968; Rosenthal, 1968). However, beyond providing the opportunity for the rebuttal of the more entrenched miscon-ceptions, their reappearance would be a regressive step for our critical under-standing of McLuhan. Instead I want to offer another response, developing a critique of McLuhan through precisely those traditions he has inspired and in particular through the work of Baudrillard, his most important interpreter. In Baudrillard we find a suitably McLuhanist extension and reversal of McLuhan, one allowing, following McLuhan's own metaphor, new light to be shone not on but *through* McLuhan's ideas, bringing with it also a clearer insight into Baudrillard's own project.

'ARCHAIC MAN *PLUS*'

McLuhan's media theory is well known although standard readings of his work typically ignore much of his later output which contains many important ideas that would complicate these accounts. Nevertheless, certain points are uncon-troversial. He begins with an Innis-inspired philosophy and history of tech-nology as a mediation of human will (Innis, 1986, 1995), extending and amplifying physical or mental capacities (McLuhan, 1994:3–4, 152, 42–3), and creating specific 'sense ratios' and 'patterns of perception' (1994:18). Any new extension reorganizes 'the whole psychic and social complex' (1994:4), hence

McLuhan's claim that 'the medium is the message' (1994:7) or 'the massage' (McLuhan and Fiore, 1997a:26), as the form of the media imposes itself 'upon all levels of our private and social lives' (Benedetti and Dehart, 1997:106). He later describes this process as creating a complete surrounding sensory 'environment' (Molinaro, McLuhan and Toye, 1987:308–9; McLuhan, 1968:131), as invisible to us as water is to fish (McLuhan, 1966a:70) as a result of its programming of our senses, its familiarity, and the 'shock' of our sensory auto-amputation. Just as Narcissus was numbed and fascinated by his extended image, so too are we, McLuhan says (1994:41), becoming 'servo-mechanisms' of our own technology (1994:46).

From this philosophy, McLuhan develops a triphasic history of our extension, from the oral-acoustic tribal world, to the phonetic-literate, mechanical world, to the contemporary electronic world. He pictures the first as a rich, tribal world of inter-involved, direct, face-to-face communication creating 'a seamless web of experience' from the interplay of all the senses (1994:335). He sees it as possessing stronger and more emotionally invested and involving relations than those which replaced them when the phonetic alphabet was developed (McLuhan and Zingrone, 1995:240). Its visual specialization and stress broke these relationships, abstracting and reducing shared experience and knowledge to place it within external signs manipulated by individual readers, creating a private experience and individual consciousness (McLuhan and Zingrone, 1995:240–4). These processes accelerated again with the invention of mechanical typography in the mid fifteenth century, which paved the way for the modern, industrial world and its mechanical 'explosion' across the globe (McLuhan, 1994:3). The invention of the electric telegraph in the mid nineteenth century brought the west into an electric age and constituted, McLuhan says, 'a total and near instantaneous transformation of culture, value and attitudes' (Benedetti and Dehart, 1997:22).

As an extension of the electrical central nervous system and consciousness these 'organic' electrical media (McLuhan, 1994:248) allow a direct sensory experience to replace a mechanical mediation, operating at 'electric speed' to negate and 'implode' the world's temporal and spatial dimensions into a 'global village' (1994:93). Thus they also instantly create a field of simultaneous events, producing a 'total field of interacting events in which all men participate' (1994:248) and a total involvement in the lives of all others' (1994:254). Organic technology, therefore, produces organic social bonds as 'the human family becomes one tribe again' (1994:172), and it is here that we find the real meaning of 'implosion' as a transformation not of dimensions but of *relations*, as we become, not just physically, but also *affectively* closer. When McLuhan writes that 'we wear all mankind as our skin' (1994:47) he should have added that we wear our hearts there too. This is an age of 'participation' in which our imploded relationship to the 'cold' electric medium – as we complete its operation and meaning (1994:22–32) – reflects our imploded relationship to all others.

Televised events such as President Kennedy's funeral (1994:335–7) provide evidence of this participation in demonstrating 'the unrivalled power of TV' to unify 'an entire population in a ritual process' (1994:337). Far from encouraging passivity, television produces an intense involvement, enabling people 'to get together and enjoy the . . . group emotion. Its like being at a ball game. A big group emotion' (McLuhan, 1998a:3). McLuhan draws on key anthropological terms to describe these processes, referring to the 'sacred' character television imbues in its participants (1994:336), and its 'ritual' character, reuniting humanity as a 'tribe' (1998a:2) and allowing us to live 'mythically' (1998b:4–5) and as 'hunter-gatherers' of information (1967:100–1). Electric society involves, therefore a retribalization and a return to its shared experience and strong social bonds, an idea echoing Durkheim's claims for the raising of individual life in tribal societies through communal festivals and rites. TV, for McLuhan, brings the same communion and emotion, hence his critique of Eliade's Durkheimian *The Sacred and the Profane* for its pessimistic interpretation of the loss of the sacred (Eliade, 1959). The sacred and profane here are not metaphysical categories, McLuhan argues, but products of our technological extension and mode of communication. Far from losing the sacred, 'modern man, since the electromagnetic discoveries of more than a century ago, is investing himself with all the dimensions of archaic man *plus*' (1962:69).

Despite this secular basis for the sacred, McLuhan himself was a Catholic convert and his work demonstrates an ambivalent theology influenced in part by Teilhard De Chardin's own Catholic, evolutionary, technological mysticism. His comments veer accordingly between a celebration of man's electronic extension as an almost spiritual unification of consciousness drawing us closer to God (E. McLuhan and Zingrone, 1995:268; Davis, 1998), and the possibility that this might be an electronic simulacrum of the divine and 'a blatant manifestation of the anti-Christ' (Molinaro, McLuhan and Toye, 1987:370; Davis, 1998:254). In one reading, however, electronic media produce not merely a rediscovery of the Durkheimian sacred, but its electronic amplification into the sacred *plus*.

ARCHAIC MAN *MINUS*

Baudrillard's first response to McLuhan, his 1967 review of *Understanding Media* (*UB*, 39–44), already reflects an ambiguity towards his work. On one level Baudrillard is critical, reproaching McLuhan for his failure to consider the historical and social context of media and for a 'fundamental determinism', 'technological idealism' and optimism (*UB*, 43). But read more closely we also see that Baudrillard has already begun to adopt and rework McLuhan's ideas, combining the emphasis on technological form with his own Barthesian semiological analysis. Following McLuhan, Baudrillard sees the message of television as lying, not in its content, but in 'the new modes of relations and perception that it imposes' (*UB*, 42) and its replacement of lived relations with semiotic relations. Television's 'precise result (if not function)', Baudrillard says, 'is to neutralize the lived, unique eventful character of that which it transmits, to turn it into a discontinuous "message", a sign which is juxtaposed among others in the abstract dimension of TV programmes' (*UB*, 42). From the beginning, therefore, Baudrillard adopts McLuhan's ideas, but turns them towards his own Durkheimian critical project. Far from transporting us into the real, for Baudrillard electronic media represent a process of semiotic distantiation, with McLuhan's 'the medium is the message' standing as the expression of this process and consequently as 'the very formula of alienation in a technological society' (*UB*, 43).

As we have seen, throughout his early works Baudrillard begins to develop the central opposition that informs his career – that of the semiotic and the symbolic – and the theme of the latter's reduction and transformation by the former. In *The Consumer Society* he explicitly applies these ideas to the electronic media (pp. 99–128), expanding on his earlier review and retaining his central concern with the transformation of experience. Again 'we have to accept . . . McLuhan's formula that "the medium is the message" ', but the most significant effects of the form involve, he says, 'the disarticulation of the real into successive and equivalent signs' (p. 122), neutralizing 'the lived, unique, eventual character of the world' (p. 123) to substitute for it a universe of self-referential media (p. 124). Hence we consume today a 'fragmented, filtered world', 'industrially processed' by our media 'into sign material' (p. 124).

While Baudrillard adopts McLuhan's emphasis on form, his primary concern is with the sign-form, not technology per se, and the only effect he is interested in is its destruction of the symbolic. Hence Baudrillard positively employs McLuhan (despite rather caustic personal reservations), but in doing so transforms his meaning, turning 'the medium is the message' into his own claim that 'the essential medium is the model' and that the key process is the production of the sign-form and the dominance of its models in the code of signification (RM, 175–6). Thus Baudrillard is led to the anti-McLuhanist conclusion that the media do not communicate, but rather abolish real, symbolic 'communication' in their very form (RM, 169). Indeed, his claim that they offer only 'simulated' forms of 'participation' explicitly targets and rejects one of McLuhan's key tropes (RM, 170–1).

This adoption and extension of McLuhanism to opposing conclusions can be seen again in Baudrillard's discussion of 'operational semiurgy' (*CPES*, 185–203), a concept that has affinities with McLuhan's concept of 'massage', both describing the working over of our sensory and psychic lives by our own technologies (Genosko, 1999:64–76). For Baudrillard, however, 'semiurgy' is only concerned with one medium – the sign – and with its permanent effect of reducing the complex meaning of the symbolic into simplified semiotic elements within 'the general code of signification' (*CPES*, 187, 190). It primarily describes, therefore, the violence of the semiotic upon the symbolic, a theme absent from McLuhan's work. Even when Baudrillard accepts McLuhan's description of the 'environment' as a product of our surrounding communicational technologies (McLuhan, 1994:295; 1974), as 'a network of signs and messages' and a branch and product of 'mass communications' (*CPES*, 200), he foregrounds the sign and the 'semiotic revolution' rather than electronic media as its cause and constituent element.

Baudrillard's central concern, therefore, is with the semiotic transformation of the symbolic. The fact that he sees the electronic media as a primary agent in this semioticization places him in stark opposition to McLuhan, although his claim that the semiotic takes the former symbolic as its significatory content (*SO*, 200) echoes McLuhan's belief in new media taking older forms as their content. For Baudrillard, in contrast to McLuhan, the electronic media do not merely rearrange or 'massage' perception, consciousness and experience, they *replace* them with their simulacra (*CS*, 33–4). 'So we live', he says, 'in the denial of the real', consuming 'the simulacrum of the world' and its 'alibi of participation' in the comfort and security of the home (*CS*, 35).

This is a clear and complete reversal of McLuhan, rejecting his claim of an electrically extended, organic participation in the real as merely simulacral. This conclusion is extended in Baudrillard's discussion of the event's production not 'from shifting, contradictory, real experience', but as a finished semiotic artefact fashioned '*from elements of the code and the technical manipulation of the medium*' (*CS*, 125). As we have seen, this constitutes a vast process of simulation taking place 'over the whole span of daily life', with the semiotic product taking on material force as a 'neo-reality', abolishing the real (*CS*, 126). If, as Baudrillard says, everything has changed 'in *form*' (*CS*, 126), a consideration of their respective anthropological influences demonstrates that this conclusion has little in common with McLuhan's.

McLuhan turned to anthropology as the basis for his critique of western literate society, drawing on work by the psychiatrist J. C. Carothers on tribal oral societies (McLuhan, 1962:18–20) and criticizing Eliade's claims of a loss of the sacred to argue instead for a contemporary electronic revival of its communal mode of experience (a view of the media's unificatory power – especially at times of national crisis or significance – that has since become commonplace). As I have argued, Baudrillard also turns to anthropology for his critique of the contemporary semiotic system, similarly identifying a mode of relations, communication and meaning in tribal societies which he sees as superior to that system. Baudrillard, however, draws on precisely that Durkheimian tradition that argued for *a contemporary waning of the sacred*, extending this to see the media as the primary mode of its destruction and replacement.

We have already traced Baudrillard's debts to this radical Durkheimian tradition, his unification of their privileged conception of human relations in the idea of 'symbolic exchange' and his adoption of their claims regarding the historical destruction of this mode in the west. The same society that eliminates the symbolic must also, however, provide an outlet for its lost energies, he says; hence our media 'create the illusion of electronic participation', simulating 'symbolic integration' (*MP*, 144, 145–6). Thus, for Baudrillard, the 'participation' and sacred, collective unity McLuhan finds in electronic media is only its semiotic simulacrum, domesticating the symbolic mode to offer its signs without its presence, scene, transformative energies or even any effort. Whereas McLuhan sees electronic media as 'organic' and thus implicitly more human, Baudrillard sees them as reducing our humanity, replacing our fundamental symbolic experience and relations. For him, electronic man is not 'archaic man *plus*', but archaic man *minus*.

As Genosko argues (1999:94), Baudrillard follows a McLuhanist strategy of pushing ideas into new meanings and to the point of their reversal, and this is a strategy he also applies to McLuhan. This is especially seen in his treatment of McLuhan's concept of implosion. Contrary to McLuhan's view of it as an affective psychic and social result of electronic technology, Baudrillard sees implosion as an absorption, contraction and collapse of differential poles (*SSM*, 102; *PS*, 31). He links it from the first to the signform, which is born from an original implosion of the symbolic relationship (*CPES*, 65), and later describes a further internal implosion of its referent in the 'structural revolution in value' wherein the sign's reality effect becomes the product of the play of signifiers (*MP*, 127; *TE*, 7–8). For Baudrillard, therefore, implosion is a semiotic process, and, indeed, is '*where simulation begins*' (*PS*, 31), as the semiotic simulation of the real is predicated on these prior implosions and as its efficacy results in a further experiential implosion of real and sign. Baudrillard applies the same arguments to the electronic media, whose processes represent, he says, the 'macroscopic extension' of the sign's implosion (*SSM*, 100) in transporting us not into the real but into a simulacrum imploding the distinction of 'real' and 'image'. Thus implosion becomes an anti-McLuhanist process.

Despite his conclusions, however, Baudrillard retains a radical appreciation of McLuhan's work, following McLuhan himself in returning constantly to 'the medium is the message' to mine new meanings from a concept 'the consequences of which are far from exhausted' and whose meaning 'must be envisaged at its limit' (*SSM*, 100, 102). 'More McLuhan than McLuhan' (Genosko, 1999:77), Baudrillard recognizes that electronic implosion results in the very disappearance of the medium: 'the implosion of the medium itself in the real, *the implosion of the medium and the real* in a sort of nebulous hyperreality where even the definition and distinct action of the medium are no longer distinguishable' (*SSM*, 101). Hence McLuhan provides 'the key formula of the era of simulation' (*SSM*, 101), describing the abolition of the 'traditional status' of the media as mediating user and reality: in the implosion of medium and message, Baudrillard says, 'the medium itself is no longer identifiable as such' (*PS*, 30). Baudrillard's example is the early reality TV filming of the Loud family (*PS*, 27–32), which produced a mutual 'dissolution of TV in life' and 'dissolution of life in TV' (*PS*, 30). The medium does not dissolve away to give a direct experience of the real, but dissolves instead *into* the real, into a state of simulation. Even an increasing perfection of electronic technology and its representation of the real would only represent the perfection of this simulacrum: as Baudrillard argues, 'the more closely the real is pursued with colour, depth and one technical improvement after another, the greater does the real absence from the world grow' (*CS*, 122).

Baudrillard, therefore, extends McLuhan's insight into the media's production of our cognitive and sensory experience in order to problematize the reality they offer as simulacral and hyperreal. This 'hyperreality' is itself a semiotic effect, being marked by the eclipse of original symbolic experience by the elevation, excessive realization and technical perfection of its semiotic replacement. Far from the electronic age bringing the dominance of high-participation, 'cold' images, as McLuhan believes, Baudrillard instead sees an increasing loss of participation as their semiotic hyperrealization abolishes the participative relationship. Faced with their unilaterality and excessively realized hyperreality we have nothing left to do other than stare 'fascinated and dumbfounded' at the empty banality of the real (1983f:42–3).

Baudrillard's most systematic reversal of McLuhan, however, is found in *In the Shadow of the Silent Majorities* of 1978, central to which is the argument that the electronic media do not produce affective relations and 'the social'. For Baudrillard, 'the media do not bring about socialization, but just the opposite' (*SSM*, 100). Although the history Baudrillard develops here has affinities with McLuhan's (1962) in similarly focusing on transformations in human relations and meaning, his conclusion is very different. Where McLuhan sees electronic implosion as ending the separation of literate man and as *producing* sociality, Baudrillard sees it as *abolishing* sociality – albeit an already simulacral sociality (*SSM*, 66–7) produced by modernity on 'the ruins' of symbolic society and as a replacement for its relationships (*SSM*, 16, 65). As both the mode of production of the social and the cause of its implosive collapse, the electronic media's attempts to save this sociality only exacerbate its loss, devouring its 'essential marrow' (*SSM*, 65, 66). Even Baudrillard's figure of this implosion, 'the masses', moves beyond their initial McLuhanist definition as a product of electronic media and their speed (McLuhan, 1967:96–8) to become a 'black hole' and force of neutralization (*SSM*, 3, 4, 9), earthing and destroying 'the electricity of the social' (*SSM*, 1–2). Instead of being unified and social denizens of a global village they are an indistinct mass created by, refusing and imploding with the circuit of communication (*SSM*, 90). Baudrillard's final 'mass (age) is the message' thus departs significantly from McLuhan (*SSM*, 44).

Baudrillard's reworking of McLuhan's 'hot' and 'cold' tropes repeats this picture of a loss of experiential reality and relations. As in McLuhan these terms are used to describe our relationship with and participation in each medium, but Baudrillard reverses their meaning, employing 'hot' for the dramaturgical scene of highly participative symbolic relations, and 'cold' for the present phase of semiotic culture (*SSM*, 35). Hence, in *Seduction*, his contrast between the 'emotional charge' of the live event and the 'cool', processed 'television event' (p. 160). Attempts to reheat this 'cold' social and stimulate the energies of the symbolic through the media fail, he argues, as the 'cold media' themselves produce the 'freezing' of every message and 'the glaciation of meaning' (*SSM*, 35). His example is *Holocaust*, the 1978 NBC television series, which tried to rekindle a cold historical event through a cold medium for cold masses. Television, that 'cold monster of extermination', could not recapture the heat and meaning of that time, Baudrillard says, only freezing it – and us – further (*SS*, 49–51). In Baudrillard, therefore, 'cold' becomes a stark metaphor for the entropic heat-death of symbolic relations and experience, and, ultimately, of society itself. The electronic media extend not *life*, as McLuhan claims, but *death*.

'MORE REAL THAN THE REALITY'

The close association of McLuhan and Baudrillard is easy to understand. McLuhan's hyperdepiction of electronic society and outlaw position clearly anticipate the style and content of Baudrillard's work and his own intellectual status. Both provide remarkable descriptions of the contemporary experience of electronic media and its culture, both frame these within a dense, aphoristic writing style and both take their place on the edge of the academy and of theory. However, while the links between the two are important, they are overshadowed by the fundamental differences in their critical project. Thus, while McLuhan's influence on Baudrillard develops through the 1970s and 1980s, so too does Baudrillard's strategic reversal of McLuhan. As well as being a critical reaction to McLuhan, this reversal also stems from the positive influence of another media theorist: Daniel J. Boorstin. This influence has gone unnoticed in the critical literature but it plays a significant role in Baudrillard's early discussion of simulation and his critical position on the media. Though later references to Boorstin by Baudrillard are rare (*UB*, 72; 2001c), his first major treatment of media in *The Consumer Society* draws heavily on his 1961 book, *The Image* (Boorstin, 1992).

The Image is the only book on media written by the American historian Daniel J Boorstin. It stands as an idiosyncratic, now neglected, but highly engaging text at the margins both of his own bibliography and of North American media and communication studies. As one of the first books to emphasize the perceived transformation of experiential reality by contemporary media, it remains prescient in its insight and influential if only in its influence on both Baudrillard and Guy Debord. Debord's (often overlooked) debt to Boorstin was, however, equivocal. His *Society of the Spectacle* of 1967 castigates Boorstin's failure to recognize the economic and political basis of our spectacular world (Debord, 1983: paras 198–200), while liberally borrowing his concept of the 'pseudo' world and critique of media and 'celebrity' (1983: paras 2, 19, 25, 51, 59, 60–1, 68, 192). In contrast Baudrillard's adoption of Boorstin was less troublesome because their approaches were more sympathetic.

Boorstin's *The Image* was concerned with the mid to late nineteenth century's 'graphic revolution' (p. 13), and its creation of 'a thicket of unreality' replacing reality for us (pp. 3, 5, 6). Central to this process are those 'pseudo-events' (pp. 7–44) produced by the media to fulfil our constant demand for ever more spectacular diversions (p. 9). Boorstin describes these as 'planned, planted, or incited . . . for the immediate purpose of being reported or reproduced', being arranged 'for the convenience of the report-ing or reproducing media', announced in advance as if they have already occurred, and judged for their success or significance in terms of 'how widely it is reported' (p. 11). Becoming true events by their appearance in the news (p. 12) and spawning in turn other pseudo-events (p. 33), they dominate our experience (p. 12) as 'the work of the whole machinery of society' (p. 36).

Though he doesn't use the term, Boorstin foregrounds the same simulacral processes as Baudrillard. Thus the pseudo-event makes the 'original' of any event impossible to trace, 'reshaping . . . our very concept of truth' (p. 205), in producing 'new categories of experience . . . no longer simply classifiable by the old common sense tests of true and false' (p. 211). In being planned for maximum publicity, drama and public interest, it also contains the power to eclipse ordinary events (pp. 37, 39–40), reducing complex experience to reassuringly intelligible and simplified images (pp. 185–94) which are 'more vivid, more attractive and more persuasive than reality itself'(p. 36). This is a world, therefore, 'where the image, more interesting than its original, has become the original', and where 'the shadow has become the substance' (p. 204). As in Baudrillard, Boorstin sees advances in technology as blurring rather than sharpening our picture of reality (p. 213) and as impacting on social relations and lived experience. Indeed, his comment that 'we make, we seek, and finally we enjoy, the contrivance of all experience. We fill our lives not with experience, but with the images of experience' (p. 252), could serve equally well as a summary of Baudrillard's own position.

Boorstin's hope for an individual response and liberation from media illu-sions (pp. 260–1) highlights both the weakness of his work and the question that remains over the exact fate of the real in his work. If at times he claims that it has been hidden by a media 'unreality', being recoverable in theory (pp. 250, 240), then other comments suggest instead its definitive loss, eclipsed by images that are, in a phrase Baudrillard would explicitly co-opt, 'more real than the reality' (p. 249). More radical and more sensitive to the problem of simulacra, Baudrillard cautions us of Boorstin's discourse of the 'pseudo' in a simulacral world that has passed 'beyond the true and the false' (*CS*, 126–7). Despite this, however, as I have argued, Baudrillard himself retains a lingering faith in the real in that concept of the symbolic that he raises against simulation.

In their shared critical content, methodological use of contemporary exam-ples, extreme interpretation of evidence, caustic tone and engaged, polemical writing style, Baudrillard's affinities with Boorstin arguably surpass those with McLuhan. Even if their philosophical conception of the real differs, they share the belief that something is lost in the social and technical advance of the con-temporary media, and that the latter do not merely transform experience but *kill* it. Thus, whereas McLuhan reads the Narcissus myth as explaining our numbing by and fascination with our technological extensions, Boorstin emphasizes instead *the languorous death of Narcissus* through this fascination (1992:257).

Boorstin's ideas were enough of a threat for McLuhan to repeatedly target him in the early 1960s. 'Professor' Boorstin's literate and learned status (Moos, 1997:32; McLuhan, 1994:52; Molinaro, McLuhan and Toye, 1987:506) is sufficient to expose him as a backward-looking figure responding to the new electronic world with a 'moral panic' charting a perceived 'decline in values' (Moos, 1997:29). In response McLuhan argues that we are not experiencing a loss of reality but only undergoing another in a series of historical transformations linked to changes in our media. Thus all media have a 'pseudo . . . character', McLuhan says, because they 'exist to invest our lives with artificial perception and arbitrary values' (1994:212, 199). As this is lost with familiarity, we must expect all new media 'to be classed as *pseudo* by those who have acquired the patterns of earlier media' (1994:199). For McLuhan, Boorstin is a 'cultural reactionary' (1994:199) who fails to understand the new reality formed in the electronic world.

Interestingly, this McLuhanist critique of Boorstin could apply equally well to Baudrillard, whose genealogical sketch in 'The order of simulacra' (pp. 50–76) privileges an anterior symbolic era representing a, now reduced or destroyed, reality. In contrast McLuhan offers a competing history of the technological 'simulation' of human powers (1966b:100–1) in our extended 'images', which we serve as 'idols' (1994:45). His history of simulacra, however, refuses to privilege any era, containing an implicit critique of any theory referring to an original and lost reality, being sensitive instead to the recurring nature of this transformation.

Except, of course, a closer reading of McLuhan complicates this because, in privileging the oral–acoustic world, he does offer a 'lost', primary scene and experiential reality. He also frequently resorts to the value judgements he claims to avoid (Benedetti and Dehart, 1997:147), in, for example, his celebration of electronic retribalization and his later, far from optimistic, critique of electronic media for the 'violence' of their 'disincarnation' of humanity and destruction of individual identity and meaning (McLuhan, 1976; Benedetti and Dehart, 1997:72-101). In private, at least, McLuhan was more openly judgemental, suggesting that, as 'a very good electrical engineer', Satan could be at work in the technology (Molinaro, McLuhan and Toye, 1987:370). At this point, therefore, McLuhan's work becomes indistinguishable from the critical position adopted by Boorstin and by his own French inheritors, Baudrillard and Virilio (1997a).

'TRACES ON A MONITORING SCREEN'

If Baudrillard is indebted to the work of both McLuhan and Boorstin, then how do these influences develop in his later work? In a 1984 interview Baudrillard says McLuhan's is 'still the best analysis' of the media (*BL*, 87), but this claim is made on the basis of Baudrillard's own 'more interesting' reading, which, he admits, extends it and inverts his hypotheses (*BL*, 88, 90). Although references to McLuhan become rarer in Baudrillard's later work he remains a central influence, especially as Baudrillard increasingly foregrounds electric media and technology. Again, however, Baudrillard deploys McLuhan only to reverse his critical conclusions.

From *Fatal Strategies* of 1983 onwards, Baudrillard escalates his description of our contemporary society, charting the 'metastatic' exponential growth and acceleration of its systems (*FS*, 32) and 'obese' overproduction of information (*FS*, 28). The centrality of the media in this process and Baudrillard's emphasis on its form and effects reinforces his McLuhanism, although he again reads these processes in terms of their destruction of the symbolic 'scene' (*FS*, 55). The consequence of the global village is indeed the instant availability of all times, places and experiences, but for Baudrillard this 'obscene' transparency leads to the erosion of all meaning, relations and participation. The scene of the symbolic is replaced by 'the smooth and functional surface of communication', reducing us to 'terminals of multiple networks', unable even to define the limits of our being and merged with our electronic connections (*FC*, 16, 27). If McLuhan had begun to suggest this (1976), Baudrillard makes the reversal clear: today we become the extension of technology. Most of Baudrillard's later references to McLuhan revolve, therefore, around his attempt to push and reverse this concept of extension (*CM*, 110; 1992c:17; *TE*, 30, 117; 1992d:12–13; *PC*, 35, 71), questioning McLuhan's 'subjective' interpretation of technology.

Baudrillard's most important later critique of McLuhan comes in his 1992 lecture 'The vanishing point of communication' (1992d). As I argued in chapter 1, Baudrillard here rejects the idea that we have always communicated, arguing that 'communication' is 'a modern invention', arising only when speech and symbolic exchange are abolished (p. 3). Thus today a formal, technical apparatus and 'a huge network of information' are necessary to organize human exchange (p. 4). Hence his claim that the essence of media remains 'non-communication', in replacing human relations and resurrecting them in a simulacral form in the 'strange structure' of electronic communication, where we pass 'like commuters', avoiding all the violence of exchange (p. 5). This represents a final, dystopic reversal of McLuhan's 'global village': instead of our media bringing people together through them we avoid all contact with the singularity of the self and its exchange, passing like blind particles on our individual, programmed trajectories (pp. 5, 11).

Baudrillard's later discussion of the 'other' provides another reversal of McLuhan's 'global village'. Baudrillard increasingly discovers the exiled symbolic surviving in the 'radical otherness' of non-western cultures, from the Aboriginal Australians to Islamic culture (*TE*, 111–74), and his critique of the west's historical attempt to incorporate these cultures into its own semiotic system through 'a discourse of difference' sees the electronic media as contributing towards this global homogenization and control (*TE*, 128). Despite, therefore, McLuhan's use of a tribal scene to illustrate his electronic global village (McLuhan and Fiore, 1997a:66–7), for Baudrillard its technologies bring not a 'retribalization' but a systematic *detribalization* and incorporation of the global 'other'. The same McLuhanist concerns and anti-McLuhanist reversal can be found in all of Baudrillard's later work on the media, his emphasis on technological form and electronic implosion repeatedly ending in claims of the abolition of participation, sociality, human relations and meaning. His more recent writings and interviews such as *The Perfect Crime, Paroxysm, The Vital Illusion, Impossible Exchange*, and essays (1997b, 1997h) extend his critique to 'virtual reality' – that assemblage of everyday technologies which produce the virtualization of the world in their drive for its 'unconditional realization' (*PC*, 25) – but his discussion of their effects, even when it is reframed around the loss of 'illusion', is consistent with all that has gone before.

In contrast, although rarely referred to, Boorstin's ideas continue to play a positive role in Baudrillard's later work. This is especially obvious in the increasing prominence given by Baudrillard to the issue of the contemporary media 'non-event', an idea explicitly appropriated from Boorstin and first used by Baudrillard in *The Consumer Society* as the basis of his discussion of media simulation and the semiotic production of events (pp. 125–6). In the 1990s he returns to and radicalizes these ideas, seeing *all* events as non-events in their instant passage into the media, rather than, as in Boorstin, only those produced by and for the media.

For Baudrillard, today, 'things no longer really take place, whilst nonetheless seeming to' (*The Illusion of the End* (*Ill.*), 16) – a disjunction between the spectacular dissemination of apparent 'events' and their lack of meaning and significance. Where once events 'happened', today they are 'designed to happen' (*TE*, 41), having passed, like Benjamin's artworks, from an original production with an 'aura' to a simulacral reproduction with 'no more significance than their anticipated meaning, their programming and their broadcasting' (*Ill.*, 21). Their preprocessed meaning and real-time appearance erase personal or historical meaning, with each non-event blazing momentarily on the screen of the media before its instant disappearance and supercession. In the implosion of medium and message the site of the event 'becomes an extension of the studio', a 'virtual space' producing a 'definitive confusion' and uncertainty (*Ill.*, 56). Source and information interfere here, Baudrillard says, creating a feedback effect casting 'a radical doubt on the event' (*Ill.*, 5–6, 57). 'The real object is wiped out by news . . . All that remains of it are traces on a monitoring screen', he concludes (*Ill.*, 56).

Boorstin is the inspiration, therefore, for a theory of the 'non-event' directly challenging McLuhan's belief that global 'events' are occurring and that they are electronically experienced and shared. For Baudrillard, there is no event, only its simulacrum, imploding the distinction of reality and image, message and medium, and site and studio. There is no shared, organically extended experience, only individual viewers, isolated in their technologically mediated experience, avoiding all contact or exchange. There is no shared reality, only the vicarious consumption of the signs of the real in the comfort of one's distance and pleasure of their guaranteed reference, with the individual propelled on their sofa not live into the event but only into a succession of spectacular images. There is no global consciousness or awareness, only a real-time experience and scene imploding meaning and short-circuiting historical resonance. There is no participation, only its simulacrum, and no involvement, only a detached fascination for the corpse of a reality that is exterminated. Ultimately, Baudrillard says: 'Television inculcates indifference, distance, scepticism and unconditional apathy. Through the world's becoming-image, it anaesthetizes the imagination, provokes a sickened abreaction, together with a surge of adrenalin which induces total disillusionment' (*Ill.*, 61). This 'total disillusionment' stands as the antithesis of McLuhan's electronically retribalized family of man. As this chapter's opening quotation – one of Baudrillard's most devastating attacks on a McLuhanist position – suggests, ours is an indifferent and discriminatory form of global empathy.

Paradoxically, Baudrillard finds the best examples of the non-event in the most heavily mediated and apparently important world events such as the 1991 Gulf War (*GW*). Baudrillard's discussion of the non-event will be explored in detail in the following chapters, but what is important here is the gulf between Baudrillard's analysis of the simulacral nature of these 'events' and McLuhan's faith in their real, extended experience and participation. When compared with the latter, Baudrillard's arguments appear counter-intuitive, being refuted by popular experience and belief. McLuhan's argument that our media involve us in depth in events, producing a remarkable empathetic and emotional response and a communal experience akin to an electronic rediscovery and amplification of the Durkheimian sacred, will seem for many a more accurate picture of their effects (McLuhan, 1994:337). The outpouring of collective grief in Britain for Princess Diana in September 1997 and the Queen Mother in March 2002, in America at 9/11, and globally after the 2004 Asian tsunami, would all seem to disprove Baudrillard's claims regarding the apathy and indifference inculcated by television.

Baudrillard's McLuhanism highlights, however, how this involvement is an effect of the medium rather than of its content or referent and any relationship we have to the latter. As the implosion of our sentiment with the media image makes it impossible to separate out or claim any real relationship, our feelings remain suspended in a hyperreality. They are a luxury of our distance and of our consumption of the content as a simulacrum; a form of pleasure and catharsis requiring only a suitable soap opera plotline, weepie film, human interest news story, celebrity death, or reality TV show and the correct lighting, editing, soundtrack and romantic or courageous denouement as their prompt. The depth of our involvement and its uncertain object and reality signals only the extent of our prior separation and distance from our proximate experiences and relationships, our empathetic response indicating only our simulacral 'participation' in the world and corresponding 'indifference' towards any actual symbolic experience.

This is a conclusion McLuhan himself suggested in his later reworking of the concept of 'global village' into a 'global theatre' full of 'actors' (Benedetti and Dehart, 1997:65). Baudrillard's reversal of McLuhan ends, therefore, with his radicalization of this claim: acting and spectatorship and event and mediation all implode to leave us as actors in a 'reality show' (*IE*, 137). 'All are immersed in the same reality,' Baudrillard says (*IE*, 138), but this is not McLuhan's electronically extended reality, only the extended simulation of a global theatre. Baudrillard, therefore, reverses McLuhan into the simulation operating at the heart of his media theory.

FISH MEETS WATER

At the close of the last chapter I introduced the issue of Baudrillard's methodology and this issue comes to the fore again when considering his relationship with McLuhan. Comparing their academic reputations and intellectual style and form, their affinities are obvious. Both have exasperated the academy with their provocative, apparently absurd analyses, popular success and media profile. Both eschew accepted perspectives, drawing on wider sources in anthropology, literature and philosophy, and developing ideas that threaten their parent disciplines. Both bypass traditional academic form and avenues of presentation to appeal to a wider public, attaining a popular success and fame, and both have been criticized for this, being seen as intellectual showmen, sound-bite specialists and gurus of charlatanistic movements. Twenty years before *Marxism Today* described Baudrillard as 'the high priest of postmodernism' (Baudrillard, 1989d:54) *Playboy* described McLuhan as 'the high priest of pop-cult and metaphysician of the media' (E. McLuhan and Zingrone, 1995:233), while a decade later he was still, for *Macleans*, 'the high priest of electronic insight' (McLuhan, 1977:9).

If Baudrillard's critics have yet to hit on an equivalent term to 'McLuhanacy' the sentiment is recognizable. Like McLuhan, Baudrillard has been taken up both by the establishment, as a key figure taught in contemporary universities across a range of subjects, and by the counter-culture. For the latter he has come to occupy the same niche, becoming a media and pop-cult sign to be name-dropped by the avant-garde and intellectual cognoscenti, his books being bought, unread, dipped into and misquoted, his epigrams gracing all and any argument, and his virtual cameo in the film *The Matrix* in 1999 even echoing McLuhan's own in *Annie Hall* in 1977. Both McLuhan and Baudrillard have paid for this position, both being seen as celebrating the society they describe and suffering academic accusations of undertheorization and superficiality.

McLuhan and Baudrillard also share a similar writing style, both employing the form of their writing as part of their philosophy. McLuhan draws on an avant-garde tradition of meaning creation by using puns, satire, verbal acrobatics, metaphors, quotation and misquotation, changes of context, connections, juxtapositions, and the reuse and reworking of ideas to provoke 'insight' in a 'cool' body of work requiring close reader participation and completion. Hence his use of 'non-linear' and 'mosaic' styles and graphic and typographical experimentation in which the reader as content produces the meaning in an 'interface' with the medium (Benedetti and Dehart, 1997:109). As Gane (1991a, 1991b) and Genosko (1997:199) have noted, Baudrillard also employs a specific writing style to reflect his critical project and prompt a particular mode of receptivity in the reader. Like McLuhan too, he employs many forms for this, from reviews and journal essays, academic treatises, essay collections, polemical essays, extreme theoretical works, political interventions, poetry, journals and aphorisms, interventionist journalism, interviews, lectures, and even photography. As in McLuhan, critical content and form are inseparable as part of a coherent and unified, career-long strategy of writing and thinking.

More importantly, however, Baudrillard and McLuhan share an anti-empiricist methodology. For McLuhan, empiricism is defunct in our electronic world since the 'shock' of our amputation (1994:42–3), environmental invisibility (1968:131) and our own rear-view mirror response (Benedetti and Dehart, 1997:186–7) all make perception unreliable. As McLuhan is fond of quoting, 'although we do not know who first discovered water it was almost certainly not a fish': that which surrounds us is always too familiar to be visible (1966a:70). Thought has to leap ahead, therefore, not to predict the future but to predict the present (Benedetti and Dehart, 1997:186): 'what has already happened' (E. McLuhan and Zingrone, 1995:257). As a result McLuhan denied any content to his work, declaring himself willing 'to junk any statement' he had ever made. He laid claim instead only to a method, the 'probe' which worked, like safe-cracking, by experimentation, using a speculation and escalation, 'extrapolating a current process to its logical conclusion'. Its aim is not to reflect the world but 'to map new terrain', pushing things further to spark new insight and reveal new meanings where fish, finally, meets water. Against the 'ostrichlike' denial of the electronic revolution and our daily slavery to its forms, McLuhan recommends direct confrontation, arguing we should 'charge straight ahead and kick them in the electrodes' (E. McLuhan and Zingrone, 1995:236–9, 257, 267).

The affinities with Baudrillard's methodology here are strong. Baudrillard similarly rejects a simple empiricism, in order to present theory as a simulation and challenge and speculative, escalatory process rather than a passive, objective reflection of truth. In this space between the imaginary and real, he argues, meaning is created, to circulate as a challenge and provocation (*BL*, 122–3). As a conceptual weapon against reality, theory fails when it is realized, though this fate is hard to avoid in a world where 'everything' – even invented quotations – 'falls back unfailingly into truth' (*Fragments: Cool Memories 3, 1990–5 (CM3)* 8). Like McLuhan, therefore, Baudrillard claims only a form: 'I don't have any doctrines to defend, I have one strategy that's all' (*BL*, 82). This is his strategy of 'theoretical violence', of a 'speculation to the death' seeking insight through escalation (*SED*, 5).

It is this 'violence of interpretation' that Baudrillard employs to remodel the system's carefully constructed and materialized reality, using the symbolic event of thought and the 'poetic singularity' of its analysis to rupture its processes (*Par.*, 69; *PC*, 103). Like McLuhan, Baudrillard believes 'we have lost the lead which ideas had over the world', and 'we are lagging behind events' in their acceleration (*PC*, 101). 'Thought has to be exceptional, anticipatory, and at the margin', therefore, to outpace the real and regain its advantage (*Par.*, 36, 42). An extreme world calls for an extreme response: 'to think extreme phenomena, thought must itself become an extreme phenomenon,' Baudrillard concludes (*PC*, 66).

But Baudrillard's McLuhanist methodology contains a final anti-McLuhanist reversal. As his comment on Borges's tale makes clear (PS, 1–2), we no longer have the option of mapping new territory. Today it is the map itself – the precessionary, modelled simulacrum – that must be opposed. In Baudrillard, therefore, the McLuhanist breakthrough to understanding becomes a 'break-in' and effraction of the dominant processes (Genosko, 1999:90). His theoretical violence is intended to be used *against* this world, to push things to the point of collapse and reversal (*SED*, 4). Only a 'radical thought' can achieve the 'critical mass' for this task, he says (*CM3*, 91; *Par.*, 24). This requires a collusion with its object (*CM3*, 48–9; *Par.*, 116), but this deceit is powerful in producing a simulacral 'parody' of it, both using truth and striking at it from outside its distinctions (*Par.*, 113). Baudrillard returns repeatedly to this hope of a single crippling strike on the system (*CM*, 46; *CM3*, 34), highlighting that for him escalation and reversal are not simply analytic tools but a means to attack the system: 'giving all it's got' to imagining and hastening its end (*Par.*, 23). In conclusion, therefore, Baudrillard's aim is not, like McLuhan, to understand media, but to oppose and transform them and it is here that we rediscover the influence of Boorstin. The latter had few qualms about a moral condemnation of the media, employing in *The Image* a strategy of escalation of the world of 1961 that, in its aim of critical transformation, directly anticipates Baudrillard's own work. For all his McLuhanism, Baudrillard has never left this project, or the influence of Boorstin, behind.

4 The delirious spectacle of the non-event

we, at the height of reality – and with information at its peak – no longer know whether anything has taken place or not . . .

Baudrillard, *The Vital Illusion*

when time has ceased to be anything other than velocity, instantaneousness and simultaneity, and time as history has vanished from the lives of all peoples; when a boxer is regarded as a nation's great man; when mass meetings attended by millions are looked upon as a triumph – then, yes, then, through all this turmoil a question still haunts us like a spectre: What for? – Whither? – And what then?

Heidegger, *An Introduction to Metaphysics*

On Saturday 28 November 1992, a British TV channel achieved a minor coup: an exclusive live broadcast by Channel 4 of the 'biggest band in the world', U2, on the British leg of their 'Zoo-TV' tour. Anchor person Rona Elliott introduced us to the evening's entertainment: 'what is expected to be the most significant and exciting TV event since the Gulf War'. As Sweeting's television review in the *Guardian* noted on 30 November, her description was significant in suggesting 'that thousands of dead Iraqis and a rock group from Dublin carry equal weight inside the self-regarding balloon of the mass media'. But it also went further, intimating also that war and concert were indistinguishable at the level of spectacle and of their televisual consumption: that, ultimately, both were *media events*.

Today the idea of a 'media event' has permeated popular, academic and journalistic discourse, being variously used to describe the media's complicity in organized publicity, official events produced to be publicly broadcast, an undue prominence given to a minor news item or popular cultural phenomenon, stories involving major celebrity, or any story where the media's presence or the weight of coverage alone becomes noticeable. The term itself may be applied neutrally, as if stating a fact, or positively or negatively, with an implicit value judgement either confirming the event's real significance or indicating a scepticism towards such claims. Despite its rapid passage into the mainstream, the simplification of its meaning and divestment of its critical content, important analyses and applications of the idea are increasingly emerging within media studies. As I hope to show, however, a still more radical formulation of the concept may be found in Baudrillard's work.

His discussion of the 'non-event' constitutes one of his most important contributions to media and communication studies, highlighting the value and relevance of his arguments, the critical project underlying his work, the practical operation of his methodology and all the pleasure of following his ideas. In an analysis that is more subtle, more paradoxical and more insightful than conventional academic approaches emerging on this theme, Baudrillard reveals a mediatic operation extending beyond the mere production or inflation of 'news'; one encompassing and implicating our entire epistemological relationship to the wider world.

It is this question of the event that I want to consider in this and the following chapters, beginning here with an introduction to Baudrillard's theory of the non-event, distinguishing it from other analyses within media studies. The next chapter will consider his most controversial example, the Gulf War, while chapter 6 will consider his later reformulation of his theory of the event and his discussion of the 9/11 attacks on the World Trade Center and of the Afghan and Iraq wars. As I shall argue, these discussions return us again to the question of methodology, with Baudrillard's analyses functioning not simply as diagnostic, but as *critical tools* intended to challenge media processes and our understanding and acceptance of them. Thus his 'speculation to the death' becomes not only his analytic method but the only appropriate response to the processes he describes.

'THINGS NO LONGER REALLY TAKE PLACE'

Originating in his early critique of semiotic media and continuing through to his contemporary pronouncements on world events, Baudrillard's theory of the event can be seen to run throughout his work. Inspired by the McLuhanist strategy of reworking ideas to reapply and rediscover new meanings and possibilities within them, he returns repeatedly to the issue, developing many different and often contradictory analyses of the idea. Though it would be difficult to map every twist he introduces, the broad outline of his theory can be traced and evaluated. I want to consider here the chronological development of his theory of the event in three phases: his critique of the semiotic media in the late 1960s to early 1970s; his developing and complex reflections on the event and history through the 1980s into the 1990s; and his critique of virtuality and real-time from the 1990s to the present.

The first 'events' Baudrillard analysed were those of May 1968, in his early essays, 'Police and play' of 1969 (*UB*, 61–9) and 'Requiem for the media' of 1971 (RM, 172–7). Already his emphasis here is on the media's role in disarming the challenge of this 'symbolic' explosion (*UB*, 67; RM, 174), describing how, in following the media reports, students consumed themselves as signs during the revolt (*UB*, 66). It was this mediation that administered the movement 'a mortal dose of publicity', he argues, depriving it of 'its own rhythm and meaning', its national extension leading to its local 'decompression', 'asphyxiation' and collapse (RM, 174, 176). From the first, therefore,

Baudrillard sees the mediated, simulacral event impacting on and abolishing the ground level event, an argument he develops as a natural extension of his critique of the semiotic processes of the media.

This critique is developed at length in his discussion of electronic media in *The Consumer Society*. Again the foundational process is the media's transformation of the real 'into successive and equivalent signs' (p. 122), and their substitution for 'the lived, eventual character of the world' of a 'multiple universe' of media 'signifying each other reciprocally' and becoming each other's content (p. 123). These media, therefore, impose their single pattern of reception on us, that of consumption: the semiotic segmentation, fragmentation and transformation of the world and its interpretation, experience, apprehension and appropriation as a sign (pp. 124, 122). It is this exchangeable, commutable signifying material that the media combine and model into those simplified semiotic structures that define our experience and knowledge (p. 122), leading to 'a world of history, events, culture and ideas not produced from shifting contradictory, real experiences, but *produced as artefacts from elements of the code and the technical manipulation of the medium*' (p. 125). The media, therefore, industrially process the 'raw' event into a finished consumable product, eclipsing reality in favour of that realized simulacral model given material force by the medium.

As we saw in the last chapter, Baudrillard's acknowledged debt here is to Boorstin's theory of the pseudo-event (Boorstin, 1992). Boorstin discusses many of these media-produced forms but his example of the 1951 parade to greet General MacArthur in Chicago is more radical because it implies that the very process of mediation gives rise to the pseudo-event, in producing its *eventness* for its audience. Here television's selection of views, editing, orchestration and commentary created the impression of continuously cheering crowds throughout the parade, producing a superior event for the viewer than for the bored crowds. Many of the latter, he says, had only turned up to be 'actors' in the performance, responding appropriately when the camera turned towards them (1992:26–9). This is Baudrillard's starting point: for him all events are pseudo-events by virtue of their instant passage into the media and their semiotic transformation and modelling. The latter turns all events and behaviours into simulations, 'already inscribed in the decoding and orchestration rituals of the media, anticipated in their presentation and possible consequences' (PS, 21). The simulacral processes of the mass media represent, therefore, a significant escalation of the totalitarian, semiotic programming of everyday life.

As I have argued, this simulation involves an implosion of real and image and also of the medium and the real – 'in a sort of nebulous hyperreality where even the definition and distinct action of the medium are no longer distinguishable' (*SSM*, 101). Implicit in this idea is the implosion also of the event into its precessionary, coded model and its media recording and transmission in a 'dissolution of TV in life' and 'dissolution of life in TV' (PS, 30). Thus, as I have argued, Baudrillard recasts McLuhan's 'implosion', not as a path to the real, but as a process operating on and coalescing with it to produce a hyperreality: a 'real' consumed in the comfort, distance and security of the sign, giving a vicarious *'alibi* of participation' in a world whose semiotic actualization and dramatization represent instead a systematic distantiation (*CS*, 33–5). We see here the paradox of simulation: just as the height of communication reverses into an isolated 'non-communication', so the hyperreal heightening of experience reverses, in its 'neutralization' of the symbolic, into an 'indifference' and 'disaffection' with a 'dissuasive' effect on reality (*SED*, 9; *OS*, 74). Equally paradoxically, the simulacral loss of certainty is accompanied by an increased determination through the modelling and programmed production of the real. Hence television offers both 'the truer than true', the experience of being there without being there, and a reality that lacks all the defining dangers, personal investment, relationships and experience of actual presence (*CS*, 34). All that is consumed is a 'cold', processed 'television event', without any of the 'hot' symbolic affect of real experience (*CS*, 35; *Sed.*, 160). All attempts to technologically perfect this simulacrum only increase 'our real absence from the world', Baudrillard argues (*CS*, 122).

Baudrillard applies the same hot-symbolic, cold-semiotic distinction to the media reconstruction of historical events and in particular to NBC's television drama *Holocaust*. Instead of promoting an awareness of the Nazi genocide as it had hoped, this programme had the opposite effect, he argues, in attempting to resurrect a lost, 'cold' event, for 'cold' masses, through a 'cold' medium (*SS*, 49–50). The 'cold monster of extermination', television, functions in the same way as the gas chambers, Baudrillard says, in eclipsing, replacing, *and effectively exterminating*, the lived memories and the singularity of the historical event. Its dramatized simulacrum produces the 'same process of forgetting, of liquidation, of extermination, same annihilation of memories and of history, same inverse, implosive radiation, same absorption without echo, same black hole as Auschwitz' (*SS*, 49). We might add that Steven Spielberg's film *Schindler's List* of 1993 has had the same effect: the Holocaust that many claimed to 'know' after watching it was only its aestheticized hyperrealization and so the real event was even more effectively eclipsed and forgotten. Caught in the western dream of approaching reality through the perfection of its representation, the film employed period detail to signify and hyperrealize 'History' itself, as well as monochrome stock to simulate media of that era and a range of cinematic, documentary, newsreel, photographic and televisual styles to enhance its 'realism' (Loshitzky, 1997:111), and thus transport us into a 'reality' that was only its effective and convincing simulation.

Baudrillard rejects the defence that these reconstructions serve a moral purpose in increasing awareness. For him they are actually *complicit* in the extermination process, with our role as tortured witnesses functioning to absolve ourselves and dissipate the horror (*TE*, 92). These films provide, he says, 'a tactile thrill and posthumous emotion', allowing us to 'spill into forgetting with a kind of good aesthetic conscience of the catastrophe' (*SS*, 50). We can only hope to understand events in their lifetimes, he adds. Now, when 'the whole of whole reality is filtered through our media' the conditions of understanding have changed (*TE*, 90–1). All discussion only adds more layers of simulacra, obfuscating the original, making it ever more remote (*Screened Out* (*ScO*), 18), dissolving all facts into uncertainty (*TE*, 90) and thus creating the conditions for 'Holocaust revisionism'. For Baudrillard the Revisionist's claims are a 'perfect reflection' of a culture whose hold on historical reality and collective memory is so tenuous that it even enters into this debate (*TE*, 93).

Baudrillard's work of the 1970s to early 1980s includes many case studies of events. Of these, two in particular stand out: his discussions of nuclear deterrence and of popular cinema. Inspired by the arms race's orbital hyper-realization that excludes, he says, any real explosion at ground level (*PS*, 32), Baudrillard begins to adopt and develop the concepts of 'deterrence' and 'dissuasion'. Understood as *what causes something not to take place*, Baudrillard uses these ideas to describe the wider process operating throughout our societies of the deterrence of the real by its own simulacral programming and effect. Central to this, therefore, is a questioning of what it means for something to 'happen' or to 'take place', with the idea emerging that simulation prevents these processes. If, as Baudrillard says in *Cool Memories*, the fact that something cannot but be as it is takes away from it 'the ring of truth' (p. 118), then the playing out of a programmed event cannot constitute its occurrence. In freezing and neutralizing the symbolic and absorbing all 'living energy', in excluding any other meaning or eventuality not contained within its model, in deterring anything that would disturb its operation, and with its 'reality' lying in the unfolding, playing out and predictable materialization of this programming, can such a reality be said to 'happen' (*PS*, 33–4, 39; *SS*, 56)? As Baudrillard says, whereas 'in earlier times an event was something that happened – now it is something designed to happen. It occurs, therefore, as a virtual artifact, as a reflection of pre-existing media-defined forms' (*TE*, 41).

For Baudrillard, popular cinema provides an example of this deterrence. The film *The China Syndrome* of 1979, for example, so anticipated the events of Harrisburg and the accident at the Three Mile Island Nuclear Power Plant on 28 March 1979, as to deter reality by its prior dramatization, homoeopathically distilling the spectre of nuclear catastrophe in 'molecular doses' throughout everyday life (*SS*, 57). Playing out the scenario before it can occur empties the real event of its significance and originality, the implosion of media simulacrum and reality producing a 'marvellous indifferentiation' in which 'all of the energy of the real is effectively swallowed' (*SS*, 54–5). Thus we can see that simulation plays a 'regulative role' here as a means of social control and pacification (*OS*, 70). This is especially clear in the 1979 film *Apocalypse Now*, Baudrillard argues, as it operates retrospectively on a war itself enacted as 'a succession of special effects', one 'filming itself as it unfolded' (*SS*, 59). Thus film and war implode for us – 'the war becomes film, the film becomes war' – providing America with a glorious, simulacral 'global victory' erasing and deterring the historical reality (*SS*, 60).

The first phase of Baudrillard's critique of the event develops, therefore, out of his early critique of the media and its semiotic processes. The second phase develops out of his work of the 1980s to early 1990s, being found in *Fatal Strategies* of 1983, *The Transparency of Evil* of 1990, *The Illusion of the End* of 1992, and related essays of the period (1987e, 1989b, 1989c, 1992c), all of which build on his critique of western 'productive' culture introduced in *Forget Foucault* of 1977. Central to this phase is the claim of a fourth order of simulacra, traceable to the account in *Fatal Strategies* of the exponential, 'metastatic' growth of the western system to the point of excrescence, a phase marked by a potentialization to the point of saturation, and orbital circulation in which all categories lose their determinate form (*TE*, 6). This constitutes a 'fractal' or 'epidemic' stage of value, Baudrillard argues, in which value 'radiates in all directions' (*TE*, 4–6; 1992c:15). This second phase is concerned with tracing the impact of these developments on our concepts and experience of the event and history. Again, Baudrillard provides many examples of this, providing analyses of the 'virtual catastrophe' of the 1987 financial crash (1989c; *TE*, 26–35) and of 'superconductive events' such as AIDS, terrorism, drugs and cancer, all of which beset the system as anomalous, internally produced, reversive forces (*TE*, 36–43, 60–70).

Baudrillard's most important discussions of the event in this period are inspired, however, by Canetti's claim that 'past a certain point in time, history has not been real', the human race having 'suddenly left history behind' without realizing it (*FS*, 14). The appeal of this for Baudrillard lies in the positing of a beyond of history avoiding any simplistic end-of-history approach, suggesting instead an undetectable 'curve' in history and passage into simulation. For Baudrillard, the 'real scene' of history, its symbolic stakes, rules and meaning, has been left behind (1989b:34). We pass from a linear history – itself only a simulation erected on the ruins of cyclical societies (1987e:41) – into a space beyond the end where 'everything has happened' (*FS*, 70). After the explosive liberation of modernity, where every concept and category was realized, either actually or in principle, we have nothing left to do, Baudrillard argues, except endlessly revive and hyperrealize their exhausted forms (*TE*, 4). History's events are behind us, he says, and today's are only 'inconsequential simulacra', absorbing their sense into themselves and reflecting and presaging nothing (*FS*, 16–17).

But Canetti's appeal also lies in the freedom it allows to model various interpretations of this critical picture of an exhausted and indifferent west, inspiring in particular three competing hypotheses by Baudrillard for the event's disappearance (1987e; *Ill.*, 1–9). Whereas the first asks whether the acceleration of modernity has propelled the event into the void, beyond that sphere of gravity in which its space and time could crystallize into that weight and meaning we call 'history' (1987e:35–6), the second hypothesis suggests the opposite, that the event decelerates and is lost when its light touches the 'black hole' of the masses (see *SSM*). Here history 'chills' around 'the cold star of the social', around the masses who act as a screen of absorption for events which exhaust themselves in their staging and special effects (1987e:37–8). Or perhaps, Baudrillard says, just as music disappears in its technical perfection – as we listen to the sound rather than the song (*Sed.*, 30) – so history might similarly disappear at the height of its realization and 'informational diffusion' (1987e:39). And just as in music too close a proximity of source and receiver creates a feedback effect, so history similarly experiences a 'disastrous inter-ference' in the overproximity of the event and its mediation (1987e:39).

This interference is the macro-extension of that experienced by the phys-ical sciences, Baudrillard argues, where subjective observation implodes with the object, annihilating the possibility of objective knowledge to produce a fundamental uncertainty. In similarly attempting to reflect and capture the objective reality of empirical phenomena, the media also implode with their object, leading to the event's disappearance 'on the horizons of the media' and a state of simulacral uncertainty (*FS*, 85). For Baudrillard, this 'uncertainty revolution' is 'the revolution of our time'. As 'there is no longer any such thing as an act or event which is not refracted into a technical image or onto a screen' (*TE*, 57), we shall never now know what anything was before it dis-appeared into the screen and 'into the fulfilment of its model' (*Ill.*, 6). As in that spectator-less football match whose broadcast he describes, 'the "real" event occurs in a vacuum, stripped of its context and visible only from afar televisually' (*TE*, 79). Here we see an anticipation of future events, he adds, events 'so minimal that they might well not need to take place at all', together with their 'maximal enlargement on screens' (*TE*, 80).

To these explanations of the waning of events, Baudrillard adds another in his discussion of the 'virus of commemoration' accelerating this loss (1992b:233). The aim of commemorations is to arm us against the future with an 'artificial memory' (1987e:43), but this memorialization only con-tributes towards its loss, celebrating and signifying 'the *absence* of something' (1992b:233). Thus, Baudrillard says, history is exterminated by its 'spectacu-lar promotion' into 'the space of advertising' (1992b:233) which allows us 'to take leave of the actual historical event' (1992b:234). His example is the celebration of the bicentenary of the French Revolution in 1989 which transformed its still-dangerous historical outburst into a safe simulacrum and positive event, viewed within a liberal-democratic vision of 'the rights of man', erasing both the glory and the terror of its explosion (1992b:234–5). Celebration, therefore, centres not on what took place, 'but what will never again take place' – what *must not* take place again – Baudrillard argues. Only 'whitewashed events' whose historical effects 'have already been neutralized' can be celebrated and thus dissuaded (1992b:236). The failure of the May 1968 celebrations in 1988 gives us some hope, he suggests, that some sym-bolic forces may still resist these processes.

This commemorative culture occupies much of Baudrillard's thought in the 1990s. Building on his interpretation of Canetti, he argues that we are unable today either to produce a new history or to ensure the symbolic reproduction of the past (*Ill.*, 23). Instead we revisit it, 'endlessly trawling' the 'dustbins' of our culture, condemned to 'the infinite retrospective of all that has preceded us': to an 'indefinitely recyclable' history (*Ill.*, 25, 27). Hence his mischievous claim in 1985 that the year 2000 would not take place (1987e), an idea incorporating his claims of our dissuasion of historical progression and the symbolic event, our fears of this end-date, and our immersion in a culture of recycling and archivization preventing any futural movement (*VI*, 34). By 1992 he could present a vision of the west's 'collective flagellation' and 'blanket revisionism', as it tried to settle its accounts before the century's end, erasing in the process the 'glory, character, meaning and singularity' and irreversibility of its history (*Ill.*, 12–13). Baudrillard's theory of the non-event coalesces, therefore, with a critical, cynical and pessimistic depiction of a western culture that is so unable to look towards the future that its own 'millennium clock' performed a negative countdown, ticking off the seconds before an end-point that is already played out and passed beyond in this programmed subtraction (*VI*, 34–7). Even the fall of the Berlin Wall, 'the last great "historic" event' (*VI*, 39), was part of the century's regression, giving rise, he says, only to 'ghost events' and 'phantom-events' (*VI*, 49–50).

In this 'strike of events', events must be produced instead by that 'system of information' that has substituted itself for history (*VI*, 51). Thus where McLuhan sees an electronic maelstrom of global events, Baudrillard sees instead 'a storm of events of no importance' (*Ill.*, 14–15), of produced 'media events' imploding with the real in 'an empty *actualité*' in which only 'the visual psychodrama of news' unfolds (*Ill.*, 16). Their 'speculative inflation', he says, leaves everyone 'both overexcited and indifferent, riveted and apathetic' (*Ill.*, 17); hence his claim that in this spectacular production and promotion of media events, 'things no longer really take place while nonetheless seeming to' (*Ill.*, 16). We have instead only 'vanishing events': events that accelerate away, superseding each other in their spectacular procession (*Ill.*, 18) and moving towards 'their vanishing point – the peripheral point of the media', hollowing before them 'the void into which they plunge', intent 'on one thing alone – being forgotten' (*Ill.*, 19). The Gulf War was one such event, producing the 'delirious spectacle' of a war that never happened (*GW*, 77).

'What has been lost', Baudrillard says, 'is the glory of the event, what Benjamin would term its aura' (*Ill.*, 21). Like the artwork, therefore, the event has passed from a sphere of authorial production and cult value to a sphere of technical reproduction and its 'exhibition value' (Benjamin, 1973:217–220). And just as the artwork's authenticity is outside of technical reproducibility, with the dissemination of its copies shattering tradition (Benjamin, 1973: 214–15), so, Baudrillard argues, the 'glory' of the event and 'history' are similarly lost in its instant reproduction across the screens of the world. All the key auratic properties – its creation, unique existence in space and time, duration, tradition, authenticity and posthumous testimony – wither in reproduction. Thus, Baudrillard argues, 'the prodigious event' – that which 'creates its own stage and its own dramatic effect' – has been lost, with history being reduced to the field of current events in real time (*Ill.*, 21). With 'no more significance than their anticipated meaning, their programming and their broadcasting' (*Ill.*, 21), these predictable, instant, spectacular events occur 'with the strange aftertaste of something that has already happened before, something unfolding retrospectively' (*Ill.*, 19) – their apriori modelling again reducing their 'eventness'.

Again, however, simulacral predictability is also accompanied by uncertainty as today's events remain 'symptomatic but ambiguous', being 'fundamentally undecidable' at the level of their 'representation, meaning and significance'. 'Credibility' in the moment has replaced 'truth' as the test and guiding principle of news in an era when events happen so fast, when the news implodes with its own message and when the live event brings only confusion and speculation. Even a discredited report 'can only be refuted virtually', on air and within 'a reality which is now uncertain, paradoxical, random, hyperreal, filtered by the medium, cut adrift by its own image' (*Ill.*, 54). 'Nothing is now news if it does not pass through the horizon of the virtual,' Baudrillard says, and today's events remain 'unverifiable other than through the screens' (*Ill.*, 55).

Again, medium and event implode here: as in *in vitro* procreation, Baudrillard says, 'the embryo of the real event is transferred into the artificial womb of the news media' (*Ill.*, 19–20) so that 'television becomes the strategic site of the event' (*Ill.*, 56). The street is transformed into 'an extension of the studio, that is of the *non*-site of the event, of the *virtual* site of the event', the site of 'the real-time confusion of act and sign'. 'The real object is wiped out by news,' Baudrillard says, its traces on the screen representing not 'the pulsing of events', but only the '(flat) encephalogram' of their dead form (*Ill.*, 56). Where once 'actions had a real resonance within a limited field, a field of organic proximity', our globally disseminated events have a 'zero' resonance as our electronic media 'reinforces us in our exile and immures us in our indifference' (*Ill.*, 58). Baudrillard's conclusion is again that television only 'inculcates indifference', 'distance' and 'unconditional apathy' (*Ill.*, 61). Immured with our plasma screens, home cinema systems, satellite interactivity and surround sound, for us the world's events fail to take place.

The final phase of Baudrillard's theory of the event emerges out of his increasing interest in the 'virtual' and in 'real-time' technology that develops through the 1990s to find its most coherent expression in later works such as *The Perfect Crime, Paroxysm, The Vital Illusion, Impossible Exchange*, and other essays of this period (1997b, 1997h). In chapter 2 I introduced Baudrillard's discussion here of a prior state of the 'vital' or 'radical illusion' of the world and his belief that this was dispelled by the drive to produce 'reality' before this was itself threatened by the passage into hyperreality (*PC*, 16). This hyperreality is now rethought as 'the virtual', a concept Baudrillard separates from that of 'virtual reality' (with its implications of a separate and inferior reality), explaining it instead as a reversal of Aristotelian logic. Whereas the virtual was once that which would become 'actual' now, for Baudrillard it is that which deters it, preventing its occurrence (*VI*, 50). For him, electronic technology produces this deterrent virtuality in its drive for hyperreality – for an absolute realization of the real eclipsing all experience.

The revolution in 'real-time' is central to this. This is not the lived time of human existence but the 'high definition' of temporality – the instant, live time of electronic technology (*PC*, 29). This real-time accelerates us into the instant, Baudrillard says, imploding with and ultimately dissuading the real in its 'technical perfection' (*PC*, 30). Just as it leads to the 'short-circuiting' of 'real life' (*PC*, 27), so Baudrillard argues, it also annuls the world's events. With instant information 'there's no longer any time for history itself. In a sense it doesn't have time to take place' (*Par.*, 8). Thus, Baudrillard says, real-time functions as 'our mode of extermination today', as a 'form of the inhuman', abolishing 'any past-present-future sequence', erasing the past in its instant passage, and foreclosing the future in its privileging of 'the present of the screens' (*Par.*, 30). Real-time's instant precession and absolute realization of the real, he says, prevents the real emerging (*Par.*, 31), ending it 'by its promotion of every single instant' (*PC*, 29).

For Baudrillard, in trying to pack in 'the total information' of the event (*PC*, 31), real-time misses the delay and distance necessary for thought, speech and all symbolic exchange:

There is a profound incompatibility between real-time and the symbolic rule of exchange. What governs the sphere of communication (the interface, immediacy, the abolition of time and distance) has no meaning in the sphere of exchange, where the rule is that what is given should never be returned immediately. It has to be returned, but never right away. That is a serious mortal insult. There must never be immediate interaction.

(*PC*, 31)

Again, therefore, electronic media are marked by their abolition of communication and its time, space, rhythm, meaning and rules. Real-time's reality, Baudrillard says, is a combination of 'artificial insemination and premature ejaculation': instant, spectacular, but ultimately empty, unsatisfying, offensive for its recipient and forgettable for all concerned (*PC*, 31).

This virtuality has seeped 'into real-life' (*PC*, 27), Baudrillard argues, leading to the 'deep-seated virtualization of human beings' (*PC*, 28). Not only do we live before an array of real-time technologies capturing our life processes, but we have 'swallowed our microphones and headsets', Baudrillard says (1997b:19). Today 'the virtual camera is in our heads', investing real-life 'from the inside' (*PC*, 26); thus we all become Duchampian-like 'ready-mades' (1997b:22), performing in our own generalized 'reality show' (*PC*, 28). Reality TV, itself, he argues, is only 'a spectacular version . . . of the transformation of life itself, of everyday life, into virtual reality' (1997b:19). Today, therefore, 'we are no longer spectators, but actors in the performance', and with this all Debordian hopes for a critical opposition to the spectacle end.

'We are defenceless', Baudrillard says, 'before the extreme reality of this world: before this virtual perfection' and its 'new form of terror' (*PC*, 27).

Baudrillard's discussion of virtuality and real-time technology represents an extension of his critique of semiotic media and their impact on the symbolic. It also represents an escalation of his belief that what threatens us is not the absence of reality, but its *excess*: our very 'ultra-reality' (*PC*, 66). Today, thanks to our technologies, 'reality is at its height', though far from reassuring us, Baudrillard says, this leaves us 'far more anxious and disconcerted' than would its lack (*PC*, 64). What he succeeds in identifying here is 'the collective, panic-stricken sense that by wishing the world ever more real, we are devitalizing it' (*PC*, 46). Against this Baudrillard can only restate his belief that this process will never be completed and his hope for a symbolic force to reverse it (*PC*, 53).

Baudrillard's last major analysis of the event in *Impossible Exchange* (pp. 132–8) confirms his career-long critique of the media's semiotic processes and his defence of 'the singularity of the event': of all that 'is irreducible to its coded transcription and *mise en scène*' and all that 'which quite simply *makes it an event*' (p. 132). But he also reworks his theory of the event here, now considering the possibility of a 'fated' symbolic event occurring or irrupting within this world of non-events, responding to our 'desire' for something significant to shake its predictability (p. 134). This 'double game' of events and the spiralling within them of symbolic and semiotic will be the subject of chapter 6; at the moment, however, I want to offer an evaluation of his theory of the non-event, positioning his ideas within those emerging in the field of media studies and defending his methodology and its critical application.

'A TOTAL RECEPTIVENESS IN THE VOID'

It should be clear from this overview that when Baudrillard employs the concept of the non-event at no point is he denying the physical existence of events or promoting a philosophical idealism or scepticism. His positive *identification* of non-events and discussion of events that he says aren't 'happening' should alert us that something else is going on in his work. In his theory of the non-event Baudrillard develops an interlinked, often contradictory and complex set of arguments which, like McLuhanist probes, all pick at and push the meaning of the 'event'. What unifies these arguments is a concern with the impact of developments in electronic technology on the event, the question of our experience and knowledge of mediated events, and the issue of their 'eventness', their 'happening' and their very 'occurrence'. In radically problematizing these issues he raises some of the most important questions today of experience, knowledge, memory, temporality and history, highlighting also issues of semiotic production, programming, predictability, uncertainty, credibility and social control.

Within media studies the literature on the media event is traceable back to the 1950s and in particular to Shils and Young's pioneering analysis of the BBC broadcast of the Queen's Coronation (Shils and Young, 1956).

New developments in the technology, scale, spectacle, ubiquity and realism of media coverage and changes in broadcasting structures have led to a renewed interest in this field in recent years, leading to a proliferation of research dealing with issues around media events or analysing specific events and the development of new interpretative approaches. The result is that 'media events', 'live events', 'live broadcasting', 'media spectacle' and 'media ritual' are attracting increasing – and multidisciplinary – attention in the field.[1] Texts in this literature draw on a wide variety of methods, approaches, theories and modes of analysis, but several perspectives remain popular and dominate theoretical discussions – in particular the new paradigm of 'broadcast talk' and neo-Marxist and Durkheimian approaches. Despite the relevance of his ideas to these areas and his own development of a theory of the event, Baudrillard's work has so far gone almost entirely unnoticed within this literature.

The 'broadcast talk' perspective which came to prominence in the 1990s explicitly opposes the disciplinary dominance of encoding–decoding models and Saussurean linguistics, emphasizing instead questions of 'liveness', 'embeddedness in the here and now' and 'particularity', and 'the cardinal importance of context and audiences' (Scannell, 1991:11). Its broad theoretical approach owes much to Goffman, Garfinkel and Schutze, allying an interactionist, ethnomethodological approach with sociolinguistics, phenomenology and cultural studies and applying this to contemporary media products. It focuses on the detailed micro-analysis of the production and performance of events by actors and the creation and interpretation of meaning in the moment. Marriott's work can be considered typical here, her discussion of British media events such as the 1997 election and 1999 solar eclipse (2000, 2001) providing impressive and important analyses of the implosion of medium and event and the spatio-temporal transformations produced.

In its focus on the construction of the event (Marriott, 2000:146) and on the simultaneous simulation of 'aura' and undercutting of this experiential dimension (2001:741), this perspective echoes elements of Baudrillard's work. Ultimately, however, the methodological and theoretical differences between the two are significant, with Baudrillard's McLuhanist emphasis on form, Boorstinian critique of the pseudo-event and structural analysis of the production of the individual, and Marxist analysis of the processes of social control all placing him in opposition to this position. Arguably, however, his resulting analysis of the media's operation and its implosive processes is more radical, pushing the interpretation of their experiential and epistemological effects further to develop a broader critique of the event and eventness lacking in this perspective. Indeed, it is this methodological strategy of theoretical escalation to the point of identifying non-events and charting their simulacral non-effects that places Baudrillard beyond the entire mainstream discipline. Rather than devaluing his work, however, it is this strategy that provides the basis for his radical critique.

This is clear if we compare his work with the contemporary Marxist theory of the media event. Douglas Kellner has provided the most recent, systematic analysis within this perspective. Drawing on the work of Adorno, Horkheimer and Debord, he offers a reading of events such as the global culture of McDonald's, along with Michael Jordan and Nike, the O. J. Simpson trial, *The X-Files* and Presidential politics, developing a broad ideological critique of 'media spectacles' (Kellner, 2003; see also 2000). Kellner's argument is that 'the construction of media spectacle' is 'one of the defining characteristics of contemporary culture and society' (2003:x–xi), these spectacles permeating 'throughout the major domains of the economy, polity, society, culture and everyday life' and 'every field of experience' (2003:10). But to this analysis he adds the claim that our 'infotainment society' (2003:11) also produces 'megaspectacles' such as 'sporting events, world conflicts, entertainment, "breaking news" and media events such as the O. J. Simpson trial, the death of Princess Diana, or the sex, murder and related scandals of the moment' (2003:vii).

Despite his stated aim to simultaneously develop 'a diagnostic critique and transformative practice' (2003:30), Kellner's analysis remains caught in the Debordian bind of both recognizing 'the triumph of the spectacle' (2003:1) and attempting to retain a privileged site of critique and a project of the real. Moreover, his Debordian analysis makes no mention of Debord's own later Baudrillardian theorization of an 'integrated spectacle', permeating and collapsing all reality and abolishing the site of critique (Debord, 1990:9). This bleed into Baudrillard, however, is one that Kellner cannot avoid and, in a remarkable volte-face, he is now forced to admit the 'brilliance' of Baudrillard's analyses and employ his ideas (Kellner, 2003:22, 37, 42, 44). Unfortunately Kellner's own readings lack the same brilliance, demonstrating no knowledge of Baudrillard's theory of the event and being ideologically unable to pursue any more radical questioning of media 'eventness'. As a result his critique is more conservative and predictable. Under the guise of a committed political critique he provides a legitimating eulogy for the megaspectacle by accepting its occurrence, failing to heed Debord's warning that 'when analysing the spectacle one speaks . . . the language of the spectacular itself' (Debord, 1983: para. 11). Baudrillard's theory of the non-event is an explicit response to this problem – an attempt to refuse rather than consecrate its status.

The dominant perspective on media events in media and communication studies has for a long time been the neo-Durkheimian approach, explicitly or implicitly influencing the work of Shils and Young (1956), Warner (1962), Chaney (1983), Cardiff and Scannell (1987), Alexander (1988), Handelman (1990) and Scannell and Cardiff (1991). Its dominance was reinforced with the publication of Daniel Dayan and Elihu Katz's *Media Events: The Live Broadcasting of History* (1992) which has now become the classic text in the discipline. Dayan and Katz approach live media events as a 'festive television' (p. 1), seeing them as functioning like religious festivals in collectively uniting, raising and integrating society, renewing social bonds and commitment and producing a Durkheimian 'mechanical solidarity' (p. viii). As 'the high holidays of mass communication', such 'television ceremonies' (p. 1) interrupt the profane world of routine television and everyday life (p. 5) to restore a 'sacred time' (p. 89) offering a communal sacred experience reversing the trend towards individualization (p. 205). This is, they say, 'television with a halo' (p. 4).

Dayan and Katz classify media events into three categories – 'contests' (such as in sport and politics), 'conquest' (stories of human achievement) and 'Coronation' (all ceremonial or quasi-ceremonial occasions), tracing their production, 'scripting', and reception to describe how mass communication achieves a 'social integration of the highest order' (p. 15). Such events unify society 'in a collective heartbeat', evoking 'a *renewal of loyalty* to the society and its legitimate authority' (p. 9). Television, therefore, provides a sacred, collective experience, transforming the home into sacred, festive and public space, reuniting families and friends (pp. 120, 205), recreating the communitas of neighbourhood in the shared experience of the event, and creating new modes of festive viewing behaviour. Here, as in religious festivals such as Christmas and Passover, the home itself is converted into 'a ceremonial place, focused on the centre and aware of all the other homes in which the same thing is taking place at the same time' (p. 131). In the attendance and celebration 'in small groups congregated around the television set, concentrating on the symbolic centre', media events, they conclude, recreate religious 'diasporic ceremonies' (pp. 145–6).

Television, therefore, does not offer a diminished experience or flattened 'spectacle' compared to actual presence, but 'an altogether *different* experience' (pp. 78, 146), allowing new ways of 'participating', qualitatively transforming public events themselves and offering 'a substitute for "being there"' (pp. 60, 78, 79). It may even offer more as it provides the TV viewer with 'the totality of an event', drawing them 'into the symbolic meaning of the event even more than is the primary audience on the spot'. Hence, they argue, actual presence is an impoverished experience compared to the television broadcast (pp. 94–95). For Dayan and Katz, therefore, television succeeds in its attempt 'to simulate ceremonial participation', producing the experience of the sacred and compensating for not being there 'with the uniquely televisual "experience of not being there"', or rather, we might suggest, with *more than the experience of being there* (pp. 92, 100).

Baudrillard is already well positioned against such arguments. As we have seen, he draws on the same Durkheimian tradition as Dayan and Katz, though he follows its radical path of development through Mauss, Bataille, Caillois, and the College of Sociology. This tradition argues instead for a *waning* of the sacred: for the destruction of its powerful forces and its survival only in attenuated, controlled forms as a safety valve for a permanently profane world. In a society increasingly intolerant of any break in everyday accumulation and fearful of the forces it unleashes, our festivals, Caillois says, 'symbolize less and less the magnitude and total character that made the ancient effervescences a complete suspension of institutional interaction and a basic challenge to the universal order' (1980:131). Caillois's conclusion, that 'general disorder is no longer admissible. At best, only a facsimile is tolerated' (1980:132), finds its direct echo in Baudrillard's critique of the simulated 'participation' and 'communication' of our semiotic media. For him, our individual, isolated consumption of the world through our 'cold' media has nothing in common with the 'paroxysm of society' offered by the festival's communion or those 'hot', symbolic powers that Caillois describes (1980:125, 119).

Rather than the irruption of the sacred into the profane, the 'media event' is only a continuation of the profane by identical means. Even major national or global events lack the extreme participative and expressive qualities that define the Durkheimian sacred. To prove their 'sacred' character by comparing them to the domestic 'diasporic ceremonies' of Christianity and Judaism fails to take into account the historic process of the reduction and control of the sacred found in these religions (see Bataille, 1992), while highlighting the attenuation of the sacred today if its experience is now identical to that of watching television. The uncritical ethnographic valorization of all behaviours in front of the screen as survivals of the sacred succeeds only in the generalization and banalization of this concept: in the zero degree of the sacred. Compare this with the sacred Durkheim and Caillois describe – its radical separation from the profane and the 'extraordinary powers' it unleashes that excite people 'to the point of frenzy' and abandon (Durkheim, 1995:220; Caillois, 1980:97). In comparison we can only agree with Caillois's claim that contemporary festivals follow the same needs but emerge 'out of the grey background, symbolizing the monotony of contemporary existence', providing, at best, 'some miserable vestiges of the collective euphoria that characterized the ancient festivals' (1980:97).

If Durkheim's 'real communion' is missing from contemporary 'television ceremonies', so too is its counterpart: that confrontation, excess, violence and passion forming the other pole of the symbolic. Nowhere in this analysis can we find anything of the participative 'frenzied agitation', 'frenetic and orgiastic' behaviour, 'debauchery', 'ostentatious expenditure' and 'destruction and waste' that are at the festival's heart (Caillois, 1980:121, 98). Nowhere is there evidence of such intensities of excitement that all moralities are laid aside in a physical and sexual licence (Durkheim, 1995:218), nor of that violence and real sacrifice that binds a community in the glimpse of its continuity (Hubert and Mauss, 1964; Bataille, 1962, 1992). What is absent is any recognition that the sacred is that which destroys as well as gives life; that which we are fearful of and which our instinct is to flee (Caillois, 1980:135). As a 'privileged moment of communal unity' and 'convulsive communication' (Bataille, 1985:242), the sacred is not only a unifying euphoria it is also a collective terror and life-threatening confrontation. Its 'abiding truth', Caillois says, 'resides simultaneously in the fascination of the flame and the horror of putrefaction' (1980:138).

In contrast to the ancient festival whose meaning lay precisely in its transgression of the sacred, modern festivals remain within the law, opposing transgression. For Caillois the festival reversed time to the point of creation, before rules and taboos were set, to partake of its fecundating powers and repeat this act of creation and renew the world and its order (1980:97–127). If such festivals were marked by disorder, ours are marked by order, as epitomized by their television scheduling, presentation and mediation through a newsreader. Caillois has argued that the religious 'masks' of 'vertiginous society' ultimately gave way to the police 'uniform' whose 'official, permanent, regulated' and visible mode of power transformed its wearer into 'a representative and servant of an impartial and immutable rule': into the official face of 'calm and rationality' (1961:132). Today this describes the formal suits of our newsreaders. They mediate and narrate all events through their calming, rational front, representing the immutable and unflappable, regulated and dignified behaviours of the profane order, condemning any outburst of disorder and public excess or violence in which a truly sacred communion might break through. As Baudrillard argues, therefore, the media event represents a processed semiotic experience, a simulation of the symbolic which is consumed as a sign in the comfort and distance of this form. It is a simulation of the sacred producing and maintaining rather than overturning the profane order, functioning, once again, as a means of social control and semiotic integration.

If Dayan and Katz rein in the sacred, to present a sanitized, functionalist version of its powers, they simultaneously limit the simulacral processes of the media. Their work contains many references to the media's fictionalization and cinematographization of the ceremony (1992:114, 118, 210), questioning the real place of the event, detailing examples of the media's intervention in events, and even acknowledging the simulacral participation produced (1992: 76, 51, 92). But they immediately dismiss such issues as 'conceptually distracting', describing the problematics of truth and falsity as 'almost irrelevant here' (1992:78). Thus, whenever they might be forced to consider the implosive effects of the simulacrum they retreat into a naive conception of a 'true' ceremony and its equally 'true' mediation. Most importantly their entire analysis is limited to the produced ceremonies they describe, ignoring all news events. For all their emphasis on the 'live' event, they offer no analysis of the semiotically produced and processed news event, no account of implosion and no discussion of real-time broadcasting, proving conceptually unable to question either mediation or the event, or offer any critical account of its operation. Ultimately they remain caught in its pomp and enraptured by its spectacular occurrence.

Ironically, therefore, the strength of Baudrillard's work lies in questioning the event and in precisely the claim *that the event did not take place*. Rather than representing a nihilistic position, it represents instead a coherent radical Durkheimian perspective, building on and extending this tradition's analysis of the historical transformation of a mode of meaning and communication. Developed through McLuhan and Boorstin and radicalized by his own Barthes-inspired theory of the sign, Baudrillard offers a defence of the symbolic and a critique of our semiotic media, of their epistemological effects on us and of the event's occurrence, reception and eventness. It is this questioning that distinguishes his position from all other perspectives on the media event, save those of Boorstin. The latter implicitly accept and promote the media event, legitimating their functioning as a mode of social programming and control.

Baudrillard's theory of the non-event is clearly intended to perform a critical as well as a descriptive function, and this issue returns us again to the question of methodology. We have already seen Baudrillard's rejection of empirical theory, not only on the grounds of its impossibility in a world of simulacra, but also because it represented the capture of theory by the real as its passive reflection. In his aim of reversing this, to capture the real and reduce it to theory's reflection, Baudrillard conceives of theory as a simulation attempting to remodel the real, and a challenge to this real to enter into a potlatch whose end result is either the realization of the idea or, he hopes, the escalation and the destabilization and possible collapse of the system. This, I argued, is his strategy of 'theoretical violence', of that 'speculation to the death, whose only method is the radicalization of hypotheses' (*SED*, 5). His aim, therefore, is essentially critical – for an implosion of theory with its object that might push the latter towards instability and its own point of implosion.

In the last chapter I considered the resemblance of this method to McLuhan's probes which escalated hypotheses to catch up with and predict 'what has already happened' (E. McLuhan and Zingrone, 1995:257). We can see here that Baudrillard follows the same method but reverses McLuhan again to predict, retrospectively, *what has not happened*. In each case insight depends on an escalation of ideas and a desire to push towards the extreme, past obvious, settled and commonsense interpretations. Again, only an extreme thought can capture an extreme world. Hence, faced with events that appear to happen only in the media space and which are immediately eclipsed to disappear from the historical stage, Baudrillard's response is to push this further: if it is as if they haven't happened then *they haven't happened*. Describing something as a non-event becomes a strategic attribution, not denying its physical existence but following its own processes to the point of reversal to deny its occurrence. So if all the weight of evidence is desperately accumulating the evidence of the event, reverse this at its limit to see the non-eventness at its heart; if the weight of coverage eclipses the event itself then reverse its claims to recognize its non-eventuality. Erase the entire event not in the absence but in the *excess* of its appearance.

In his *Cool Memories* series Baudrillard reflects on the process of writing and the relationship of thought to the event. Instead of foretelling events, the more original move, he says, is 'to assume it has already occurred', to overcome their futural pull by projecting them backwards to place us in the more interesting situation of being after the event (*Cool Memories 2* (*CM2*), 68). Or, alternatively, we could deny their occurrence, to overcome the retrospective lack of pull of events by placing us in the original position of being after the non-event. Either strategy will do: his aim, he says, is not to be part of the event, 'but to be part of the imminence of the event, the change it brings, anticipating it, divining it', to 'wrench events away from their media miscarriage'

(*CM2*, 22). This requires, he says, 'a total receptiveness in the void' (*CM3*, 8). Against the void of events, therefore, he aims to create his own void (*CM2*, 64) into which events will fall to shine out 'with a silent abstraction' (*CM2*, 64). And just as he aims to kill off the concepts he projects into this void, so too the event itself will die with them (*CM2*, 71).

While Baudrillard's analysis of the non-event represents one of the most radical critiques found in the literature, it is not without its own problems. As we have seen, his critique rests on the ground of the symbolic, a category itself undermined by the simulacral processes it seeks to oppose. Even accepting the ground of his critique, however, Baudrillard's method risks falling into several traps. The first of these, and the fate of his Gulf War essays, is the reader's hyperconformity to the claim of non-occurrence and a 'hyperreaction' to its perceived nihilism (*BL*, 154). Provocation succeeds too well here, reversing into a consolidation of the event's public status: as Baudrillard says, ours is 'a society of icy intolerance, where the slightest diversion from, the mildest breach of, the reality principle is violently repressed' (*CM3*, 26). A second problem lies in the diminishing critical returns of this strategy; hence Baudrillard's more recent interest in the 'fated' event and his discussion of 9/11 which renews his work through its own extension and reversal. A final problem, however, would arise from the success of his critique. If, as Baudrillard suggests, when reality merges with the idea then the game is over, then we should be wary of the day when claims of our world of non-events brings not an anti-postmodernist backlash but a resigned agreement.

Luckily Baudrillard admits 'I anticipate a little': the processes of virtualization are not complete and, 'as in the best detective novels, the crime is never perfect. Some traces can still be found' (*VI*, 63). Where once he turned to Borges's fable of an empire whose 1:1 map of the world was left to rot, with traces of it discoverable in the desert to describe the usurpation of the real by the simulacrum (*PS*, 1–3; see Borges, 1975:131), so, he now says, on this map of the virtual 'some fragments of the real are still floating and drifting' (*VI*, 63). 'We need a paradoxical way of thinking' to meet the challenge of 'this paradoxical state of things', he argues (*VI*, 68). We need a collusive theory that partakes of the evil it exposes (*CM3*, 48–9), a theory that will discover the 'chain reaction' of concepts for their 'critical mass' (*CM3*, 91), and that will work, 'like acupuncture, by the faintest touching', to trigger the system's implosion (*CM*, 46). This theory proceeds by a violence of interpretation, systematically venturing 'the opposite hypothesis to the one accredited by governments and the media, or even by enlightened criticism' (*Par.*, 69). Nowhere would this violent thought be tested more – and nowhere would it both fail and succeed so well – as in his denial of the Gulf War.

5 Shreds of war rotting in the desert

The fact that an event has taken place is no proof of its valid occurrence.

Ballard, *The Atrocity Exhibition*

In 1920 Johannes Baader, Dadaist shock-meister, media manipulator, direct-action provocateur, 'idiot-savant messiah' (M. Green, 1993:viii), and self-proclaimed President of the Republic of Germany, President of the Globe, and *superdada* – a man whose 'innate unreality' led Raoul Hausmann to declare him 'capable of driving his head through a brick wall in the service of an idea' (Richter, 1965:125) – exhibited his five-storey sculpture *Plastic-Dada-Dio-Drama* at the Dada Fair. In its accompanying essay he declared, of the recently concluded World War:

The World War is a newspaper war. In reality it never existed. The figure of History, whose severed head of genuine Bavarian beeswax has been hung in front of the remains of a royal Prussian 'Rex' pressure-cooker, would never have allowed a paroxysm as maniacal as the World War to become a reality. So one should never believe newspapers. It's all eyewash. From the first reports of the mobilisation, to Liège, the battle of the Marne, the retreat from Russia and the armistice – the press has created the World War. Superdada will put an end to it all.

(M. Green, 1993:101)

It was not Baader's first such provocation. During the November revolution he and Hausmann had declared a Dada republic in Nikolassee, a rich suburb of Berlin, announcing the expropriation of all villa owners. Panicked, the mayor called a regiment of 2,000 troops to defend the suburb from the two Dadaists (M. Green, 1993:ix).

Baader's denial of the war was an explicit response to, and cannot be understood apart from, a war whose insanities had created the conditions for Dada's emergence and for their equally meaningless retorts and provocations. This Dada bluff was 'a purge, a flood of ambivalence and rawness aimed at snapping the solid citizen out of his complacency and decontaminating culture' (M. Green, 1993:ix). Its strategy of 'taking the absurd swindle of the surrounding world and, by extending it ad infinitum, presenting the real dichotomy and discord' (1993:ix) would be central to the twentieth-century artistic and intellectual avant-garde – a tradition which Baudrillard's debt to the pre-Dadaist excesses of Alfred Jarry (see Genosko, in Stearns and Chaloupka, 1992:146–59), Situationist inspiration, and speculative, 'theoretical violence' places him squarely within.

Given this background and his personal history of rejecting contemporary events we should not have been surprised, therefore, at Baudrillard's declaration in *Libération*, on 29 March 1991, that 'the Gulf War did not take place'. He had been leading up to this conclusion since the arguments of his first contribution, 'The Gulf War will not take place', on 4 January, had been spoilt by the launch of the coalition air campaign against Iraq on 16 January. Rather than backing down Baudrillard instead escalated his claims, asking on 6 February, 'Is the Gulf War really happening?' Now, a month after the end of the three-day ground offensive that began on 24 February and ended with the liberation of Kuwait on the 27 February, Baudrillard felt confident enough to reject the war completely.

Whereas earlier claims that the Vietnam War was a simulacrum (PS, 36–7) or that World War III had already happened (*CM*, 182) had attracted little attention, this time – like establishing a Dada republic in the middle of a real revolution – his provocation paid off. Baudrillard was surprised at the strength of the critical reaction. His denial caused more outrage than Baader's and still stands as the most famous and controversial claim of his career. Despite the later availability of his essays in translation (*GW*) and a series of non-wars since, many academics retain a hostility towards Baudrillard's claims, often even without having read them. It is widely perceived that it was this issue that finally exposed Baudrillard's absurd 'postmodernism', that his arguments are outside serious debate and that they are indefensible in the face of real suffering.

This reaction was closely tied to the contemporary reception of Baudrillard in the English-speaking world and the growing left-wing backlash against the academic and popular success of postmodernism. With Baudrillard identified as postmodernism's leading light, his Gulf essays were targeted by Norris in his 1992 polemic *Uncritical Theory: Postmodernism, Intellectuals and the Gulf War* (1992). The appearance of Baudrillard's most obvious provocation yet was a gift to the left, enabling it to draw on the war's reality as a moral high ground to attack French theory and postmodernism. With only one of Baudrillard's essays available in translation ('The reality gulf', 1991), Norris's arguments went unchallenged, being accorded an academic credibility they did not deserve (Wood, 1992; Mann, 1993).

Though effective defences of the essays have since appeared (Merrin, 1994; Patton, 1995, 1997; Genosko, 1992, 1994a:98–104; Gane, 2000a:77–87), Norris's views remain tenaciously popular in the academic community since those who did not read Baudrillard then have equally failed to follow the critical literature since. Add to this Baudrillard's own eventual embarrassment at the episode, his only occasional attempts to defend his claims, and their limited discussion within the thriving literature on contemporary media-war – on the contemporary relationship between war, its technologies and its mediation – and we can see that the current reputation of the essays is low. This chapter aims to reverse this, to defend his analysis of the Gulf War as a non-event and to argue that, far from constituting an apolitical or nihilistic response, Baudrillard's denial fits within his wider critique and strategic, theoretical assault on western culture, media and society.

'GOD SAVE US FROM THE ILLUSION OF WAR'

Retrospectively, Baudrillard's first essay arguing that the Gulf War would not break out – at a time when its occurrence was far from certain – can be seen as a satirical extension of his picture of western society and of that inertia and deterrence he sees as dominating its processes (*GW*, 23–8). As he admits, its argument is a 'stupid gamble', though one whose opportunity has to be seized. For him the war would not break out due to war's entropic heat death since 1945, passing from a 'hot war' to a 'cold', then a 'dead war'. War itself had been plunged into crisis in the post-Soviet world as the deterrence of the 'other' had given way to the west's own 'self-deterrence' – that wider dissua- sion of the real preventing it from employing its own strength or any passage from the virtual to the actual.

Though these claims would prove easy to dismiss later, the essay contains many significant points in the light of the war that resulted. Baudrillard's rela- ting of the western audience to the human shields, claiming, 'we are all hostages of media intoxication, induced to believe in the war' and 'strategic hostages *in situ*' whose site 'is the screen on which we are virtually bombarded day by day' (*GW*, 25), is particularly insightful. So too is his suspicion towards the replacement of 'the declaration of war' with a UN-mandated 'right to war', which represents 'the disappearance of the symbolic passage to the act', and thus of war itself and the distinction of winners and losers. 'Since it never began', he presciently says, this war has become 'interminable' (*GW*, 26). Finally his claim for the 'virtualization' of war and for an operation 'the aim of which is to present a face-lifted war' achieved a foresight few commenta- tors at the time rivalled (*GW*, 28).

Faced with the beginning of the air campaign and the deployment of the greatest conventional military arsenal in the history of warfare, Baudrillard could have forgotten his claims or revised his argument. Instead he went on the offensive, questioning, from inside the war itself, whether it was taking place (*GW*, 29–59). Much of his argument depends on the definition of 'war'. In describing the Gulf War as '*the absence of politics pursued by other means*' (*GW*, 30) he reverses Clausewitz's famous definition of 'war' (1976:87) to argue that a 'non-war' is taking place instead. This is 'a preventative, deterrent, punitive war' to prove the west's power (*GW*, 56) and to domesticate and eliminate the symbolic 'alterity' of the Arabic 'other', he argues (*GW*, 36–7). But this is also not a 'war', Baudrillard claims, in the absence of that symbolic relationship the concept contains. Echoing that simulation model of 'communication' where sender and receiver do not meet, the military similarly exclude all contact, refusing to recognize or engage the enemy in 'annihilating him at a distance'

(*GW*, 43). 'Any dual or personal relation is altogether absent', Baudrillard says, from the 'clean relation' of this technologically mediated combat (*GW*, 44–5). This is war conducted according to the media model: war as a technological relationship – unilateral, indifferent, and founded on the abolition of symbolic exchange and the simulation of real communication.

This leads on to Baudrillard's third explanation for the war's non-occurrence. The programming and the predictability of the coalition's success renders it 'both terminated in advance and interminable', he argues (*GW*, 36). As in Matton's film *Italien des roses*, where the suicidal deliberations of Bohringer's character use up 'the real event' in advance for us (*GW*, 35), so 'having been anticipated in all its details and exhausted by all the scenarios' it is as though this war 'has taken place ten times already' (*GW*, 35). Can something so meticulously programmed and demonstrated still occur or have a chance of being true, Baudrillard asks, or does this precessionary effect deprive it of 'the ring of truth'? For Baudrillard, therefore, what is happening in the Gulf is a unilateral military production and imposition of war from its precessionary model: a simulation of war materializing its signs and excluding anything not contained in its programming. As its success lies in 'the victory of the model' (*GW*, 55, 42) – its predictable realization without disruption or resistance – the simulation of war is more lethal for its enemy than a real war, the latter holding the possibility of survival. 'God save us from the illusion of war,' Baudrillard writes (*GW*, 49)

If the military simulation of war provides one reason for its non-eventness, the media's processing and production of the conflict is another. For Baudrillard the audience experiences only a 'virtual war' in 'the absence of images', the 'profusion of commentary', the 'speculative' coverage, and the 'uncertainty that invades our screens like a real oil slick' (*GW*, 30, 29, 30, 32). Thus the image of 'that blind sea bird stranded on a beach' becomes for him the symbol of all that we are 'in front of our screens, in front of that sticky and unintelligible event' (*GW*, 32). This remains a 'symptomatic' war, 'the object of an endless speculation' and uncertain reading by professional pundits (*GW*, 41). In this filling of the screen by commentary that is instantly 'amnestied by the ultra-rapid succession of phony events and phony discourses', we feel 'the emptiness of television' as never before, Baudrillard says (*GW*, 51).

The 'real-time' broadcast of this war – that hyperrealization 'furnishing the images of pure, useless, instantaneous television' to fill the hole of the screen (*GW*, 31) – is also central to its non-occurrence. The live 'acting' produces 'an involution in real-time . . . an involution of the event in the instantaneity of everything at once, and of its vanishing in information itself'. This involution precipitates us, Baudrillard says, 'precisely into the virtuality of war and not its reality'; thus 'what we live in real-time is not the event' but only 'the spectacle' of its degradation and 'its spectral evocation' (*GW*, 47–8). Again, therefore, all attempts to capture 'the live and real-time' only further our simulacral distancing (*GW*, 48–9). Like communication, signification and history, 'war implodes in real-time', Baudrillard concludes (*GW*, 49). He ends his essay on a moral note, urging a 'sceptical intelligence' against all those who accept its existence and fail to interrogate 'the event itself or its reality' (*GW*, 58). 'The real victory' of the war's proponents, he argues, is having 'drawn everyone into this rotten simulation' (*GW*, 59).

This anger and moralism dominates Baudrillard's final essay (*GW*, 61–87), where his argument for the war's non-occurrence centres again on its pro-grammed, unilateral enactment and the success of its realization. 'This war was won in advance,' he says, and 'we will never know what an Iraqi taking part with a chance of fighting would have been like'. Lacking that symbolic 'antag-onistic, destructive but dual relation between two adversaries', this was not a war but 'a matter of war-processing in which the enemy appears only as a computerized target'. It was 'an ultra-modern process of electrocution', elim-inating an enemy 'with no possibility of reaction', allowing nothing to occur 'which would have metamorphosed events into a duel' (*GW*, 61–2, 73). Hence the two wars in the Gulf – Iraq's 'traditional war', lost in advance, and America's 'virtual war', won in advance, never met (*GW*, 62).

Baudrillard's argument also draws again on his reversal of Clausewitz (*GW*, 83), though his claim of a lack of political aims appears more credible in the aftermath of a war which ended in the exchange of 'the perfect semb-lance' of victory and defeat by America and Saddam, leaving him in power with nothing changed in the region (*GW*, 70–2). This result reveals its real aims, Baudrillard argues: the production of a 'transpolitical war' to overcome global 'hegemonic rivalry' to the west, imposing its democratic worldview (*GW*, 83–5), and domesticating the resistant surviving symbolic forces of other cultures which threaten us in their very existence and vitality (*GW*, 85–7; *TE*, 81–8). *See WOOTON*

But Baudrillard also reaffirms the media's role in this non-event, likening its effects to America's fuel-air explosives, its virtuality devouring 'all the oxygen of war'(*GW*, 68). Quoting Brecht's *Dialogues d'exiles* – ' "This beer isn't a beer, but that is compensated for by the fact that this cigar isn't a cigar either. If this beer wasn't a beer and this cigar really was a cigar, then there would be a problem" ' – equally, he says, 'this war is not a war but this is com-pensated for by the fact that information is not information either' (*GW*, 81). The non-war with its non-victory and non-defeat, and the non-information and non-communication of the media resolve themselves as 'equally unreal, equally non-existent' (*GW*, 82). Thus the military and media processes were complementary: the media's simulation of the experience of war followed the military's own simulation of a dual conflict. If the war performed the role of global social control, then the media coverage represented a domestic social control, 'our training in the unconditional reception of broadcast simulacra' being 'the complement of the unconditional simulacrum in the field' (*GW*, 68). Though we are complicit in this process, he adds, with our 'collective demand for intoxication' leading to 'a suffocating atmosphere of deception and stupidity' (*GW*, 74, 68). Since we lacked the taste for 'real

Exposal no war

drama or real war', this war fulfilled our need for its simulation, our 'hallu-
cinogenic pleasure' in the spectacle and indifference to the deaths highlighting 'our definitive retreat from the world' (*GW*, 75).

In simultaneously moving towards and withdrawing from its point of
explosion this war was like a 'bad striptease', Baudrillard says. Just as Barthes
said of striptease that the woman is desexualized at the point of nudity
(1973a:91), so Baudrillard also sees this process of laying bare as eliminating
our engagement and relationship. Quoting Nietzsche's claim that truth does
not remain true 'when all its veils have been removed', Baudrillard argues that
war is no longer war when it is finally exposed (*GW*, 77). His final attack,
therefore, is on the war's aftermath and nudity, and on the logic that left us
unable to consider anything except its occurrence. 'To be for or against the
war is idiotic', he says, 'if the question of the very probability of this war, its
credibility or degree of reality has not been raised even for a moment'
(*GW*, 67). Our response should be to reimmerse the war back into its own
virtuality, to 'be more virtual than the events themselves' (*GW*, 66). This
critical challenge was central to the essays but it was soon annulled by a very
different interpretation of their meaning and project.

'I WATCHED TELEVISION AND I'M PROUD OF IT!!!'

Baudrillard's claims attracted much attention in the English-speaking world.
The most famous response, Norris's *Uncritical Theory*, was specifically conceived of as 'a brief polemical rejoinder to Baudrillard's postmodernist
musings on the Gulf War' (1992:184), though its critique owed less to an
actual reading of the essays than to his own earlier simplistic reading of
Baudrillard as an anti-Enlightenment, idealist, anti-realist, relativist sceptic
(1990:164–93). Hence Norris's entirely unsupported claims that Baudrillard
believed the war was a media 'illusion' existing 'only as a figment of mass-
media simulation' taking place 'in the minds of a TV audience' (1992:11).
Baudrillard's belief that this is 'a fictive or fabulous war' highlights his
'thorough-going cognitive and epistemological scepticism' (1992:193, 196).
Baudrillard's 'moral and political nihilism', Norris concludes, is akin to a
'Berkeleian transcendental idealism': 'a piece of "unresisting imbecility"' to
which only Dr Johnson's response is appropriate (1992:194, 196).

There are many problems with Norris's reading, including his failure to
read Baudrillard's second Gulf essay and his definition of what Baudrillard
means by the idea of 'the reality gulf' – 'a condition of existing in a permanent hiatus, a twilight zone between war games illusions and the unthinkable
event itself' (Norris, 1992:14) – a phrase that Baudrillard never used but was
the headline given a translation of his first essay (1991). More seriously,
Norris's characterization of Baudrillard as a nihilist denying physical reality is
lazy, unsupported and philosophically simplistic, while his assumption that
Baudrillard promotes the simulacrum woefully misreads his critical project.
Baudrillard had even given prior notice of the lethality of simulated wars,

arguing in 1978 that 'moralists of war . . . should not be too discouraged: the war is no less atrocious for being a simulacrum – the flesh suffers just the same and the dead and former combatants are worth the same as in other wars' (*PS*, 37–8). Concerned only with attacking a straw man of postmodernism, Norris displays no understanding of Baudrillard's media theory, although he is not alone in his misinterpretation. Surprisingly, given his own stronger claims in 1991 for the virtualization of war (2002a), Paul Virilio has pursued an equally literal interpretation of Baudrillard's Gulf essays, condemning the denial of its occurrence (1999:99)

Significantly, Baudrillard's critics have all overlooked a key reference essential for any understanding of these essays, Jean Giraudoux's 1935 play 'The Trojan War will not take place' (Giraudoux, 1955; see *Ill.*, 64–5; PS, 33).[1] Giraudoux's drama expressed his fear of the movement towards war he'd experienced as a professional diplomat after the First World War. From its opening line, 'There's not going to be a Trojan War, Cassandra!' (1955:1), we know, with the benefit of hindsight, classical education and the ironic reference to the prophetess of doom, that this war is inevitable and that, as the last line declares with war erupting, 'the Grecian poet will have his word' (1955:74). Everything in the play moves towards this point as we watch, after the event, the opening declaration of its futural non-occurrence, knowing that it has already happened; that even 'the Trojan War' in its title is a product of the Greek victory, and that the mythical characters we are watching only appear for us through the posthumous story of its occurrence. As Ulysses says to Hector before the battle, 'the future has never impressed me before with such startling clarity. There's nothing to be done. You're already living in the light of the Greek war' (1955:69).

Reversing Giraudoux in seeing the outcome as a non-war, Baudrillard's essays similarly play with temporal expectations and knowledge, passing from a claim about the future, to a present questioning of the event, to the denial of the past after it has occurred. Just as Giraudoux's and Baader's claims are based on and draw their power from our shared knowledge of a war's occurrence, so Baudrillard's arguments only have meaning in the light of this war. And just as Giraudoux's warning of a future war that would not happen but that we know already has can be read as a warning for his age, justified retrospectively in the light of the world war that followed, so we can read Baudrillard's essays warning of a past war that did not happen but that we know did as a warning for our own age: one justified retrospectively in the light of the war's failure and historical erasure by its sequel. If the Trojans were living before the event in the posthumous light of the war's occurrence, so are we living after the event in the posthumous light of its non-occurrence.

In this retrospective light many of Baudrillard's claims for the war's non-occurrence are defensible. This was not a Clausewitzian 'collision of two living forces' each aiming for the other's defeat (1976:77), but a programmed, modelled, technical realization of an ideal of war whose success in achieving its aims and in eliminating all serious contact and opposition reversed into the absence of a 'war'. Following the war with Iran, the war which Iraq prepared for – a war of the exchange of arms, land, munitions and casualties – did not happen. The overwhelming supremacy of the coalition military, its mediated combat excluding all contact, the ferocity of its bombing, and the collapse or annihilation of the Iraqi army, all testify to the one-sided nature of this war.

Evidence of this unilaterality is found in the coalition air supremacy and its physical and electronic control of the theatre of war. Examples include the night-vision videos of Apache helicopters gunning down blind targets on the ground (Balzar, 1991), and the lightning ground offensive against which Iraqi resistance was useless. Here we find the most horrifying images of unilaterality as, over seventy miles of trenches, front-line Iraqi soldiers were bulldozed and buried alive. Already *dead in advance* before the American forces they were not worth engaging, only burying. Colonel Moreno later reported, 'For all I know we could have killed thousands. I came through right after the lead company . . . what you saw was a bunch of buried trenches with people's arms and things sticking right out of them' (Sloyan, 1991). Similarly on the 'highway to hell' fleeing Iraqis trapped without cover were helpless against repeated coalition air strikes. Even the pilots, queuing to fire and desperate to have seen action before the war was called off, described it as 'a turkey shoot' or 'like shooting fish in a barrel' (Bulloch, 1991:13).

The ground offensive, therefore, was a 'walkover' (Freedman and Karsh, 1993:397), involving minimal or ineffective Iraqi resistance, the devastation of all engaged forces, and the mass surrender of Iraqi troops, including to unmanned drones and camera crews. Coalition losses of 240 throughout the war, many from 'friendly fire', look uncomfortable next to estimates of over 100,000 Iraqi dead from a 'hyperwar' employing 'the latest generation of area impact munitions . . . designed to kill and maim over the widest possible area' (Rogers, 1991). This was not a 'war' but 'a series of massacres' (Knightley, 2000:498).[2] From a military perspective the maximization of enemy casualties, minimization of losses and rapid achievement of all war aims count as a highly successful war, but Baudrillard's argument shows us that the *hypersuccess* of this war – its precessionary victory, its unilateral enactment and the 'walkover' of the ground offensive – produces its own reversal, opening up the possibility of questioning its occurrence. This argument is not without historical precedent. Recall the observer who commented on the Polish cavalry's futile sabre charge against the tanks of the German blitzkrieg in 1939: 'It's beautiful, but it's not war.' The aesthetics may have changed, but the sentiment has not.

Baudrillard's position even finds support from Gulf War veterans: in the 'war memoirs' of a soldier for whom the war finished before he could fire a shot (Swofford, 2003), and in the defence of a British veteran charged in 1996 with battering his child whose counsel said he blamed it on his trauma – 'His view was that he was not taking part in a war at all, but in a massacre of young conscripts. And he was having to advance with his unit effectively through fields of dead bodies' (*Guardian*, 6 Aug. 1996, p. 6). In the opening scene of his 1999 film *Three Kings*, set after the Gulf ceasefire, David O. Russell satirized the obsolescence of the infantryman in a war won by high-tech. 'I didn't think I'd see anyone get shot over here,' one soldier says, looking down unbelievingly at the dying Iraqi they'd just hit, while his comrade, with no experience of war, compares it to a scene from *Predator* (Russell, 1998). As individual heroics were absent from this war, its makers instead contrived the postwar, bullion-robbing escapades of George Clooney, Mark Wahlberg, Ice Cube and Spike Jonze to rescue the war film genre, supplying the necessary heroism and individuality lacking in its real operation. In contrast to those made-for-TV movies rushed into the schedules, Russell realised that the Gulf war film could not take place.

As Baudrillard suggests, this war was a clash of two eras: the first world's third-world-war versus the third world's first-world-war. A coalition war won in advance met an Iraqi war lost in advance and not even fought – not only because of Iraq's helplessness but also because much of its military remained uncommitted. Together with America's overestimation of the success of Iraq's weaponry and air strikes, this cast a retrospective question mark over the war's victory (see Cockburn, 1993b; Weiner, 1993; Walker, 1993, 1996, 1997). Again, it was the success of this war that led to its premature conclusion as George Bush, alarmed at the mounting evidence of Arab casualties, agreed a cease-fire leaving much of the Iraqi military intact. Hypersuccess reversed into failure as the survival of Saddam, his repressive policies and weapons programmes necessitated a military watchfulness that would not have been required had Iraq been defeated. As Baudrillard had warned, the war that never began and that ended with the simulacrum of victory and defeat became interminable.

This was apparent within days with Saddam's crushing of the postwar internal insurrection. The following years saw a 'cheat and retreat' policy of obstructing UN weapons inspections; the continuing repression of Kurdish and Shia groups and all suspected political opponents; and the use of chemical weapons against the Shia and the draining of their marsh homelands. A series of provocations led President Bush to launch air strikes against Iraq in January 1993, followed in June by a cruise missile response by Bill Clinton, newly elected president, to an alleged plot to murder Bush in April. Iraqi troops massing again at the Kuwait border prompted another American build-up in October 1994, and in September 1996 Clinton responded to Iraqi troops entering Kurdistan and ending a CIA-backed coup attempt with another major cruise missile assault, a regional build-up and plans for a full-scale air campaign. The air strikes that Iraq had narrowly avoided that February and November returned in December 1998 as Clinton launched 'Operation Desert Fox' which, in its seventy hours, fired more cruise missiles than were fired in the entire 1991 war, being described in the British press, like previous assaults in 1993 and 1996, as 'Gulf War II'. During all this time air strikes had continued against air defences and missile sites in the northern and southern no-fly-zones, themselves constituting an 'undebated and virtually unreported . . . low level

but determined war against Iraq' (Vulliamy, 1999). These skirmishes continued, alongside more air strikes on Baghdad in February 2001 ordered by US
president George W. Bush with UK prime minister Tony Blair, until, after
Afghanistan, Iraq became the next US target in its 'war on terror'. Finally, in
March 2003, President Bush launched 'Operation Iraqi Freedom', otherwise
known as 'the Iraq War' or 'Gulf War II', removing Saddam from power
in April.

Baudrillard's claim that the Gulf War represented 'the absence of politics
pursued by other means' was vindicated in its aftermath. Refusing to set regime
change as a war aim, frightened of a regional power vacuum and an Iran in the
ascendant, and wanting to avoid a long-term military commitment, as Peter
Galbraith of the Senate Foreign Relations Committee, admitted, America had
'no contingency plans for peace, no idea of what might happen or how they
should react' (Bulloch, 1991:13). It was this absence of victory, of defeat and
of policy that necessitated continued military action, and eventually Gulf War
II – that final admission that the Gulf War, as Baudrillard said, had had no
effect, no consequences and had solved nothing (*BL*, 207), being historically
replaced by its sequel. But everything here was in order: the victory was not a
victory, the defeat was not a defeat and the peace was not a peace.

Further confirmation of this non-war as non-event can be found in the
media coverage. This remains one of the most memorable aspects of this war,
attracting considerable critical attention, though Baudrillard's McLuhanist
emphasis on the form and epistemological effects of the media stands outside
the mainstream analysis in the discipline, which concentrates instead on the
pool system, the control and censorship of reporters, coalition and Iraqi
propaganda, and the professional failure of the media to see and report what
actually occurred (see Taylor, 1998; Knightley, 2000; Kellner, 1992; Hudson
and Stanier, 1997; Carruthers, 2000). While Baudrillard's approach may
be criticized for avoiding conventional questions of media and state power,
ideology, representation and media content, he nonetheless raises a range of
important issues absent from mainstream accounts.

If, for Baudrillard, this war was a military simulation, the media produced
and globally disseminated another simulacrum: that 'war' produced for its audience from rolling news coverage, scattered reporters, real-time commentary,
studio speculation and analysis, military briefings and footage, and electronic
graphics, virtual maps and sand-pits. We see here exactly that disarticulation of
the real and its transformation into signifying material to be combined and produced as a semiotic event for an audience's consumption that Baudrillard
describes. And we see also that simultaneous actualization and dramatization
of the real, in the breathless, live CNN reports from Baghdad and reports from
Tel Aviv from gas-masked journalists waiting for the Scud missiles to land, and
its deactualization and distancing, as we are served up war at 'room temperature', for our pleasure, in the comfort and security of our home.

As Baudrillard argues, our 'cold' TV transports us into the heart of the
event while neutralizing its heat, producing both a heightening of experience

and a profound indifference to the symbolic reality on the ground. Thus no 'war' was 'happening' for a western audience, whose electronic extension entailed no risk, no relationship and no involvement. *They* would not be shot, wounded or bombed. There was no McLuhanist, globally extended empathy but only an affective and moral distantiation in the scopic thrills of watching the Baghdad skyline being bombed and the grainy, smart-bomb video footage. As Aksoy and Robins argue, our 'screen culture' led us into 'a blind and complicit fascination' with the technology (1991:328): 'Engulfed by images of the western military machine, we seemed to forget how murderous and destructive those weapons were. It was as if our moral senses had been taken out and neutralized' (1991:327). Comparisons to watching a 'video game' would soon become common and by February 1998 CNN could be found taking out full-page newspaper adverts for another expected war as if they were publicizing the highlights of their new television season (*Guardian*, 17 Feb. 1998, p. 8).

The absence of images of war also means that no war happened for its TV audience (see Taylor, 1998). For all the real-time reports, little was seen of the conflict or its aftermath and effects. The speed and success of the ground offensive, the occurrence of the most ferocious fighting away from the reporters, the overt censorship of the material and the self-censorship of footage of smart-bombs, with their pictures being cut off at the point of impact, all ensured that this 'clean' war was a war cleansed only of the images of violence. A Steve Bell cartoon soon after showed a penguin grandson asking his grandfather what he did in the war: 'Me? I watched television and I'm proud of it!!!' (*Guardian*, 24 May 1991). This was the dominant western experience of and mode of public participation in a war that took place far from their home comforts, entailed no personal effort and was brought back to them for their viewing pleasure. We all watched television but we didn't see a war in the Gulf: we saw nothing of the battles or massacres that occurred, being offered instead war as a build-up, as a mobilization and as an edited aftermath. Only a single Iraqi casualty was seen in Britain when the *Observer* published the picture of a charred face at the windscreen of a vehicle (3 Mar. 1991). The real disaster in the Gulf, we were told, was ecological. We saw more dead birds than we did dead bodies.

And yet we also saw so much *more* of this war. The coverage was marked by a technological hyperreality, epitomised by real-time broadcasts accelerating us across continents to the Saudi border, to the launch of missiles from Gulf ships and then to the centre of Baghdad to follow their progress. Here the real dissolved into the hyperreal – an excessive mode of perception and experience instantly realizing and heightening the moment to hold us hostage, as Baudrillard says, before empty actuality and the visual psychodrama of the news. The defining images of this hyperreality come, however, from the inhuman perception of 'the bomb's-eye view' (Broughton, 1996), offered by the nose-cams of smart or guided munitions.

Long before it became common to talk about the 'pornography' of war coverage, Baudrillard had applied this concept to the operations of media devoted to the realization of an absolute hypervisibility and transparency (*Sed.*, 28–36). 'One sees in close-up what one has never seen before,' he says, aptly describing the smart-bomb cam and its images of the flight, the sight and the *experience* of this bomb as it closes on its target. In this bomb as image, spectacle, news, warfare, advert, and video press release (Cumings, 1992:122), a McLuhanist implosion into the event is superseded by a further implosion as *the watching audience becomes the bomb*. This smart-bomb was designed to mobilize the home front (Cumings, 1992; Wark, 1991:15–17). If its explosive power was aimed at the Iraqis, its implosive power was aimed at us to produce an identification with the bomb rather than its anonymous victims (Broughton, 1996; Robins and Levidow, 1995). In its hyperrealization of experience and simultaneous distancing from the symbolic reality of its effects, nowhere does Baudrillard's comment, the more closely the real is pursued 'the greater does the real absence from the world grow' (*CS*, 122), find more horrific support.

More support for Baudrillard's analysis can be found in the title of his book, whose literal meaning was so important to his critics' interpretation. As Genosko points out, the actual literal translation of 'la guerre du golfe n'a pas eu lieu' is 'the Gulf War has not had (a) place' (Genosko, 1992:52); a connotation Baudrillard intends as he explicitly refers elsewhere to the 'non-place' or 'not-here' ('non-lieu') of memory and of the event (1998b). The Gulf desert is one such non-place: a featureless, geological space and site of both the extermination of human scale and meaning (*Am.*, 5–6), and the extermination of a non-war whose explosive force left the Iraqi families without a place to mourn. But this non-place is also that of speed. As Virilio says in *Speed and Politics* of 1977, today geographic space has been surpassed by the speed of electronic systems: '*the strategic value of the non-place of speed has definitively supplanted that of space*' (1986:133). In the Gulf the non-place of the speed of the coalition technology and their ground offensive surpassed that territorial space defended by the Iraqis. Baudrillard, therefore, reverses Sun Tzu's claim that 'speed is the essence of war' (Virilio, 1986:133). Now speed is the essence of non-war: war as pure speed, pure unilaterality, pure non-confrontation.

This war also lacked a place in its global extension, the coverage imploding with the event, with the television becoming its 'strategic site', wiping out the real event to leave only traces on the screen (*Ill.*, 56). The war we watched took place in the electronic non-place of this global broadcast, whose vectors ranged across Baghdad, Riyadh, Washington, London, Paris, New York, the Saudi border, Jerusalem, Tel Aviv, Kuwait, southern Iraq and all the regional and international diplomatic, military and command centres. As Wark argues, 'the terminal site' of this vector 'is the terminal in practically every living room of the western world', that television that was 'the centre of the construction of the event' (1991:5–6, 11). Even the war's operation took place in this electronic non-place, with satellite information being relayed between stations and command posts to the front line. As the 'flows' of this event crossed borders instantly with impunity, where then was its place (Wark, 1991:7)?

Baudrillard's claim that the implosion of medium and event does not transport us into the real but into a 'nebulous hyperreality' also finds support in a war coverage dominated by uncertainty. Information was impossible to verify, often contradictory or later contradicted. Official military reports were censored and pooled reporters knew only what they were told, while reporters interviewed live from the region remained confused not only as to the wider picture but often even as to what was happening to them. The military was subject to the same problems, overestimating the damage it had caused, the success rate of its smart weapons and Patriot missiles, the success of its search for Scud launchers and the damage it inflicted on an Iraqi military whose strength had been underestimated (see Walker, 1993, 1996, 1997; Cockburn, 1993b; Weiner, 1993). But Baudrillard is right: the failure of Patriot missiles in reality to hit a single Scud or of the US air-force to destroy a single launcher were less important than *the credible appearance* of destruction in the moment of the broadcast.

This uncertainty surrounds even the issue of casualties, with sources disagreeing as to both sides' losses, with Iraqi deaths entering into a numerical hyperspace, inflated or deflated according to need (see Freedman and Karsh, 1993:408–9; Taylor, 1998:265; Rogers, 1991; Cockburn, 1993a; Knightley, 2000:499). Does the absence of corpses prove the lack of Iraqi casualties or a ferocity of bombing that annihilated their bodies? Were the vehicles in the 'highway to hell' really mostly empty, as Freedman and Karsh claim (1993:408), or do we believe the photographs and eye-witness reports of the aftermath (O'Kane, 1995; Taylor, 1998:246–64; McCullin 2003)? These issues cannot be settled: each has long been immersed in the fog of war, in the nebulous hyperreality of its reporting, and in the confusion of all accounts since.

Finally, few contemporary events encapsulate as well as the Gulf War Baudrillard's description of a 'phantom', forgettable, vanishing event pursuing its own trajectory into the void. Within days the global spectacle was replaced by the 'humanitarian crisis' of the abandoned and persecuted Kurds, and a year later Cumings could even ask, 'Does anyone still remember the Gulf War?' (1992:128). If we do, what we remember is the coverage and its images, though even these now merge and blur in the déjà vu of a media model re-experienced since in attacks on Kosovo, Afghanistan and Iraq. Like that bloody 'Gulf War' fought for eight years between Iran and Iraq that it replaced, it itself has now been surpassed by its own sequel, its only consequence being that of its own simulacral repetition. Forgotten soon after, and now erased from history by the success of the latest campaign, this war barely took a place in our memories.

DREAMING OF A STEALTH IDEA

In his *Cool Memories 3* Baudrillard describes J. G. Ballard's 'War fever' as the counterpart to his book *The Gulf War Did Not Take Place* (CM3, 75–6): where he describes the non-occurrence of a war that everyone knows about and sees, Ballard describes the occurrence of World War Three without anyone realizing or remembering it. The reference – actually to the 1988 short story 'The secret history of World War Three' (Ballard, 2001:1116–23) – is apposite, but we can find a greater resonance with Baudrillard in another Ballard story, 'The greatest television show on earth' from 1972.

In this story Ballard describes a future void of events as the world's population, its appetite whetted by live transmissions from the battlefields of Vietnam, devotes itself solely 'to watching television' (2001:806–10). To satisfy this market the television companies turn to time travel, broadcasting 'instant history' nightly to huge ratings. Soon they are offering the 'live' assassination of Kennedy, and the major battles and highlights of the second World War, before moving back to prepare for 'their most spectacular broadcast to date . . . live coverage of the defeat of Napoleon Bonaparte at the Battle of Waterloo'. Scouting out the battle, however, the producers are disappointed to discover that it fails to live up to its reputation. As they face a ratings disaster, a nameless assistant producer has the idea of remaking history – that 'first draft screenplay' – to boost its audience appeal, and so the companies step in, scouring the countryside for extras, providing military supplies, and revamping the entire choreography of the battle to heighten its drama. The show is a success: 'the Battle of Waterloo, when finally transmitted to an audience of over one billion viewers, was a brilliant spectacle more than equal to its advance publicity of the past two hundred years.' As Napoleon ends his days in 'baffled exile', bemused by the turn of events, the television companies begin to eye the stories of the Bible. . .

In his introduction to *Crash*, Ballard strikes a Baudrillardian note, describing a 'communications landscape' governed by advertising and pseudo-events, the governance of our lives by fictions of all kinds and the pre-empting of all original response by the television screen. This has changed the relationship of fact and fiction, he says. It is now unnecessary to invent the latter: 'The fiction is already there. The writer's task is to invent the reality' (1995:4). Reinterpreting the point, Baudrillard quotes this approvingly: 'Ballard: when the imaginary merges with the real, the task of fiction is to invert the real' (*CM2*, 84). Invention and inversion, the simulation of an empirical theory describing the real that simultaneously invents, inverts and reverses the real, this is Baudrillard's method too: that mode of doing violence to the real to remodel and to challenge our experience and conceptualization of it.

We can see, therefore, that Baudrillard's admitted invention of the Gulf War (*BL*, 188) was a strategic, critical reading of the conflict. It was intended as a challenge to the occurrence, meaning, credibility and historical place of the war, albeit one based on its occurrence, responding, like a counter-gift, to the overwhelming evidence of its reality to invert its processes, aiming to 'contest the very self-evidence of war, when the confusion of the real is at its height' (*Ill.*, 64). Baudrillard's Gulf essays describe the same implosion of media and event and the same production and live recording of the historical truth and reality of this war for western audiences as Ballard's story. Stripping away the hired extras, the excessive munitions and the media's dramatic choreography of the war, Baudrillard exposes the paucity of its production and reverses the event itself.

In contrast to both left and right who accepted the truth of this 'war', Baudrillard's strategy refused to legitimize its historical status. He succeeded in opening up the space for an original critical engagement with a war whose unilateral, semiotic processing and imposition refused such a position, to problematize the categories, assumptions and knowledge that constituted our experience of it. Far from being a nihilistic denial, his essays were both a Baaderist provocation, aiming at shocking their audience out of their complacency by extending the absurd swindle – or '*schwindel*' (*Ill.*, 62) – of this war, and a genuine, impassioned, sustained polemic infused with an anger, wit, scepticism and power. They were premised on an opposition to the war and to the western project of destroying the symbolic alterity and singularity of other cultures, from a critical position grounded in, not this western system, but the realm of the symbolic, emerging from it and staking all on the gamble of its own method to strike against the military and media operation. Compare this both to his critics, who merely used the war as an opportunity to renew their insular academic grudge with postmodernism (Patton, 1995:15), and to ourselves who, like Steve Bell's penguins, did nothing but watch television. Faced with depression or rage at the 'vile' reality of the war, Baudrillard attempted to transform it through the only means available: writing (*BL*, 181). His aim was to transfigure the event through its escalation (*BL*, 180), working on the event as it happened to produce a new kind of journalism: not one reporting with hindsight what has happened but reporting 'with the distance of anticipation' what is not happening (*CM3*, 33).

Baudrillard's Gulf essays, therefore, represent the best example of his method of theoretical violence, containing some of his strongest work and most fruitful ideas, activated by a powerful engagement with and critique of this war. Considered closely, his most paradoxical and counter-intuitive claims become defensible and his critical value for a radical media studies becomes obvious. However, these same essays also stand as the most spectacular failure of his method. Their provocation, like the war they critiqued, was *too successful*, leading to their reversal and neutralization in his critics' own invention and inversion of his ideas. If, like Ballard, his aim was 'cautionary' (Ballard, 1995:6), his critics ensured that it would only be his own work that the public would be warned against. Despite his dreams of 'a stealthy idea' that, like the bomber, would slip through all detection systems 'and unfailingly reach its target' (*CM3*, 34), this one set off every claxon possible before being shot down. Baudrillard was clearly stung by this. Despite defending his essays in his next book as having fallen into the same black hole as the war (*Ill.*, 64), his attitude towards the laughter that even the concept of the simulacrum evinces has been defensive (*PC*, 95). Explaining his prophetic strategy in a 1998 essay, he finally conceded, for his weaker interpreters, that 'the Gulf War did take place' (1998b).

Since 1991, however, stronger claims than Baudrillard's for the virtualization of warfare have become commonplace in popular, journalistic and
academic discourse as the Gulf model of media-war has been repeatedly
replayed. Today the description of the Gulf War as a 'deadly video game' is
used without controversy by respected sources (Knightley, 2000:483), and the
idea of a 'Nintendo war' (Robins and Levidow, 1995:122), of a war watched
as screen entertainment in which only virtual targets are hit, has become a
popular cliché. The spread of satellite TV and 24-hour news channels has
exacerbated these processes, and newspapers now regularly comment on the
implosion of media and war and the hyperrealization of warfare for its domestic audience (Katz, 1993; Anthony, 1998). By 2000 Michael Ignatieff could
publish his own sub-Baudrillardian ruminations on 'virtual war' without
attracting any of the opprobrium the same ideas received when expressed by
Baudrillard (Ignatieff, 2000), while, by 2003 and Gulf War II, it was routine
to compare its production and presentation to dominant contemporary paradigms in reality TV and cinema (Kampfner, 2003; Bennett, 2003; Patterson,
2003). As Iannucci acknowledged, these insights were only an extension of
Baudrillard's own in 1991 (Iannucci, 2003).

Somehow, therefore, Baudrillard's stealth idea had hit its target, though it
had done so years too late for its explosive power to have any consequences.
More 'unscrupulous' than even Baudrillard had suspected, the reality that had
abandoned him in 1991 surreptitiously realized his ideas years later to posthu-
mously rob them of their critical force and leave us once more lagging behind
events (*PC*, 101). As Baudrillard has said, a worse fate than being 'proven
wrong' is to be proven right since the value of thought lies precisely in its
differences with the real, in its 'vital' challenge to truth (*PC*, 94), and 'the
singularity by which it constitutes an event' (*PC*, 96). Only this 'event' of
thought can compete with the non-events of this world, its realization and
confirmation representing 'the death throes of the concept' (*PC*, 101). For
Baudrillard that confirmation may now have happened. In 1997 he wrote that
the simulacrum had ceased to be an event in the world, becoming instead our
everyday banality and obscenity (1997h:11) and this has also been the fate of
our simulacral wars. Whereas it was dangerous to expose their simulations in
1991, today it is not only popular knowledge but, given television ratings, our
everyday-obscenity-of-choice. So what can we do, Baudrillard asks, 'in a
world won over to the craziest hypotheses' (*PC*, 102)? Unless this escalation
of simulacra can be met with an escalation of an opposing force then our
acceptance of these simulacra will represent not just the confirmation of
Baudrillard's work but its death throes too. In the Gulf, this force may be hard
to find.

As Baudrillard has said, 'the consequences of what did not take place may
be as substantial as those of an historical event', the flesh suffers just the same
(*GW*, 70). Refusing to report from the war zone, Baudrillard asked, 'what
would I have seen?' (*BL*, 188). He would have seen the same horizon as he
did in America: 'desert for ever' (*Am.*, 121). This is a scene of a physical and

significatory disappearance and radical indifference: of a nudity delivered from all culture, nature, depth and scale, and of a 'visual silence' and a horizontal, geological time (*Am.*, 5–6). If anything the Gulf deserts are older and more indifferent. In *Aftermath: Kuwait 1991* (1993), French photographer Sophie Ristelheuber's collection of images, we discover that same desert of extermination – the extermination both of warfare and of the war itself. Her photos show immense, empty, horizontal sandscapes traversed with tracks or pock-marked with bomb craters; they are scarred with trenches, dug-ins, sandbanks and earth fortifications and lined with spiralling geometrical patterns, abstract shapes and alien, aerial doodlings traced in the sand. Here, in landscapes without horizon or reference and in the visual silence of their vastness, the Gulf War is lost. As Ristelheuber acknowledges, the instant of the shutter captures its aftermath; the *fait accompli* of the war: the instant of its realization and of its disappearance. Baudrillard would later find in photography a technological path to the symbolic (1997e:38), reversing his critique to discover its ability to wrench the object 'from the thunderous context of the real world' to restore to it an immobility and silence equivalent to the deserts (1997c). Ristelheuber also takes the object as her project: her work reveals the disappearance of the subject, the traces they leave behind, and the objects that remain after their withdrawal. Though there are no corpses here, the subject's absence is revealed more profoundly in the alterity of the objects that survive than in the torrent of real-time news and speculation or the few images of death that have since emerged.[3] In Ristelheuber's photography the 'art of disappearance' exposes the extermination of this war.

At the end, therefore, we return to the desert, just as Baudrillard returns repeatedly to Borges's tale of that arch cartographic folly, a 1:1 scale map covering the land before being left to rot, with its fragments last seen blowing in the eastern deserts (Borges, 1975:131; *SS*, 1–3). For Baudrillard it is the territory that blows over the expanse of the map, with vestiges of the real persisting in its deserts (PS, 1). Though he immediately escalates this to see in the simulacrum's victory the abolition of this sovereign difference, he also later admits that this 'perfect crime' of the murder of the real is never perfect as traces of it still remain (*VI*, 63). As he says in *The Gulf War Did Not Take Place*, 'today we see the shreds of this war rot in the desert just like the shreds of the map in Borges' fable' (*GW*, 68). It is these shreds of the real blowing through the deserts that Ristelheuber captures. It is these shreds that the American troops would pass by the roadside over a decade later in their advance on Baghdad, outlasting their own war as it was erased by its sequel, to be joined in the deserts by the shreds of this new campaign. Perhaps only these traces can oppose the everyday obscenity of the simulacrum.

6 'Total screen': 9/11 and
The Gulf War: Reloaded

Are you wholly intent on demoralizing the West . . . ?
                                        Philippe Petit to Baudrillard, in *Paroxysm*

If Baudrillard wanted to find overwhelming evidence of a world of 'non-events' he could have turned to our contemporary media and its popular productions. Today, sports, popular culture, and entertainment are all presented as 'events' worthy of news headlines, with the concept becoming generalized to include a range of phenomena from 'water cooler' TV and 'reality television' shows, to movies, websites, popular adverts and soap opera characters and plotlines. As Baudrillard says, the simulacrum has become our 'absolute banality and everyday obscenity' (1997h:11). While his newspaper articles often comment on current events and phenomena such as mad cow disease (see *ScO*), it is noticeable that his critique of non-events largely eschews an easy attack on the media–culture industry in favour of high profile, frontal assaults on the most heavily mediated and apparently politically important events of our age. His aim in this is primarily critical, in seeking to problematize the media's processing and production of our experience and knowledge, to demonstrate its functioning in support of a code of power, and to challenge these processes in both the form and content of his work.

Hence, instead of targeting popular culture, Baudrillard challenged the entire media and military simulacra of the Gulf War, an act derived from and confirming his career-long commitment to a specific critical position and project. For him traditional or mainstream interpretations cannot produce this challenge: only the violence of extreme thought can capture and make visible extreme phenomena and push them further towards their reversal. Though Baudrillard has always retained a belief in this symbolic challenge, the great paradox of his career is its eclipse by the popular assumption of his nihilism. For many the stylistic power and insight of his description of our nihilistic world overshadows his own critical position, leading to the common belief in his hyperbolic celebration of contemporary phenomena and his pessimistic rejection of all forms of resistance or hope or means of transformation.

Though erroneous, these claims are in part products of Baudrillard's symbolic challenge and, in particular, of its methodological failure. For his challenge to succeed, Baudrillard's counter-intuitive claims must negotiate a delicate balancing act. They must simultaneously double the world and push it further, producing a simulacral representation that resembles yet avoids domestication as a good reflection. They must simultaneously capture the spectacular form of this world while avoiding their own integration, speaking the language of the spectacle without providing its consecration. They must explore the perfections of this totalitarian system while searching for modes that survive and resist it, and they must simultaneously coincide with the world and retain the distance and dual relationship required for that critical play that allows theory to become an *event* in the world to challenge the latter's non-events. At its best, this challenge produces a highly original and provocative analysis and an effective critique, but when it fails – when the doubling of the world is too effective, losing the critical distance, and when the description appears as an elegy – these misinterpretations gain popular currency. Baudrillard, however, also risks a more serious failure than this; one caused not by his own doubling of the world but rather by the world's escalation to and doubling of his own theory. It is a struggle he may be losing as, in *Cool Memories 4*, he laments the pace of the world's realization of his ideas: 'The simulacrum hypothesis deserved better than to become a reality,' he says (p. 92).

But the misinterpretations surrounding Baudrillard's critical project are also the product of attempts by hostile commentators to discredit his work. The belief that Baudrillard rejects all hopes of transformation is traceable to Kellner's early Marxist critique of what he derogatorily titles Baudrillard's 'postmodern carnival' (1989:93). Taking Marxism as a gold standard for all claims of radicality and resistance, Kellner refuses to seriously consider Baudrillard's own critical site, the symbolic, or his search for resistant, reversive forces. By side lining his critical project, mistaking his descriptive analysis of a nihilistic system for its celebration and failing to consider Baudrillard's opposition to simulation and the latter's functioning as a mode of social control, Kellner is able to condemn Baudrillard as postmodern 'nihilist', warning readers of the dangers of his reactionary thought. Hence his conclusion that 'Baudrillard no longer poses *any* social alternative, resistance, struggle, or refusal', seeing 'any sort of agent of political change' as impossible (1989:214, 216). This conclusion entirely misses the fact that from the first Baudrillard's work has been animated by the dual project of tracing the new forms of social control that govern and produce us and searching for and discovering forces which oppose and reverse this perfected system.

From his earliest analyses of the sign system Baudrillard has emphasized its role as a means of social integration and control (*CS*, 60-1, 94), allying western Marxist theories of the extension of alienation throughout everyday life with structuralist, sociological and technical analyses of the operation of this media and consumer society. Much of his early work is concerned with our socialization and training in the 'code' and our semiotic production and 'personalization' as part of the 'total organization of everyday life' (*CS*, 87–98, 29), an analysis he reaffirms in his discussion of general political economy and its role as 'a mechanism of power' (*CPES*, 66,85,87). His later redevelopment of the concept of the simulacrum does not represent a nihilistic refusal of political and ethical responsibility, as Best and Kellner argue (1991), but rather an *intensification* of his concern at the semiotic, totalitarian and terroristic programming of everyday life.

The simulacrum, Baudrillard says, serves as a powerful 'social control' (OS, 60). In only containing those possibilities 'there in advance, inscribed in the code' (OS, 59), and with its 'reality' being reduced to the materialization of these, it produces our experience, expectations, conception of the real, and behaviour. The 'diffraction' of its models and their unilateral imposition thus plays a 'regulative role' (OS, 70), in their short-circuiting, 'dissuasion' and 'deterrence' of the symbolic and of any other thought or response. Despite the radical uncertainty it introduces, therefore, the simulacrum paradoxically also leads to an increased determination. Baudrillard's discussion of our '*referendum* mode' (OS, 62), in which all our responses are precoded stimulus/ response choices that do not reflect but produce our reality to position and integrate us, illustrates precisely this. Simulation functions therefore as a 'leukaemia infecting all social substance', replacing the blood of the system's body 'with the white lymph of the media' (OS, 67).

But if Baudrillard escalates his description of social control he also escalates his hopes for resistance, motivated by his belief in the radical presence and possibility of symbolic forces opposing, spiralling with and irrupting within the semiotic. Broadly we can identify three sources of resistance in his work. The first of these is the survival of the symbolic and its 'demand' within semiotic societies. The concept appears from the first in Baudrillard's work as a site opposing the semiotic, soon being explicitly separated and defended as an ineradicable source of resistance (*MP*, 147; *SED*, 2). By *Symbolic Exchange and Death* Baudrillard's emphasis has shifted to the form of the symbolic itself – 'reversibility' – combining Mauss and McLuhan to see this form as operating *through* semiotic processes, escalating them, creating reversive forces within the semiotic system or causing its collapse at the point of perfection (pp. 1–5). This leads to a new strategy: not of opposition but of *exacerbation* – 'things must be pushed to the limit where, quite naturally, they collapse and are inverted' (p. 4) – and Baudrillard's own theory attempts to follow this, trying to produce exactly this escalation in its potlatch with the world (*IE*, 149–50). The final mode of resistance emerges in his later work in his discussion of the surviving symbolic cultures of the world, such as Aboriginals and Islam, whose vitality and beliefs pose an external threat to the west (*TE*, 81–88, 113–74).

Thus Baudrillard sees a range of forms shadowing the system and multiplying in response to its own movement towards perfection and control. His work continually allows, searches for and discovers reversive modes of resistance. Even the victory of non-events in the contemporary semiotic mediascape is not complete. In *Impossible Exchange* Baudrillard redevelops his analysis, taking a new interest in the 'double game' of events: the spiralling within them of both semiotic and symbolic elements. The world of non-events gives rise, he says, to a desire for 'an event of maximum consequence': a desire for a 'fateful' or 'fated' event symbolically 'rebalancing the scales of destiny' (pp. 132–8). Even within the non-event, therefore, another force of reversal operates.

Baudrillard's own example of this spiralling is the death of Princess Diana. His only contemporary response was a small poem, later set to music, whose lyrics – 'Frontal shock. Total screen. Full stop' – comment simultaneously on the physical impact of the crash for its victims and the media impact of the news (Baudrillard, 1998c). Now, however, he returns to describe her life and death as both a non-event (see also Merrin, 1999a) and a fated event. Thus he describes the 'positive "reality show" of her public and private life' and our own role as 'full blown actors' in this imploded sphere, while also claiming the same public as her 'virtual murderers', desiring her death and with a 'secret sense of exhilaration' at 'the unpredictable event' (*IE*, 137). The non-event of her life, therefore, gave rise to the symbolic event of her 'sacrificial death' (*IE*, 134–6), with the public mourning representing only the guilty 'moral-isation of an immoral event' (*IE*, 137).

In Baudrillard's recent work this spiral of non-event and fated event has become a major theme, being central to his reading of the 9/11 attacks on the World Trade Center and the Pentagon in 2001 and of the American response. It is this spiralling of semiotic and symbolic forces in the event – of forces of control and internal and external forces of reversal – that I want to explore here in an analysis of Baudrillard's comments on 9/11 and on the 'war on terror' and Afghanistan and Iraq wars. In particular I want to consider the media processes involved, his interpretation of 9/11 as both a non-event and a reversive, symbolic event and of the western response as an attempt to reassert a global semiotic control, before concluding with a critical evaluation of the moral implications of his defence of symbolic forces against this western system.

'THE ABSOLUTE EVENT'

In his 2002 book *The Spirit of Terrorism* (*ST*), Baudrillard describes the 9/11 attacks as 'the absolute event' (p. 4).[1] The event strike he had theorized through the 1990s was over (p. 3). Sharing the surprise at that day he not only reversed his theory but also his methodology, arguing a slower thought was required to deal with the 'speed' of such events (p. 4). For him the attacks were marked by a spiralling of semiotic and symbolic, with the western response – the 'war on terror' and the Afghan War – representing a further spiralling as the simulation of security and war was employed against the symbolic threat of terrorism. The 'double game', therefore, here forms a site of struggle between the global power of the western system and those internal and exter-nal, resistant and reversive forces that challenge its dominance.

Perversely, 9/11 also realizes many of the central elements of the non-event. Instantly passing into and imploding with its electronic transmission, this was a global media event, accelerating us into a state of hyperreality and of feedback, interference and uncertainty. Despite the audience's extension into the heart of the event – the real-time montage of close-ups, long shots, multiple angles and ground images, edited and replayed and mixed with commentary, speculation, political reaction, and the apprehension and adrenalin of the live moment – no event was 'happening' for them. Their electronic experience simultaneously actualized and hyperrealized the real, and de-actualized and deterred it, in its semiotic transformation and presentation as televisual spectacle for domestic consumption in the comfort and security of the sign. As in the televised Gulf War, *they* did not risk their lives that day.

'What stays with us, above all else, is the sight of the images,' Baudrillard says (*ST*, 26). The image takes the event hostage and consumes it, 'in the sense that it absorbs it and offers it for consumption' as an 'image-event' (*ST*, 27). So even this irruption of violence did not return us to the real, Baudrillard argues, for ours was primarily a 'fascination with the image' (*ST*, 28–9), albeit it one with the real 'superadded' to it, 'like a bonus of terror, like an additional *frisson*: not only is it terrifying, but, what is more, it is real' (*ST*, 29). This frisson is important – the vertiginous pleasures of the medium, of its technical capacities, the real-time unfolding of action and the editing and production that repeated and layered the most spectacular images, all highlight the scopophilic presentation and consumption of this event. The crucial moments and footage of the plane's explosion, the fireball's growth and the tower's collapse and spreading dust clouds were continuously repeated, blurring temporality: as Sky News unnecessarily added, relishing the detail, 'slow-motion pictures reveal *the full force* and *horror* of the crash . . .' As Žižek says, the satisfaction we got from the repeated shots 'was *jouissance* at its purest' (2002:12).

These were 'pornographic' images, motivated by the desire to materialize the real in its hypervisibility, as exemplified by the copter-cam close-ups of waving people at the windows and tracking shots of bodies in freefall down the tower's side. The press shared the same 'obscenity' the next day in their spectacular wrap-around photo-covers and pull-out photo-sections, as did the public who queued to consume it again, poring over each image and reliving the incredulity and excitement. This consumption of real-life pain and humiliation has now become a mainstream TV entertainment format, running across popular game-shows, quiz shows, CCTV, official and viewer footage clip-shows and even the news, in its coverage of disasters and wars. September 11 was the continuation of this scheduling by other means. In the mediated consumption of another's pain there is a direct line from the smart-bomb's eye-view of the Gulf War, to the accidents, injuries, embarrassments and camcorder-catastrophes of reality TV, to the impotent copter-cam close-ups of 9/11: *you've been maimed*. In 1978 Baudrillard claimed terrorism was 'our theatre of cruelty' (*SSM*, 114). By 2001 it was part of a wider media experience.

For Baudrillard, however, 9/11 was more than a non-event; it also represented a combination of internal, reversive forces and the terrorist's external symbolic challenge. His interpretation of this draws heavily on his earlier analyses of the west's development (*SO, CS, CPES, SED, FF, FS, TE*), and of its project of virtualization (*PC, IE*), its global aspirations (*GW, Ill.,*), its creation within itself of anomalous, reversive forces, such as terrorism, operating against its overprotected operationality (*TE*, 36–80), and its attempts to incorporate or exterminate surviving global, symbolic forces of 'otherness' and 'radical alterity', as well as of their resistance (*TE*, 81–8, 111–74; *PC*, 107–49). One can also find in his earlier work an analysis of the World Trade Center as the perfect sign of this system (*OS*, 69–70) and a discussion of terrorism in which the themes of his 2002 essay are foregrounded (*SSM*; *FS*, 34–50; *TE*, 75–80; 1992a).[2] All these phenomena crystallized for him in the events of 9/11.

In *The Spirit of Terrorism* Baudrillard eschews a 'clash of civilizations' thesis, emphasizing the internal as well as external forces that produced this event. One of these was our own desire to see the reversal of every absolute, hegemonic power, including the west's own. So, Baudrillard says, 'We have dreamed of this event' (p. 5), attempting to both live and exorcise it through our cinematic imaginary (pp. 5–7). It is this complicity – like that of the suicidal towers themselves (p. 8) – that gave the event a 'symbolic dimension' and 'resonance' (pp. 5–6). In the attacks, therefore, the 'visible fracture' of global hostility to the west connected with that system's own internal, reversive fracture (p. 10). 'There is indeed, a fundamental antagonism here,' Baudrillard concludes, though it is that of '*triumphant globalization battling against itself*' (p. 11). Thus terrorism is the shadow of a system that is itself terroristic, in its semiotic programming of everyday life, dissuasive media simulations and global domination (*SSM*, 50).

This system also finds itself fighting all the global 'antagonistic forces', embroiling itself in an 'impossible' 'fractal' war against all the singularities and antibodies opposing it: against the resistance of '*the globe itself*' to globalization (*ST*, 12). Just as every system devoting itself to total positivity 'signs its own death warrant' (*TE*, 106), so the west took its own post-Communist ascendancy for granted, allowing the return of an 'evil' that cannot be forced into an equilibrium by its power but that infiltrates itself globally 'like a virus' (*ST*, 15). If this opposition cannot threaten the west militarily, the latter becomes vulnerable instead in its very 'excess of power' and refusal of exchange. Hence the challenge posed by 'a definitive act which is also not susceptible to exchange', by the creation of an 'irreducible singularity' that revenges all those expelled and extinguished by the global system (*ST*, 9). The terrorists, therefore, employed the 'absolute weapon' of their own sacrifice against a system founded on the 'zero-sum' equation of 'the exclusion of death', inflicting on it nearly 3000 casualties. This, Baudrillard says, is 'the spirit of terrorism' (*ST*, 16–18).

But this act represented not only an external symbolic opposition but also an internal one, as the terrorists were part of this system. This was 'a terrorism of the rich', Baudrillard says: of those who had assimilated modernity and globalism and still wanted to destroy the west (*ST*, 23, 19). Their act multiplied 'to infinity' the destructive power of the 'symbolic weapon' of their death by combining it with the 'modern resources' of the west. Employing the global network without compromising their 'symbolic pact', their act combined 'the white magic of the cinema' with 'the black magic of terrorism', producing both 'the purest form of spectacle' and 'the purest symbolic form', the challenge (*ST*, 21, 22, 29–30). Contrary to western claims it is not this sacrifice but the elimination of enemies from a safe distance, without any contact, communication or risk, that is the real cowardice (*ST*, 26).

'The whole of visible power can do nothing against the tiny, but symbolic, death of a few individuals,' Baudrillard claims; the 'infinitesimal point' of their deaths creates 'a gigantic suction or void, an enormous convection' around which the system of power gathers (*ST*, 19, 18). The act provokes a hyper-reaction and reversal of the system, leading it to introduce the same repressive security measures as fundamentalist societies (*ST*, 31–2). Once the system has terrorized its own population with a fear of terrorism, all natural, accidental and reversive forces are experienced as terroristic – so the anthrax attacks in October 2001, the plane crashes in New York in November 2001, in Florida in January 2002 and in Milan in April 2002, as well as the American-Canadian blackouts in August 2003 were all immediately seized on as Bin Laden's work (*ST*, 33).

In his 2002 book *Power Inferno* Baudrillard extends this analysis of the interplay of western universalization and globalization and the global singularities that stand outside it (see 2002, 2003b). He argues here that the Enlightenment universalization of values that once attempted to assimilate other cultures within itself as difference (see *TE*, 124–38) has been replaced by a globalization that instead 'sweeps away all differences and values, ushering in a perfectly in-different (un)culture' (*Par.*, 14). What remains is an 'all-powerful global technostructure standing over against the singularities', the former's homogenizing power being opposed by all the 'antagonistic', 'irreducible', 'heterogeneous forces' that emerge in response (*Par.*, 14). The more it proceeds the more we see a 'resurgence' of 'increasingly intense resistances to globalization', Baudrillard argues (*Par.*, 13). September 11 represented, therefore, a violent response to 'the violence of the global' – the eradication of singularities by a fundamentalist, western monoculture (2003b).

For Baudrillard, 'globalization has not completely won . . . heterogeneous forces are rising everywhere.' Simultaneously reworking Nietzsche, McLuhan, Weber and Durkheim, Baudrillard describes the west's attempts to subjugate these resistant cultures as the *ressentiment* of an 'indifferent and low definition' (semiotic and cold), 'disenchanted', 'de-intensified' and 'de-sacralized' system against hot, symbolic, 'high definition', 'high intensity', sacrificial cultures. His Maussian view of the *exchange* of cultures leads him to the original argument that it is not the impoverishment and underdevelopment of the third world that explains their hostility to the west but rather the latter's overwhelming, unilateral gift of itself to them. It is not due to 'the fact that the west stole everything from them and never gave anything back' but to 'the fact that they received everything and were never allowed to give anything back'. September 11 was an attempt to reverse this 'symbolic obligation' through a humiliation 'the global system cannot give back'. But this western gift is also the 'curse' of its own culture, Baudrillard adds, as in turning its own populations into the perpetual receivers of its bounty it risks provoking a 'self-hatred' – 'an invisible despair' that could itself break into violence (2003b).

Baudrillard's *The Spirit of Terrorism* has become one of his most successful and famous essays. Aided by its rapid translation and dissemination on the internet, it has been largely responsible for restoring his intellectual profile and cutting-edge cachet in the English-speaking world. For once the critical reaction was serious and sympathetic, his ideas being faithfully summarized and positively received. Had he denounced the attacks, as expected, as a non-event, the reaction would undoubtedly have been more hostile. As it was his description of 9/11 as 'an absolute event' increased his readership, though in mirroring so closely the popular discourse and journalistic platitudes about an event whose historical status was being reappraised within two years (Eagleton, 2003) it risked shortening its critical shelf-life.

Hostile reactions to his essay could still, of course, be found – especially in America. Mark Goldblatt declared in December 2001 that Baudrillard had 'vaulted into the lead in the unofficial competition for Most Despicable Quote in the wake of September 11th' in claiming that America wanted these attacks (Goldblatt, 2001), comments echoed by Walter Kirn in the *New York Times* in September 2002, who awarded Baudrillard 'first prize for cerebral cold-bloodedness' for equating the experience of living and working in, with that of dying in, the towers (Kirn, 2002). Baudrillard's most critical reception, however, was in France, where he 'sparked a lively public debate' conducted in the national newspapers and earned 'many critics' (Swint, 2002). On 13 November 2001 Jacques Julliard argued in *Libération* that Baudrillard was part of 'a class of miserably anti-American intellectuals' (Swint, 2002), an accusation repeating that by Alain Minc in the strongest attack on Baudrillard in his *Le Monde* article, 'Terrorism of the spirit' on 6 November (Minc, 2002).

For Minc, Baudrillard follows a French intellectual tradition of 'standing surety for the revolution underway' – just as Foucault supported Ayatollah Khomeini in Iran in 1979 so Baudrillard now becomes the philosopher of the 'terrorist model'. By blaming American globalization Baudrillard finds an equivalence in the system to the attacks, implicitly defending them as 'one evil' responding 'to another', and so the rhetoric of this 'perverse magician', Minc says, offers only 'an apology for terrorism dressed up as an explanation'. Baudrillard, therefore, shares the French intellectual's inability to recognize the existence of 'a hierarchy of values', combining a nihilistic 'anti-humanism' in which 'nothing has value' with 'anti-American impulses, pro-Third World reflexes and Leftist reactions'. Against this Minc defends 'the absolute value' of western political and economic liberalism, its expression of an objective morality and the right of the west to defend itself (Minc, 2002).

Minc's reading of Baudrillard as anti-American, is of course too limited – Baudrillard has his eyes set on a wider target: the entire western semiotic culture. The more important criticism, that of implicitly defending the act, however, is itself compromised by Minc's own absolute exoneration of America, its globalized system and its foreign policy. Mirroring America's own amnesia of the historical context which provoked the attack, and its construction of its own innocence, all Minc offers against Baudrillard is an apology for America dressed up as an explanation of morality. His uncritical paean to western liberalism demonstrates a naivety more 'pitiful' than Baudrillard's opposition, and ends by lending support to a 'war on terror' experienced by many as globally terroristic. The estimated numbers of civilian casualties of allied actions in Afghanistan and Iraq now grossly outweigh the 3,000 killed in 9/11 and Minc's implicit defence of these deaths exposes the racist hypocrisy of the 'humanism' he claims to stand for, highlighting his own, rather than Baudrillard's, nihilism.

Much of Baudrillard's analysis is actually defensible. September 11 did represent the reversal of western power as well as the reversal in particular of the west's unilateral model of war. Just as the Gulf War was 'won in advance' (Baudrillard, *GW*, 61), so these single, unanswerable air strikes instantly crippled, humiliated and defeated American power: before Bush could even announce his 'war on terror' the war had already taken place and America had lost. As in the Gulf, military defeat was not necessary; victory on the airwaves was sufficient and this was provided by the global media's amplification of these attacks. Their endless replays created a montage effect not of a single cruise missile strike but of dozens of strikes on New York City: of an *urban storm* reversing that 'desert storm' unleashed on the Arab world in 1991. The real-time images sucked the oxygen from their imploded, urban, front-line audiences like fuel-air explosives, just as Arab civilians in the urban front-line of the Gulf War were hit by western munitions. Ultimately, Baudrillard was correct that the spectacle of this 'definitive act' was 'not susceptible to exchange'. The problem America faced was not simply one of punishment or long-term security but one of producing a response that would match these images, erasing their memory and restoring its global face. Its answer was to turn back to the model of the Gulf War, its semiotic materialization and its global deterrence.

'LET FREEDOM REIGN!'

As Baudrillard suggests, the western response employed simulation as a global social control, the non-event of the Gulf War (*ST*, 12, 34) providing the model for the unilateral 'spectacular set-pieces' of the Afghan and Iraq wars that were designed to both revenge the attacks and domesticate all resisting territory (2003b). If the American response succeeded in this, it failed, however, to ascend to the terrorist challenge and produce images equivalent to those of that day. Set against the spectacle of 9/11, America's strikes on

Afghanistan, one of the poorest countries on earth, appeared an impoverished act. Its 'repetitive, rehashed pseudo-event', in which the model preceded and dominated, could not substitute, Baudrillard says, 'for a real and formidable, unique and unforeseeable event' (*ST*, 34).

Beginning on 7 October with a cruise missile and bombing assault on Kabul, the war would always suffer from being a TV repeat of the Gulf War, lacking the spectacle, footage and novelty, waged on a country that, as the captain of the USS *Enterprise* admitted, was 'not a target-rich environment' (Borger et al., 2001). As one general commented, the military action involved 'turning big bits of rubble into small bits of rubble' (Freedland, 2001:2). Bombed, ramshackle training camps, already-razed Afghan cities, mountain warfare, and a ground offensive mostly conducted with Afghani, Northern Alliance fighters, televisually indistinguishable from the Taliban they opposed (and often had once been), came a poor second to the real-time, hypervisible spectacle of the imploding Twin Towers. American attempts to stage-manage the media spectacle of war and manufacture more dramatic footage of commando raids noticeably backfired (Harding et al., 2001).

Despite the end of al-Qaeda operations in Afghanistan and the defeat of the Taliban, the war that faded from view even before the BBC's John Simpson 'liberated' Kabul (Burkeman, 2001), and Kandahar and the Tora Bora were cleared, was a limited success. Afghanistan still lacks democracy, basic services and peace, as renewed Taliban attacks show, and Mullah Omar and Bin Laden both escaped. The latter has taken on an even more spectral presence in the tapes and videos released since 2001 (see Kampmark, 2002; Baudrillard, 2004b), his iconic status being confirmed by the sight of Eminem in a Bin Laden beard getting down in a cave in his 2002 *Without Me* video and Aaron Barschak's gate-crashing of Prince William's birthday party in June 2003. On 20 December 2001, on the day the number of dead in 9/11 was revised down to 3,234, civilian deaths in Afghanistan were estimated at 3,767 (Milne, 2001).[3]

Despite George W. Bush's promise of 'a new kind of war' to defeat global terrorism (Campbell, 2001), the Afghan War failed to produce or achieve either. The Gulf War model, so effective in the non-place of the desert, was of limited use against the non-place of al-Qaeda, while the only effective response – a networked, intelligence-led, ongoing security campaign against terrorism – could not provide the images to eclipse 9/11. Hence the turn to Iraq in early 2003. Though it offered little advantage in the fight against terrorism, it promised a more tangible target amenable to western military power, the opportunity to repeat the global spectacle and ratings success of the 1991 war, a more certain, visible and traditional victory than any in the 'war on terror', and the chance to settle old, familial geopolitical scores against an enemy whom many Americans believed anyway to be behind the World Trade Center attacks (Harris, 2003).

'Operation Iraqi Freedom' was launched on 20 March 2003 – broadcast as 'the Iraq War' or 'Gulf War II' – to deliver a global, spectacular television victory over a physical, urban centre and identifiable regime, with Saddam substituting for the absent Bin Laden as his sliding, metonymic double. If the Rumsfeld doctrine was in the ascendant militarily, the media war was still modelled on 1991. Cognisant of how real-time reports from Baghdad had captured the world's attention then, on 22 March this city became the theatre for the *son et lumière* display of 'Shock and Awe'. The repeated simulacral model of war and the real-time global spectacle of a cruise missile assault on the city to excited commentary would again function as a means of social control, reasserting America's power and pride. The attack failed, however, to 'awe' either the Iraqis or its western audience. The video-game images ('Shock and Awe' being trademarked by Sony soon after (Day, 2003)), were too reminiscent of the video-game images of 1991, and just as the 'bullet-time' fights of *The Matrix: Reloaded*, though *better*, lacked the excitement of first seeing them in *The Matrix*, so the 'bomb-time' effects of *The Gulf War: Reloaded* suffered from the same problem.

There were, however, important innovations in the media war. In Britain the access to 24-hour news channels had grown significantly since 1991, bringing a new real-time experience of war (Sherwin, 2003; Wells, 2003). Moreover what was seen was more explicit, including battlefield footage from Umm Qasr and live enemy operations on the banks of the Tigris. Satellite TV and the internet also provided access to more non-western sources as well as to otherwise censored images and personal weblogs charting civilian experience in Iraq (Hammersley, 2003; Dodson, 2003; al Yafai, 2003). Satellite TV technology also allowed a new, individually tailored experience, with interactive buttons allowing the viewer to switch between battle zones, 'to call the shot of the shots' (Lawson, 2003a).

Despite this the war coverage repeated its predecessor's simulacral dramatization and deactualization for its western audience. The *extra reality* on offer returns us again to Baudrillard's claim that all attempts to add more dimensions to our experience of the real only perfects its simulacrum, increasing our absence from the world in making us think we are closer to it (*CS*, 122). Perceptive analysts noted how much the war coverage owed to the styles of reality TV and contemporary simulated reality shows such as *24*, adding to the media's implosion with the war (Patterson, 2003; Iannucci, 2003; Lawson, 2003b). This was seen especially in the live feeds, editing, narrativization, camera shots, split-screen effects, audience voting and email feedback coverage, and the *Survivor*-style reports of the embedded journalists, epitomized by NBC's David Bloom. This was war packaged in a prime-time entertainment format as the hoped-for summer 'reality-event-show'.

The military followed the same television and Hollywood scripting (Patterson, 2003), most obviously in the ready-made for war-TV *human* drama 'Saving Private Lynch' – the dramatic rescue of Jessica Lynch from the Iraqi-help Nassiriya Hospital B9 American Special Forces – which emerged amidst a stalled campaign and growing criticism of Rumsfeld's game plan. The eye-witnesses' description of her rescue as conducted like 'an action movie' was apposite, given that, as Kampfner says, 'the Pentagon had been influenced by Hollywood producers of Reality-TV and action movies, notably *Black Hawk Down*' (2003:3). Despite later doubts, the edited video-package did its job in turning around the national mood. Hollywood may be circling around this story but any future film would already be a sequel. What this non-event highlighted was the significance the military attached to not just controlling but actively producing and directing coverage for a medium whose need to fill its air-time was felt by the allied powers as potentially destabilizing – as British Foreign Secretary Jack Straw made clear when he complained that the evacuation of Dunkirk would have been impossible with rolling coverage (Ahmed and Hinsliff, 2003; White, 2001). He had a point: the 'pause' in the first week of the war, together with unexpected Iraqi resistance, caused confusion and worry for a media and public who had never considered the possibility of a *real* Gulf War. This, however, would not happen: the victory here was as precessionary and certain as in 1991 (Borger, 2003:3).

The endgame, however, failed to provide the global spectacle America desired: the half-toppling of the statue of Saddam in Firdouz Square on 9 April was a too obvious and weak symbolic counterpart to the fall of the Twin Towers. With Saddam's disappearance, all that was left was a non-event produced and framed for our consumption as the definitive and predictable sign of the regime's end. The self-liberation of the Iraqis could not be accomplished: when it became clear that they could not quickly pull the statue down the American military stepped in to finish the job. The Iraqis did not understand the primacy of the western audience, the time constraints even of rolling news, and the networks' fear of a drifting audience and their need to deliver that 'Kennedy' moment ('where were you?' . . . 'watching television'). So the Iraqis were excluded from this act, in an implosion of media and military with the event that neutralized and short-circuited the people's efforts, replacing them with that demanded, semiotic image of the statue's fall. Believing they were the centre and meaning of the act, the Iraqis did not see that they were only the extras, providing local colour and a guarantee of authenticity and legitimacy for the western audience for whom the event really occurred. This forced, final act exposed the paucity of the war's spectacle, rushing the end of the war for the television public.

The most visible face of Iraq during the war was the Iraqi Information Minister, Mohammed Saeed-al-Sahaf. Dubbed 'Comical Ali' by the western media for his 'Panglossian' stories and lies, he became a cult figure in the west, appearing on T-shirts and websites and as a talking doll (Black, 2003; Watt, 2003). Our mirth at his lying was, however, disingenuous. Just as Disneyland's fictions serve, Baudrillard argues, to convince America that everything outside it is real (PS, 12), so the west employed 'Comical Ali' to demonstrate the abuses of the totalitarian system and the truthfulness, transparency and morality of our own media. Actually their hyperrealized, fragmentary and uncertain reports provided little more 'truth', and many of their claims were as fictive or uncertain as those of Comical Ali (Millar and White, 2003;

Millar, 2003). How many times, for example, was Umm Qasr taken by the coalition? We should reflect, therefore, on Comical Ali's last words to western journalists: 'I now inform you that you are too far from reality' (Revill, 2003). Whatever 'lies' his talking doll tells it is more truthful than the Bush doll also offered for sale in the US wearing a 'full naval aviator flight uniform', modelled on the one Bush wore on the USS *Abraham Lincoln* on 1 May 2003 as he declared the end of the war rather than the National Guard uniform he wore during the Vietnam War (Campbell, 2003a, 2003b).

If, as Baudrillard argued, the 1991 Gulf War ended with a victory that was not a victory (*GW*, 81), so too did its sequel. Whereas America's 'absence of politics' (its lack of plans for the region after the war) led to its rapid withdrawal in 1991, this time regime change necessitated a military and political presence. The same 'absence of politics' was immediately obvious, however, as mass looting, lawlessness and anti-Americanism, together with a continued and effective insurgency cast a question mark over the victory that even the capture and global display of Saddam Hussein in December 2003 could not overcome. Although this spectacle had been long anticipated, the images of a shabby old man's medical were less impressive than had been hoped, and certainly could not compete with those of 9/11. A June 2003 estimate of 5,000–10,000 Iraqi civilian deaths in the war (Jeffrey, 2003) made the figure for the World Trade Center, that had morally and politically legitimated the invasion, appear small. In October 2004 the BBC reported that *The Lancet* suggested a figure of over 100,000 'excess deaths' since the war was launched.

There were other Baudrillardian echoes in the aftermath too. The war that Bush declared over on 1 May was a non-war and it was followed by a nonpeace: by a postwar that looked more like a real war. In August 2003 the number of American soldiers killed after the war overtook those killed during it (Beaumont, 2003) and, by 16 June 2004, 694 of the 853 US casualties to date had been killed in the postwar period (Borger, 2004). Iraqi insurgents targeted the American military, foreign workers, the new Iraqi regime, the Shia community, Kurds and other ordinary Iraqi civilians, leading to a confused, insecure and bloody state of 'peace'. April 2004 also saw a Sunni rebellion centred on Falluja, and a radical Shi-ite uprising in south and central Iraq, both against the US occupation. Fighting spread, covering Iraq from north to south, much of it put down by US military force, leading to at least 600 people killed in Falluja (Chevallot, 2004:5). By the anniversary of Bush's declaration of the war's end it was Comical Ali's claims – 'we have them surrounded in their tanks'; 'they are the ones who will find themselves under siege'; 'we have drawn them into a quagmire and they will never get out of it' – that appeared most truthful.

Criticism also grew of the justification for the war. Weapons of mass destruction were not found, Iraqi 'freedom' had turned into civil and military chaos and the moral superiority of the west collapsed when photographs of the torture and sexual abuse of Iraqi captives were published in April 2004.[4] On 28 June Iraq was given sovereignty in a secret handover, brought forward to avoid attack. Bush's media-friendly response to the news on a note passed to him – 'Let freedom reign!' – bore little relation to the situation on the ground, where armed resistance, terrorist attacks and the taking and execution of foreign hostages continued. For Bush's critics the Iraq War was increasingly seen as a personalized diversion of the war on terror; one fuelling global Islamic militancy, giving al-Qaeda a foothold in Iraq and having little effect on its terrorist capacity, as attacks since 9/11 in Tunisia, Karachi, Kuwait, Bali, Jordan, Kenya, Morocco, Yemen, Saudi Arabia, Turkey and Madrid demonstrated (Burke, 2003; McGrory, 2003).

For Baudrillard, therefore, the American response to 9/11 represented a further spiral of the semiotic and symbolic processes within those events and an attempt to deploy simulation as a means of global control and homogenization. His claim that the unilateral, simulacral model of non-war was employed by the west to eradicate globally resistant forces finds support in the operations in Afghanistan and Iraq and their aftermath. These were not just conducted in order to defeat terrorists or a future terrorist threat but also to integrate these outlaw zones and their symbolic cultures within a western model of democracy and a controlled, global system. While Baudrillard's picture of a fundamentalist western monoculture imposing the global 'reign' of its own values may attract criticism, it is one that many others around the world will recognize. Either way, his claim that such a global project inevitably and continuously produces new forces of resistance to it is one that should be heeded, especially after witnessing the deterioration of Iraq.

'UNACCEPTABLE' THOUGHT

Baudrillard later admitted the problems of thinking about the 'absolute event' of 9/11, in providing 'an analysis which might possibly be as unacceptable as the event, but strikes the . . . symbolic imagination in the same way' (*ST*, 41). Baudrillard's defence of the world's singularities against the west and critique of its own semiotic terrorism will certainly be unacceptable to many. In particular his claim in *Cool Memories* that it would be 'better to feel ourselves dying, even in the convulsions of terrorism' than to disappear in our systems, condemned to their 'anaesthetized', political, social and historical 'coma' (*CM*, 5), retrospectively makes for uncomfortable reading. Baudrillard's career-long defence of the symbolic against the semiotic becomes problematic, therefore, on the issue of terrorist violence.

Minc was not the only one to feel Baudrillard's 9/11 essays represented an apology for terrorism. *Der Spiegel* opened its frank 2002 interview with him (Baudrillard, 2004b) with the question:

Der Spiegel: Monsieur Baudrillard, you have described the 9/11 attacks on New York as the 'absolute event'. You have accused the United States, with its insufferable hegemonic superiority, of rousing the desire for its own destruction. Now that the reign of the Taliban has collapsed pitifully and Bin Laden is nothing more than a hunted fugitive, don't you have to retract everything?

Baudrillard: I have glorified nothing, accused nobody, justified nothing. One should not confuse the messenger with his message. I have endeavoured to analyse the process through which the unbounded expansion of globalization creates the conditions for its own destruction.

Baudrillard's replies offer a restatement and defence of his earlier arguments on 9/11. Thus American power, focusing on visible objects, cannot erase the 'symbolism' of that day, he argues, the war in Afghanistan representing a 'completely inadequate, substitute action'. He is also equivocal about the final benefits of that war, rejecting the idea that B–52 bombers can act as 'instruments of the world-spirit'. He repeats his belief that terrorism is a product of the global system, a product that cannot be militarily defeated since its virus has penetrated everywhere to sit 'at the heart of the culture that fights it'. He criticizes especially the 'immense violence' of globalization, rejecting its self-promotion as a force for human rights and universal values as an 'advertising' at odds with its actual effects. Finally, he warns again of the inevitable counter-reaction the west's paradoxical project of forcing democracy on the world will bring (2004b).

In the interview, Baudrillard explicitly denies defending terrorism: as he says, 'I do not praise murderous acts – that would be idiotic.' When pushed on the morality of his critique, he reverses the interviewer's assumptions to point out that, in opposing the west's violent incorporation of 'everything that is unique, every singularity', *he* is 'the humanist and moralist' (2004b). We can see here his positioning both within and outside the western system he criticizes. From one perspective Baudrillard remains a western thinker, drawing on established intellectual traditions and pursuing a committed internal critique of the west's organization, operation and effects and thus adopting a clear moral position on these phenomena. But this position spirals with another with his defence of symbolic cultures from the claimed, external standpoint of the symbolic and his ironic adoption and reversal of western morality against itself (in emphasizing the contradiction between its universal ideals and the terroristic effects of its globalization), both destabilizing this same moral position.

This simultaneous actual and ironic adoption of western intellectual values is seen again in his claim for a morality in the form of his work. 'In my own way, I am very much a moralist. There is a morality of analysis, a duty of honesty.' Rejecting claims of resignation, he says, 'I don't resign myself, I want clarity, a lucid consciousness . . . In this respect I am a man of the Enlightenment.' Against a moral reading that falsifies history he argues that 'we must see the thing beyond the opposition of good and bad. I seek a confrontation with the event as it is without equivocation' (2004b). Whether Baudrillard achieved this remains open to question, but his was one of the most well-publicized, critical voices emerging in the aftermath of an event whose horror seemed to place it beyond questioning, creating a mood of respectful silence that legitimated the resulting neoconservative military response and policy. If he fulfilled here his role as a lucid consciousness and Enlightenment intellectual, confronting the event without equivocation, it was, however, the spiralling of this position with his anti-Enlightenment, anti-humanist, anti-western, symbolic critique, and its provocation and challenge, that gave his essay its power.

Thus we return to the issue of Baudrillard's defence of the symbolic. His initial response to *Der Spiegel's* first question might be seen as disingenuous. Though he does not offer the 'apology' for terrorism Minc claims, he does not offer the purely descriptive analysis he suggests either. As I have argued, Baudrillard has actively defended and promoted the symbolic and its mode of resistance and reversal from the beginning, searching and even hoping for its irruption within and against the western semiotic order. This becomes problematic when that irruption takes the form of the terrorist atrocity of 9/11. He does, of course, see this terrorism as part of the semiotic order and its processes, which complicates his positioning, but in so far as it remains a manifestation of those symbolic forces he has defended, his critical framework is implicated in a support for its actions. His concept of the symbolic explicitly draws on the radical Durkheimianism of Bataille, Caillois, Klossowski and the College of Sociology which valorizes forms of behaviour, modes of relations and violence such as ritual sacrifice as a means of disturbing the profane and opening the sacred in the communion they produce. Hence, despite the internal processes contributing towards 9/11, his description of the terrorist 'sacrifice' risks a radical Durkheimian valorization of the attacks. From within western Enlightenment morality such a position is, as Baudrillard admits, 'unacceptable', but it may be that outside that system, from the perspective of the symbolic and the order of the sacred, its horror may allow for another explanation and even a justification.

Interestingly, Baudrillard does not go that far, his identification of terrorism as part of and as produced by our system allowing him to avoid a full commitment to it as a symbolic force. The same spiralling of these forms can, therefore, be found in his own positioning because he cannot be satisfactorily or comfortably placed in relation to the morality of the terrorist attacks. Arguably he fails in the sight of both semiotic and symbolic orders. From the western perspective he does not condemn them sufficiently, while from the perspective of the symbolic he fails to offer the defence his position logically calls for. The main failure of Baudrillard's essay, therefore, is its *lack* of defence of the terrorist acts. As he acknowledges, such a defence would have been absolutely unacceptable, but arguably his philosophy demanded precisely that position. Thus, for the first time, Baudrillard failed to rise to his own challenge.

The strength of his essay, however, lies in its critique of the western order and this is how it should be read. What Baudrillard's work presents us with is a stark choice of modes of meaning, communication and relations. If the violent world of the sacred and its 'convulsive communication' is threatening or terrifying to us, immured in the hypersecurity of our permanent profane in which we consume the world through its media simulacra, Baudrillard makes clear that what is even more monstrous is a society that expels it so thoroughly to promote the semiotic reduction, processing and mediation of all relations and the neutralization, dissuasion and anaesthetization of experience. Only *that* society is capable of responding to the terrorism of September 11 with an indefinite, terroristic 'war on terror', and only that society, having declared the absolute value of innocent human life, could transmit live images of the destruction of another city into its population's home as entertainment, and care so little about the mounting casualties it creates. Ultimately, Baudrillard's media theory makes us aware, it is *we* who are the apologists for terrorism.

'Are you wholly intent on demoralising the west?' Philippe Petit asks Baudrillard in *Paroxysm* (p. 15). Baudrillard wilfully reinterprets the question in the light of the radical Durkheimian tradition's historical genealogy of the west's desacralization and nihilistic evacuation of all symbolic relations and meaning to reverse its critical intent. 'The demoralization of the west is constitutive of its history,' Baudrillard responds. 'I didn't invent it' (p. 15).

7 'The matrix has you': virtuality and social control

We are no longer the actors of the real but the double agents of the virtual.
Baudrillard, *Fragments: Cool Memories 3*

There is a scene early in the Wachowski brothers' 1999 cult film *The Matrix* where the lead character, Neo (played by Keanu Reeves), is visited by his friend Choi, who has arranged to buy some software from him:

> He closes the door. On the floor beside the bed is a book, Baudrillard's *Simulacra and Simulation*. The book has been hollowed out and inside are several computer discs. He takes one, sticks the money in the book and drops it on the floor. Opening the door, he hands the disc to Choi.
> (Wachowski and Wachowski, 2001a:10)[1]

As Neo picked up the book in the film, we could read the title. Jean Baudrillard is in *The Matrix*.

The superficial reason for his inclusion is clear: the producers of an uber-cool, big-budget, action-movie, effects fest whose theme is the virtual reality computer simulation of our entire reality get to name-check for the cognoscenti *the* theorist of simulation. Elevated by the Wachowskis to the patron saint of a knowledge, of a zeitgeist, of a complete contemporary experience of the real, and – for them – of the entire future of humanity, Baudrillard's hyperbolic title, 'the high priest of postmodernism', may now appear too conservative (Baudrillard, 1989d). Though this latest investiture repeats many of the errors of the last, it does at least serve a purpose here, his appearance in the film representing an acknowledgement of the importance of his theory of simulation. On one level, therefore, the film functions as a useful case-study of aspects of Baudrillard's media theory, its fictional projection of the path of virtual technology allowing us to reconsider his discussion of the simulacrum. But the film's status as a milestone in the development and domination of digital special effects also allows us to extend this, to explore Baudrillard's views on cinema, to consider in more detail his critique of new media and 'virtuality' and to explore again how, for him, these simulacral processes operate as a mode of social control. In this chapter, therefore, I want to offer a critical reading of *The Matrix*'s use of Baudrillard, his own views on contemporary developments in digital cinematography, his response to the film and the way he figures in it, and his wider critique of virtuality.

The plot of *The Matrix* follows the life of Keanu Reeves's Thomas Anderson, 'program writer for a respectable software company' (Wachowski and Wachowski, 2001a:20), who is by night a successful hacker going by the name of 'Neo'. Obsessed with discovering the identity of 'Morpheus' and the meaning of 'the matrix', he is contacted by 'Trinity' (Carrie-Anne Moss) who, with Morpheus (Laurence Fishburne), has been trying to find him. From them he learns 'the truth': that the entire world he has lived within is unreal and that he is actually in an embryonic sac connected to an incubation pod in a future world where machines have evolved to enslave humanity, harvesting and feeding off their energy, keeping them unconscious of this by connecting their brains to a giant, virtual reality, 'a neural interactive simulation that we call "the matrix"' (2001a:38). The world he lived within was a virtual reality illusion. Instead of it being 1999, Morpheus tells him, 'It's closer to 2199' (Wachowski and Wachowski, 1999). The rest of the story follows the guerrilla resistance of Morpheus's group and their attempt to find 'the one': a prophesied saviour whose power to internally manipulate this computer matrix will lead to human freedom from the machines.

That this prophecy is realized and that it is Keanu Reeves who achieves this Christ-like state are inevitable. That the whole is wrapped up in state-of-the-art, computer-generated special effects, the complete range of action-movie clichés, designer hyperviolence, a thin veneer of trite philosophy, the aestheticized hypercool noir of shades, black leather, mobile phones, machine pistols and military hardware, and a tacked-on hero-gets-the-girl love interest, is equally inevitable for a mainstream, summer-release, Hollywood-style 'blockbuster'. But beneath this banal, overfinanced action movie and its ultra-violent cyberchic, there is more going on: there is another film and another reality, one containing one of the most important popular representations of new media, their possible future, and the epistemological issues they raise. To get at this film one must, like Neo, follow a path that moves beyond the merely apparent.

'WELCOME TO "THE DESERT OF THE REAL"'

The stock of references employed by the Wachowskis for Neo's path to reality include, at various times, both *The Wizard of Oz* and *Alice in Wonderland* (Wachowski and Wachowski, 2001a:27–30). *Alice* it may be, but this is *Alice* read through Jefferson Airplane's acid trip, 'White rabbit',[2] where pills not cookies bring the required expansion of consciousness; though in the late twentieth century world of *The Matrix*, sunny West Coast psychedelia gives way to the thumping techno-noir of the appropriately named band Rage Against the Machine; the promised harmony of the age of Aquarius is replaced by a vision of a dystopic reality of charred nature and machinic domination, and 'free your mind' becomes not a counter-cultural mantra of creative exploration and cosmic attunement, but an evangelical statement of millennial anarcho-libertarianism. The linking of Neo's path with Alice's and Dorothy's (Felty, 1999), however, is misconceived: where they moved from the real to a fantasy world from which they later woke, Neo passes from the dream to the real world; a world from which there is no return. 'I can't go back, can I?' he asks. 'No, but if you could, would you really want to,' Morpheus replies (Wachowski and Wachowski, 2001a:42).

Descartes's *Meditations* from 1641 might, however, provide a better way to approach the Wachowskis' story (Descartes, 1968). In his attempt to discover epistemological certainty, he poses early on the question of whether we are dreaming (1968:96–7), an idea echoed in the film, with all Neo's early scenes opening with him waking and questioning whether he has been, or still is, dreaming (Wachowski and Wachowski, 2001a:11). Morpheus also poses the same problem for him on their first meeting, asking if he has ever had a dream he thought was real: 'What if you were unable to wake from that dream? How would you know the difference between the dream world and the real world?' (2001a:30–1). Once posed, however, this philosophical question is immediately dropped as Neo is awoken to the truth of his life as a crop – as a farmed animal producing energy for the machines – being greeted in the sewers with the words 'Welcome to the real world' (2001a:34).

What makes this interesting is the updating of the Cartesian problematic through projected developments in virtual reality technology. From within, a perfected sensory simulation would be indistinguishable from the real – as the 1996 script points out: 'If the virtual reality apparatus . . . was wired to all of your senses and controlled them completely, would you be able to tell the difference between the virtual world and the real world?' 'You might not, no,' Neo answers. 'No, you wouldn't,' Morpheus replies (Wachowski and Wachowski, 1996). You wouldn't, unless Morpheus, the Greek god of the underworld and dreams, wakes you from your immersion, just as he reveals the reality to Neo, who is himself destined to wake humanity by the trilogy's end.

Descartes's *Meditations*, however, soon moved beyond the problem of dreaming to pose a more important question – that of the possible manipulation of our senses by an external, malevolent force. His suggestion there of an 'evil demon' producing sensory images whose reality and reference cannot be established (1968:100) is explicitly repeated in *The Matrix*'s depiction of this world as a digital simulation created by evil, super-evolved machines (Probst, 1999). Both *The Matrix* and Descartes, however, can only be understood in relation to that longer history of images outlined in chapter 2 and the epistemological issues raised by their power to act on us as the real: to assume its force in fusing with its prototype (Freedberg, 1989). The founding philosophies of the west were aware of this problem, with Platonism and Christianity explicitly opposing this power, denigrating this world as a secondary reality tempting and diverting men's minds and as a place of confinement and illusion. In *The Republic* Plato compared us to prisoners chained in a cave, confusing shadow-play on the walls for reality (1955:316–25) and, like Christianity, explained the power of images as a supernatural force in a demonization of its simulacral properties that continues through the western tradition. As Wark argues, in returning us to this efficacious image and the enchaining of humanity to its deceptions *The Matrix* is a 'trip into Plato's cave' (1999).

The projected electronic 'virtual reality' simulation of sensory experience the film presents us with has a longer history in western media, its modern development arguably beginning with the late eighteenth century immersive, multimedia simulations of the panorama (Oettermann, 1997; Comment, 1999) and phantasmagoria (Weynants, 1998; Mannoni, 2000). Later media forms such as the stereoscope (Merrin, 2005a) and large-screen cinema (Oettermann, 1997) retained this immersive experience, though the path of developments in the nineteenth and twentieth centuries moved away from this dream (Merrin, 2005b), and it took the advent of electronic computers and significant advances in processing power, application, interfaces, networking and software before the concept of immersive simulation began to be rediscovered (Rheingold, 1991). The new modes of spatiality and social interaction offered by computers also led to a new term, 'cyberspace', coined by William Gibson in his 1984 cyberpunk novel *Neuromancer* (1995). If, to date, this cyberspace has been predominantly experienced onscreen there have been attempts to develop a more complete sensory experience either with others or with an artificial environment. These attempts typically employ a complex of technologies to cover, simulate and coordinate each sensory channel to produce 'an *experience*, the experience of being in a virtual world or remote location' (Rheingold, 1991:46). Though the nature and extent of this experience varies, for some, such as Moravec (1988), this virtual future is unlimited.

Contemporary discussions of virtual reality, however, are more aware of the current limitations, not only of the technology, but also of writing about a medium that has no final, developed, technological or commercial form or agreed applications. Given that research is conducted independently across a range of secretive governmental, scientific and business institutions, it is hard enough to ascertain its current let alone its future form. Science fiction, however, is under no such limitations and it is there that its possibilities have been most fully explored, most obviously in novels such as Galouye's *Counterfeit World* of 1964 (1965) and Dick's *Do Androids Dream of Electric Sheep?* of 1968 (1997) and *Ubik* of 1969 (2000); in TV sci-fi such as the BBC's *Dr Who* (which featured an electronic VR called 'the matrix' in 1976), in Vinge's *True Names* of 1981 (2001), in Gibson's *Neuromancer*, its sequels and the entire cyberpunk literature the book gave rise to, and in a range of films including *Tron* (of 1982), *The Lawnmower Man* (of 1992), *Strange Days* (of 1995), *The Thirteenth Floor* (of 1999), *eXistenZ* (of 1999), and of course *The Matrix*. Ironically, therefore, today's *actual* virtual reality lags behind *virtual* virtual reality, its representations attaining in the popular imagination that coherence and finality lacking in actuality, retrospectively defining the medium's completed form from the perspective of its anticipated future.

Just as actual VR has improved its simulation of the human sensorium so its representation has also left behind its crude block graphics and neon, video-game aesthetics, recognizing that the medium's potential lies in its perfect simulation of everyday reality and corporeality in an electronic hyperrealiz-ation of the real. The originality and the shock of *The Matrix* lies here, in eschewing the usual narrative movement from the real to the virtual to expose this real *as* the virtual. From within, its reality is convincing. As Morpheus explains:

Do you want to know what *it* is? The matrix is everywhere. It is all around us. Even now in this very room. You can see it when you look out of the window, or when you turn on your television. You can feel it when you go to work, when you go to church, when you pay your taxes. It is the world that has been pulled over your eyes to blind you from the truth.

(Wachowski and Wachowski, 2001a:38)

Except that this hasn't been pulled over the eyes, rather it is a VR that is plugged straight into the nervous system. Confused, Neo feels a chair in the training program and asks if it is real.[3] Morpheus replies: 'What is real? How do you define real? If you are talking about what you can feel; what you can smell; what you can taste and see, then real is simply electrical signals inter-preted by your brain' (Wachowski and Wachowski, 2001a:38). This returns us directly to the epistemological debates of the seventeenth to eighteenth centuries whose attempts to establish cognitive certainty reveal an underlying fear of deception and of being trapped in a perfect but merely apparent world. Ultimately, however, the world Descartes finally accepts as divinely guaran-teed and sanctioned (1968:168) is no different from the demonic simulation he had spent so much time querying, and for all Hume's dissection of the processes by which the senses, mind and memory collaborate to produce a coherent experiential reality and history, he admits that his immediate impres-sions alone are sufficient to dispel his sceptical 'chimeras' (Hume, 1969:316). So if, as *The Matrix* suggests, the real is only 'electrical signals interpreted by your brain,' then the perfected simulation of these signals produces not an unreal but an identical and indistinguishable 'real' sensation.

If the Wachowskis had these technological and philosophical issues in mind it was nevertheless Baudrillard's theory of simulation that provided much of the inspiration for the film (Bond, 1999), with the leading actors being given *Simulacra and Simulation* to read as preparation (Wachowski and Wachowski, 2001b). The debt is acknowledged in the opening scene and in the 1996, 1997 and shooting scripts when Morpheus introduces 'the matrix': 'You have been living inside a dreamworld Neo. As in Baudrillard's vision, your whole life has been spent inside the map, not the territory. This is the world as it exists today . . . "The desert of the real"' (Wachowski and Wachowski, 2001a:38).

If his name did not make the final screenplay, the quotation from *Simulacra and Simulation*, referencing Borges's tale of a 1:1 scale map left to rot in the

desert, survives (PS, 1–3; Borges, 1975:131). In his book Baudrillard radicalizes Borges's story to argue that today the map precedes and produces the
territory, rendering their distinction impossible, leaving us with a 'desert of
the real', a real whose vestiges can now be found in the deserts (PS, 1). So
Morpheus reveals the matrix as a precessionary map and its own and
only reality and the obliteration and replacement – the literal and physical
desertification – of the real for the unconscious remains of humanity.

The breakfast scene illustrates this simulation. Here 'Mouse' asks the crew
about the processed slop they eat: 'Do you know what it really reminds me
of? . . . *Tastee Wheat*. Did you ever eat *Tastee Wheat*?' Existing only within 'the
matrix', no one actually has. 'Exactly,' replies Mouse. How did the machines
know what *Tastee Wheat* even tasted like, he asks: 'Maybe they got it wrong'
(Wachowski and Wachowski, 2001a:60). Existing only as its own effective
reality, however, *Tastee Wheat* cannot even be wrong. Compare this meal with
the Judas Cypher's last meal before betraying Morpheus. Falling for the secondary imagic world of sensory temptations, his pleasure at eating the steak
and in his luxurious surroundings is greater than that found in the breakfast
slop and the ascetic life of a ruined world. So 'the matrix' represents a materialization of the real and its excessive hyperrealization, definitively eclipsing its
experience. As Cypher retorts when challenged that the matrix isn't real: on
the contrary, 'I think the matrix can be more real than this world.' Hence also
his mocking response of 'Welcome to the real world, huh, baby?' as he unplugs
a comrade, whose death registers more on the faces of those watching it in
the matrix than on his own outside (2001a:86).

Baudrillard, of course, was not the only influence on the Wachowskis.
They packed *The Matrix* with many other references and a minor industry
has arisen to mine the film's meanings. Foremost among these are the reli-
gious allegories, drawn especially from Gnosticism, Christianity, Buddhism,
Taoism, Judaism and ancient mythology. Despite the layering of multi-faith
symbolism, the film avoids falling into the genre clichés of *Dune* or the *Star
Wars* series since its use directly relates to the concept of the simulacrum. *The
Matrix* extrapolates from these traditions the idea of this world as a deficient
simulacral realm and illusion to be transcended in order to see, like the beatific
Neo, the streaming green code beyond the veil of the phenomenal. Just as
Christian iconoclasm was only part of a wider assault on this world as an
image, so the film declares war on our entire fallen reality, mimicking its theology of salvation in the appeal to the divine – the one – as the force to banish
the demonic simulation.

But just as the world's simulacral power is too great for Christianity to break
its spell, so the matrix is too powerful for Morpheus's crew. 'The matrix is a
system' and all those caught in it 'are our enemy', he says: most people are not
ready to be 'unplugged' and 'will fight to protect it' (Wachowski and
Wachowski, 2001a:51). If the demoniacal spell of the image cannot be broken
then iconoclasm is the answer: the entire apparent reality must be destroyed.
Hence the resort to a hyperparanoid, anarcho-libertarianism combining

Old Testament fundamentalism, new age mysticism, *X-Files* hyperconspiracy, US backwoods militia, Japanese doomsday cult and a proto-Fascistic aestheticization of violence, fashion and military hardware. Morpheus's evangelical, paramilitary terrorism sacrifices the lives of all who oppose him in the greater cause of an apocalyptic gun-battle between the demons and their minions and the saved few, between diabolical image and divine truth. His millennial redemption combines Gnostic Christianity with a Waco-style, 'Heaven's Gate' suicide cult. Nerve gas attacks on the Japanese underground and gun-battles on tube platforms, the bombing of Oklahoma federal offices and 'Government lobby' shoot-outs: all coalesce in the film's confused, evangelical politics. Morpheus is the Unabomber of the matrix.[4]

Ultimately, however, the Wachowskis play with the concept of the simulacrum, but only to domesticate it again before a higher reality. If, as Deleuze says, quoting Nietzsche, 'behind every cave . . . there is and must necessarily be, a still deeper cave: an ampler, stranger, richer world beneath every bottom, beneath every foundation' (1983:53), then it is this possibility that the film rejects. The blockbuster film needs truths to deliver and neither film nor audience could withstand the logical extrapolation of the film's premise – the 'internal reverberation' of the simulacrum that overflows into madness. But Baudrillard's response to the simulacrum is no different, appealing to the symbolic as a lived and real ground against its processes. Perhaps Neo and Morpheus have been reading the wrong books?

Morpheus's opposition to the simulacrum and its machinic masters also falters when we consider his relationship to technology. For McLuhan, following Samuel Butler's *Erewhon* of 1872 (1970:198–226), our everyday, unthinking use of technology already constitutes an adaptation and enslavement to it as the technology's 'servo-mechanisms' (McLuhan, 1994:46). Thus the crew's love of and dependence on VR chairs, mobile phones, guns, helicopters and submarines integrate them as surely as the matrix does. As they download special moves and abilities as in a video game they become identical to the 'agents', the intelligent programs policing the matrix. Neo's mastery of 'bullet-time', therefore, only emphasizes his cybernetic transformation, indicating that the future of humanity lies not, as is claimed, with those 'born free' in Zion (Wachowski and Wachowski, 2001a:43), but in a cyborg figure which implicitly threatens the ontological and moral distinction of human and machine that the film relies on (Hables Gray, 1995; 2002). It also threatens the claims of Baudrillard himself, and similar thinkers such as Virilio (1997a), who assert the value of a mode of being and relations against the contemporary technological realm. As McLuhan indicates when he says that it is the 'idols' we serve that enslave us (1994:45), it is the simulacrum that undermines their critique.

'THIS PROSTITUTION OF IMAGES'

Although we can fruitfully employ Baudrillard's virtual cameo in *The Matrix* as a lens through which to consider the influence of his theory of simulation, his relationship to the film becomes more problematic at the level of form. If we consider his comments on cinema and its path we find a very different relationship emerges, and if we extend this analysis through a consideration of his critique of new media technologies and our contemporary modes of virtuality we discover a significant reversal of the position his appearance in the film suggests.

Although Baudrillard's work has found a place in film studies his comments on cinema itself have received less attention. Though he doesn't develop a systematic film theory his discussion is still significant. Much of what he says is personal, expressing his pleasure in the medium as 'a good cinema-goer' and his belief in cinema as a 'symbolic' medium (*BL*, 29, 31) in creating that privileged Durkheimian collective communion. The cinema, therefore, is 'for sharing' as 'our own special ceremonial', a ritual and mythic form actualizing 'the imaginary' – the collective dreams – of our society (*BL*, 68). In contrast to the cold electronic light of television – which lacks that 'stage', 'depth', 'distance' and imaginary that seduces us (*BL*, 69), its hyperreality instead making the entire world instantly available (*BL*, 30, 69) – the cinema 'is a passion', its 'magic appeal' producing 'a total absorption' and symbolic relationship (*BL*, 30, 33, 67).

This preference is complicated, however, by Baudrillard's criticism of contemporary film-making and in particular of that style found precisely in the Hollywood films he even claims to prefer (*BL*, 31, 67). Film-making today has become only 'a spectacular demonstration of what one can do with the cinema' (*BL*, 23). Its trajectory, following the western desire for the absolute realization of the real, passes 'from the most fantastic or mythical to the realistic and the hyperrealistic', with each step contributing to the loss of 'the cinematographic illusion' (*PC*, 30) and a movement away from 'the secret of cinema' (*BL*, 32). Thus cinema is currently abolishing in its content that symbolic dimension that defines its experience. Hence Baudrillard's condemnation of those films whose visual perfection and absolute historical correspondence is 'disquieting' (*SS*, 45). To his list of 1970s films we could add any number of contemporary examples of hyperrealist reconstruction, such as *Schindler's List* (from 1993), *Titanic* (from 1997) and *Saving Private Ryan* (from 1998), all of which aim to produce the truth of their events through an accretion of the signs of the real. In their obsessive visual hyperfidelity to their period their details no longer stand as themselves in their symbolic interrelationships but as signs of 'history', shining 'in a sort of hyperresemblance' to the reality of their age (*SS*, 45). If this hyperrealism isn't new in a medium based on the photo-chemical and mechanical simulation of life, its elevation to raison d'être and star of the medium may be.

Since Baudrillard targeted this mode of hyperreality another has emerged with the development and rise to prominence of computer-generated digital cinematography (see Pierson, 1999; Darley, 2000). The digital production or manipulation of imagery is now commonplace, being used to clean or alter existing images, to create CGI effects, to fill in for deceased actors and even to create entirely new actors – such as 'Jar Jar Binks' in *Star Wars – The Phantom Menace* (in 1999) – and some argue that the future of cinema lies with such 'synthespians' or recreated golden age stars (Kane, 1997; Logan, 1999). Either way digital films are already with us, developing from early animations such as *Toy Story* (in 1995) to full 'd-cinema', employing entirely digital production, post-production and projection.

Baudrillard's feelings about these developments are not hard to guess. All his comments on the loss of illusion, the play of the imaginary and the symbolic dimension and relationship in the hyperclean, hyperliteral perfection of the digital image and its forced materialization apply here. As Romney argues, echoing Baudrillard, the digital image completes its quest for the real by expelling from itself all presence, particularity and uniqueness, ultimately lacking 'that element of accident, of peculiarity, that has always given screen objects their visual and mythic substance' (Romney, 1996:6). Cinema, Baudrillard concludes, has fallen into a 'resentment' of its own culture and history, becoming 'a performance game'; one displaying 'a supreme contempt for the image itself, which is prostituted to any special effect whatsoever', as well as for the viewer, who has become an 'impotent voyeur of this prostitution of images' (*Par.*, 110–11).

The Matrix represents exactly this form of film-making; indeed its reputation is based in large part on its ground-breaking effects and action sequences. More generally a technologically realized hyperrealism dominates its aesthetics as we linger scopophilically on the digital quality of the film, its effects and its *look*: on the cyber-noir tones, shades and metals of the featured fashion and technology. Arguably the stars of the film for our identification are not Neo and Morpheus but their clip-on shades, leather coats, machine guns and mobile phones. And if we identify so completely with the shade-adorned, VR-enhanced, Kung-Fu programmed and hyper-armed video-game characters, with their technology, and with the film itself and its effects, do we not thereby lose the right to side with Neo in defence of the '100% pure, old-fashioned, home-grown human'? Shouldn't we be rooting for the machines?

The Matrix revels in its effects, and especially in its own 'bullet time', introduced in two key sequences. In the first, Trinity jumps to kick a policeman, freezing in mid-air, mid-kick, with arms outstretched in a pose which is part martial arts, part praying mantis. In this freeze-framed moment, culturally and technically echoing the chrono-photography of Janssen, Marey and Muybridge, the camera whirls vertiginously around her before releasing the pause button and unleashing an 'inhumanly fast' violence (Wachowski and Wachowski, 2001a:4). In the second sequence we watch Neo, 'bent impossibly back', entering 'the liquid space of bullet time', weaving between the bullets (2001a:101). Visual effects designer John Gaeta describes bullet time as 'slowing down time to such an extent that you really see everything around you as clearly as you possibly could' (Wachowski and Wachowski, 1999), but actually you see everything *as you possibly couldn't*, in a hyperrealization of the instant, in an unreal real-time and its omniscient, mobile vision in which we move beyond human time to the time of the projectile.

We enter this kinetic, slow-motion, multispatial, digitally realized temporality again in the 'Government lobby' shoot-out where Neo and Trinity gun down a platoon of armoured soldiers in a lethal, choreographed ballet of violence as bullets, shells, impact explosions and the infinite fragments of the walls and pillars float in the air, forming dense fractal patterns, all beautifully, almost ecstatically hyperrealized, with each tiny fragment pursuing its own trajectory among the clouds of debris. For the German author and thinker Ernst Junger photography had produced a 'second, colder consciousness', a 'cruel way of seeing', creating 'a space where . . . pain can be regarded as an illusion' (Phillips, 1989:209–10). If 'the matrix' is that space in the film, allowing the indifferent annihilation of meaningless lives, for us we find it in our cinematic digital effects, our video games, and in the real-time feeds of televised war. Junger's experiential 'storm of steel' – that raging maelstrom of lethal fragments and explosions that was the battlefield of the First World War (Junger, 1996) has been replaced for us by a digital storm of bits consumed in the comfort and distance of the home.

The Matrix is dominated, therefore, by an ultra-imagic, hyperrealized style of film-making, owing much to the Wachowskis' own comic book backgrounds, to the visualizations of Geoff Darrow, to the influence of Japanese manga comics and anime films, Hong Kong martial arts movies and their wire-fighting techniques, and the American super-hero genre (Green, M. E., 1999; O'Toole, 1999; Probst, 1999). The film was even conceived of as an 'origins' story for a new breed of super-hero (Probst, 1999); hence the final scene and Neo's emergence from the phone booth to take to the air 'faster than a speeding bullet' (Wachowski and Wachowski, 2001a:122). From the story-boards of every scene and their own publication (Lamm, 2000), to the film's continuation as a comic, as an anime and a video game (Wachowski and Wachowski, 2003e, 2003a, 2003b), the imagic impact of *The Matrix* has continued. With the video game, film and spectator implode: the audience could now 'enter the matrix', playing alongside and even 'affecting' events in the sequels while participating in and enjoying the bullet-time dispatch of the mindless human minions of the machines. As Poole notes, here one cycle of influence is completed since the film itself was influenced by the look, action, narrative and audience of video games (2000b:87), recreating in its kicks, jumps and 'special moves' *StreetFighter* and *Tekken*-style beat-em-ups – a link explicitly made in the script as the crew watch Neo and Morpheus spar in the classic video-game arena of the dojo as if they are 'watching a game of *Mortal Kombat*' (Wachowski and Wachowski, 2001a:47).

The Matrix, however, goes further, mimicking our own virtualization by transforming everyday reality into a virtual beat-em-up; the location for an aspirational hyperviolence in which, in a teenager's dream come true, only computer lives are lost. In a final twist the film itself telescoped into the real, being linked to and blamed for a series of murders, as well as the Columbine school massacre and the Washington sniper (Poole, 2000b:221; Campbell, 2003c). Such links, however, are debatable and, as Baudrillard's work suggests, detract attention from the wider process of simultaneous virtualization and moral distantiation we experience every day in our news media and in war reports and our consumption of tragedies. But *The Matrix* has had a greater influence as a popular cultural phenomenon, its apocalyptic quasi-spirituality and problematization of reality speaking not only to nihilistic youth but chiming with the everyday experience and fears of the wider public. If, as Baudrillard says, our 'panic-stricken production of the real' only leads to the devaluation of its stocks (PS, 7), then *The Matrix* represents the reversive product and site of collapse of our hypermediated society. The same culture that could give rise to and even debate Holocaust revisionism (*TE*, 93) has so little faith in its own reality and history that a film like *The Matrix* could gain credence. But the film also functions as a safety net for our society, suggesting that beneath the simulacra of everyday life the real survives and can be rediscovered. It was this popular success of the film and its sequels that eventually led Baudrillard to break his silence on it.

'THE DOUBLE AGENTS OF THE VIRTUAL'

As well as the release of *The Animatrix*, *Enter the Matrix* and *The Matrix Comics*, 2003 also saw the release of two sequels, *The Matrix: Reloaded* and *The Matrix: Revolutions* (Wachowski and Wachowski, 2003c, 2003d). Just as the sequel reveals that the matrix shown in the film is the sixth version, so by the trilogy's end we are faced with a similar proliferation of the original matrix. Of these, only 'Matriculated', in *The Animatrix*, adds anything to the original high concept of virtual reality in its idea of developing a virtual reality to convert and enslave the machines. *The Matrix: Reloaded* focuses more on the threat to Zion, but the latter's privileged reality now has the effect of making the scenes set in 'the matrix' less interesting. The bullet-time effects that uncannily bent the apparent rules of reality in the first film now appear only as what they are in this film: digital special effects in an unreal realm. Whereas in the first film the narrative path and its timed revelations were effective, here, as in a video game, hasty, convoluted dialogue excerpts are sandwiched between the spectacular set-pieces we are guided through. Thus we follow effects sequences such as 'the Burley Brawl' with the multiplying Agent Smiths with an incredulity that owes too little to the remarkable technical achievement of its accomplishment.

The main plot development in *The Matrix: Reloaded* is Neo's journey of self-discovery, through his return to and path through the philosophical, criminal and even ghostly underworld of the matrix. This culminates in his meeting with 'the Architect' and the revelation of a series of matrices each with their 'one'. The latter's true nature and function is now explained as an internal anomaly who must return to 'the source' to overcome the matrix's inherent instability by reinserting the 'prime program' and restarting both the matrix and Zion. Neo, the saviour, is therefore part of the system he opposes and its primary means of social control. The final film follows the fight to save both Zion from the machine army and reality itself from Neo's 'opposite' and 'negative', the demonic, legion, Agent Smith. Its culmination, Neo's union with the machinic AI to defeat Smith, leading to peace between humans and machines, sets up a denouement as unbelievable as that reconciliation of capital and labour at the end of the 1926 film *Metropolis*. Unlike the film's positing of the return of an ever more perfect matrix, the films themselves, therefore, pursue the opposite route.

The year 2002–3 also saw the first public comments by Baudrillard on his appearance in the film in a series of interviews, most notably with *Le Nouvel Observateur* (Baudrillard, 2003a, 2004a; Staples, 2002). Here Baudrillard describes his adoption by the Wachowskis as based on 'a misunderstanding' of his work, hence his silence and his refusal, when asked, to contribute towards the sequels. The Wachowskis focus, he complains, on the reality of simulation, taking 'the hypothesis of the virtual as a fact' and carrying it over 'to visible phantasms', whereas 'the primary characteristic of this universe lies precisely in the inability to use categories of the real to speak about it'. Thus their treatment of the virtual is 'roughly done', Baudrillard says, in presenting people either as in the matrix or 'radically out of it' in the real world of Zion (2003a). As I have argued, this use of Baudrillard is most clearly seen in the training program sequence when Morpheus, quoting Baudrillard, shows Neo 'the desert of the real'. This allies Baudrillard's concept of simulation with virtual reality and implies that he similarly sees the world as unreal. Baudrillard, however, has shown little interest in VR, resenting the popular confusion of his ideas with this technology. While his discussion of digitality as epitomizing the era of third order simulacra, and producing them in its generation from models (OS, 56–7), seems to suggest a Wachowskian scenario of the virtual reality production of the real, the concept of the simulacrum threatens the virtual/actual distinction this technology rests on.

Moreover, Baudrillard's later concept of 'the virtual' is explicitly developed against the idea of virtual reality, seeing the virtual not as that which will become actual or (as in VR) exist parallel to it, but as that which 'takes the place of the real' and as 'the final solution of the real in so far as it both accomplishes the world in its definitive reality and marks its dissolution' (*Passwords* (*Pw*), 39–40).[5] VR, therefore, is only part of a wider complex of electronic technologies operating *through everyday life*, hyperrealizing and virtualizing the latter (*Pw*, 39). These technologies do not create a separate unreality because, Baudrillard argues, they have 'long since left their media space to invest "real" life from the inside', colonizing and imploding with real experience to make the distinction of real and virtual impossible (1996b:26). The result, Baudrillard says, is the 'deep-seated virtualization of human beings' (1996b:28), the diffusion of the virtual throughout real life 'in homeopathic doses, beyond detection' (1997b:20) and the 'transformation of life, of everyday life, into virtual reality' (1997b:19). As he concludes, 'All this digital, numerical and electronic equipment is only the epiphenomenon of the virtualisation of human beings in their core' (1997d:20).

There are moments, however, when *The Matrix*'s use of virtuality approaches the power of Baudrillard's own concept, fulfilling his hopes for contemporary science fiction elaborated in his essay 'Simulacra and Science Fiction' (1994b:121–27). There he returns to his three orders of simulacra (1993d:50–86) to trace the development and 'imaginary' of the orders of science fiction, from the utopian projection of the preindustrial era, with its fantastic worlds, to the mechanical and metallurgic Promethean projection of the industrial era, with its spaceships and robots, to the contemporary third order. The latter's implosion of imaginary and real in a forced hyperreality creates a problem for science fiction today, he argues, since we can no longer exceed and project beyond our world. If we now can't 'fabricate the unreal from the real' then our task instead, he says, is

to put decentred situations, models of simulation in place and to contrive to give them the feeling of the real, of the banal, of lived experience, to reinvent the real as fiction, precisely because it has disappeared from our own life. Hallucination of the real, of lived experience, of the quotidian, but reconstituted, sometimes down to disquiet-ingly strange details . . . brought to light with a transparent precision, but without substance, derealized in advance, hyperrealized.

(*SS*, 124)

Science fiction must 'evolve implosively, in the very image of our current con-ception of the universe', attempting 'to revitalize, reactualize, requotidianize fragments of simulation, fragments of this universal simulation that have become for us the so-called real world' (*SS*, 124). If Philip K. Dick and J. G. Ballard provide the exemplars of this fiction for him, there are aspects of *The Matrix* that might also qualify. While much of the film remains within the second order in its depiction of technological evolution, it does succeed occa-sionally in moving beyond this, in its uncanny revelation of the everyday world as simulation. Thus the film's epiphanic moment is not, as Wark sug-gests (1999), Neo's awakening to the real world, but rather when he returns to the matrix, watching it from the car while 'the simple images of the urban street blur past his window like an endless stream of data rushing down a com-puter screen' (Wachowski and Wachowski, 2001a:62). Like Neo, we also hallucinate on its verisimilitude, sharing his confusion. 'Almost unbelievable isn't it?' Morpheus says.

But such critical, Baudrillardian moments are rarer than the Wachowskis might have hoped. If *The Matrix*'s shelf-life fades as we leave the cinema, 'Baudrillard's vision' does not, as his claims about the world are more radical than those in *The Matrix*. For him, simulacra are not unreal media produc-tions covering a real that can be rediscovered, as *The Matrix* suggests; rather they are efficacious as the real, representing our everyday experience of the real's own volatization. Cinema itself provides an example of this, Baudrillard argues, in invading and imploding with our lives. 'Go to America', Baudrillard says in *America* (1988), and 'you *are* in a film. In California particularly, you *live* cinema', each city and town being experienced in a cinematic 'panning shot' (*BL*, 34). In America the cinema is not to be found in the theatres or the fake spectacle of the studio tours: it is 'everywhere but here', he argues (*Am.*, 55–6). 'The whole country is cinematic' (*Am.*, 56) – the break between film and reality does not exist: 'life is cinema' (*Am.*, 101). Only America has this power of the cinematographization of everyday life, Baudrillard says: 'It is there that I discover the "matrix" of the cinema' (*BL*, 34).

Here, two years before Gibson and seventeen years before the Wachowskis, Baudrillard theorizes 'the matrix'. This matrix is the power of the hyperreal image to invade, invest and excessively assume the force of the real. This matrix is the simulacrum. It is only in that panoramic shot of Neo watching from the car that *The Matrix* approaches its power. It is that moment of confusion, as Neo struggles to reconcile the ungrounding knowledge of the world's illusion with its apparent grounded reality, that articulates our own experience. This is the experience of mundane, everyday reality in all its banality at that moment when the matrix breaks through; when the lighting, the scenography and the editing are just right. It is the moment of the confusion of real and image – of the cinematographization of everyday life and the materialization of that aspirational hyperreality that simultaneously heightens life and degrades reality; of that disquieting 'hallucination' that transforms experience into imagic spectatorship and the world's 'substance' into a digitally perfect screen effect. We do not have to look to the year 2199 for this, for this virtualization of the real happens every day.

Baudrillard's critique of virtuality represents, therefore, an extension of his critique of electronic media traced throughout this book. As we have seen, influenced by Barthes, McLuhan and Boorstin, his early work offered a critique of the semiotic form and effects of electronic media in replacing the lived symbolic with their own processed and combined signs in a simulation that simultaneously actualizes and deactualizes the real and its experience. His subsequent writings develop a critique of the media's 'non-communication' (*Am.*, 164–84), of the transformation of referentiality, the precession of simulacra and the processes of hyperreality (*MP*, *SED*, *SS*), and of the implosive effects of electronic media (*SSM*, *Sed.*, *SS*). From 1977 he reorients his project around a critique of the west's 'productive' culture (*FF*), its 'pornographic' processes (*Sed.*) and its obscene and transparent exponential systems (*FS*, *TE*), leading him to an attack on our entire communicational culture, its information networks and its impact on and absorption of the individual as a 'pure screen' and terminal (*EC*).

The question of 'the virtual' emerges in Baudrillard's work in the early 1990s, especially in discussions of 'virtual war', 'virtuality', 'real time' and the uncertainty and credibility of media events (*Ill.*, *GW*). These ideas crystallize by the mid-1990s into a critique of 'the perfect crime': the 'murder' of a reality principle (itself built on the extermination of a prior radical illusion) through its own virtualization. For Baudrillard this crime proceeds by the 'unconditional realization of the world by the actualization of all data' (*PC*, 25), and by the perfection of real-time technologies which simulate, implode with and abolish the real, virtualizing everyday life (*PC*, 26–8).

This critique informs Baudrillard's writing on new media to the present and he explores the virtual across a range of books and essays (*VI, IE, ScO, PW*), increasingly linking its processes to western globalization (*Par., ST*, 2003b). The field of 'new media' is attracting increasing attention in media and communication studies, cultural studies and cyberculture studies (see Harries, 2002; Lister et al., 2003) and Baudrillard's ideas have found more favour here than in the mainstream discipline. This is mainly due to the field's interest in postmodern and cyber-theory and the revival of interest in McLuhanist questions of form and effects, although the texts typically follow the accepted mainstream positioning of Baudrillard, emphasizing his post-modernist and McLuhanist analysis of new media above his Durkheimian critique (Lister et al., 2003). This descriptive analysis does, however, have its limitations since Baudrillard lacks a practical knowledge of or interest in specific new media and their operation, while his commitment to symbolic exchange leads him to reject any interpretation of these media as producing real relations, meaning or community or increasing individual freedom and identity. The strength of his work, however, lies in his pushing of ideas to reveal new insights, his remarkable depiction of our electronic culture and his unwavering critique of its form and effects.

His early work already points to this later critique of virtuality. In *The System of Objects*, he describes 'modern man, the cybernetician', active engin-eers busy manipulating and controlling their semiotic and communicational environment (*SO*, 26, 29) and this analysis is extended in *The Consumer Society* in a discussion of 'the gadget' and its 'systematic logic' (*CS*, 113). Our rela-tionship to these objects is not utilitarian or symbolic, he argues, but 'ludic', being marked by 'a play with combinations' and with the 'technical variants or potentialities of the object' (*CS*, 114). This, for him, is the opposite of 'passion' with its concrete relationships, and 'total investment' and 'intense symbolic value', representing instead a 'curiosity', interested only 'in the play of elements' and the unilateral consumption of the form and its functions – a claim instantly recognizable to us in our own use of mobile phones, games, DVDs, etc. (*CS*, 114).

Baudrillard's 2000 essay '*Screened out*' returns to these themes, in a McLuhanist discussion of the implosive effects of 'interactivity' (*ScO*, 176–80). The user of video images and computer screens experiences an 'immersion', he argues, abolishing distance to enter into a 'tactile interaction' with the medium, playing with its elements (p. 177). This immersion, however, comes at the price of a loss of distinction of man and machine: with the machine 'on both sides of interface' humanity becomes 'the virtual reality of the machine' (p. 177). Moreover, everything produced by the machine is itself a machine, as the product of its capabilities and its operator's enthrallment to these. All we see here is 'the automatism of the programming, an automatic run through of all the possibilities' (p. 178).

For Baudrillard, therefore, we are immersed 'virtual agents, whose only act is the act of programming', controlling the form from within – 'from its matrix' – playing with its code to produce the 'ideal performance' of its possibilities. We pass here beyond the alienated spectator of Debord and Baudrillard's own theorization of us as imploded 'actors' in a 'reality show', to being the active producers and 'operators' of virtuality (*Pw*, 40). Thus, whereas *The Matrix* postulated a humanity enslaved by machines in a virtual reality policed by agents, for Baudrillard we have become machines, enslaving ourselves in our own virtualized reality, as well as the 'double agents' that ensure the virtual's continuation (*CM3*, 125). We are, he concludes, 'joyfully collaborating' in 'our disappearance into the virtual' (*CM3*, 139), no longer extending ourselves in our technologies but instead expelling and abrogating all human functions and faculties (*VI*, 37).

Baudrillard's critique of virtuality simultaneously combines one of the most radical conceptualizations of new media and their processes with a conservative response to the changes and effects he identifies. He combines an insightful McLuhanist analysis and awareness of technological form with a Boorstinian fear of their effects on the real, integrating these into his broader Barthes-inspired critique of the semiotic from the perspective of the radical Durkheimian symbolic. However, as the above discussion makes clear, this is also combined with a western Marxist sensitivity to the operation of media and technical processes throughout everyday life as a mode of social control. When Baudrillard says we face a 'virtual reality', or rather 'the horizon of a programmed reality' (*VI*, 37), the debt to Lefebvre (1971), Debord (1983) and Marcuse (1986) and their respective analyses of the programming and control of everyday life is especially clear. Baudrillard's critique represents an explicit extension of these concerns, highlighting the contemporary production and processes of virtuality and their function as a mode of social control.

Hence Baudrillard's critical reversal of *The Matrix* films on themselves because, he argues, they represent in their form – in the dominance of their spectacular but punctum-less hyperreal digital effects and programmed demonstration of the capacities of computer-generated cinematography – exactly that process of virtualization he discusses. As he caustically says, '*The Matrix* is like a movie about the matrix that could have produced the matrix.' Just as Neo in the sequels is revealed to be part of the system, as a mechanism of control and of its self-reproduction towards perfection, so too are these films for us. As simultaneously mainstream action-movie effects-fests and aspirational cult movies, they are part of a process they claim to oppose, contributing to virtuality and its domination of everyday life. Echoing McLuhan again, Baudrillard says that 'the message' of the form of *The Matrix* 'is its very propagation', its relentless contamination of daily life, spreading simulation through a claimed critique of simulation. Whereas the matrix in the film, however, is a simulacrum that covers up the real, *The Matrix* itself is a simulacrum that helps to cover its absence (Baudrillard, 2003a).

The Matrix, therefore, has us. Our consumption of the films, the merchandise, and the world and myth the Wachowskis sell us, and our collective orgasm over the effects and phones, guns, shades and leather, represent our integration into the virtuality it promotes. Our avid, ludic immersion in and consumption of the DVDs and their special features, commentary, extras and links, and of the video game and official website and fan forums, represent an enslavement to technology and its functions. The film's aesthetic has imploded with daily life, becoming a ubiquitous feature of the advertising semioscape, its effects being used to sell us anything from cameras to phones, insurance and frozen food; its trade-mark action, styles, characters and dialogue being ripped off, referenced, spoofed and reproduced throughout popular culture.

Official and fan-run websites have proliferated, as have popular tabloid, broadsheet and glossy press features and cover stories. Film and media courses quickly appropriated the film and a flood of academic and popular books and essays – my own included – rushed into print to explain its references and meaning, all adding to its cultural legitimacy and dominance (Irwin, 2002; Condon, 2003; Garrett, Garrett and Seay, 2003; Haber, 2003; Horsley, 2003; Lloyd, 2003; Merrin, 2003; Yeffeth, 2003). With its DVD release in 2000 becoming the fastest-selling disc to date, *The Matrix* became a viral meme spreading through and being mimetically absorbed into popular culture, extending our virtualization. Just as the film offered the stark choice of being in or outside the matrix so you were either *in* or outside the zeitgeist. To paraphrase Morpheus: *The Matrix* is everywhere. As Baudrillard makes clear, however, its fans and public are caught in a similarly invisible matrix that is far greater than that depicted in the film, and that the film itself is part of and extends.

This promotion of virtuality continues. The year 2005 sees the launch of *The Matrix Online* ('MxO'), a new Massively Multiplayer Online Role Playing Game (MMORPG) following the success of games such as *EverQuest*. As the website explains: '*The Matrix* will become a reality as gamers everywhere log into *The Matrix Online* to continue the saga of the Matrix movie trilogy' (Wachowski and Wachowski, 2004). Now gamers can immerse themselves in *The Matrix*, in a 'fourth matrix movie' set after *The Matrix: Revolutions*, interacting with the film's story and characters and each other in ongoing and open-ended missions and in storylines and plot arcs scripted by the Wachowskis, helping to determine the future of *The Matrix* universe (Ragaini, 2004). Users will be able to 'jack in' to the matrix in cyberspace – in Gibson's original 'matrix' – immersing themselves in and imploding with both the technical medium and its content. As the site suggests, the matrix does indeed 'become a reality' here, except that, unlike in the film, now we voluntarily plug ourselves into it. The tag-line for the game's promo-video, 'the future of The Matrix is in your hands', is telling, confirming Baudrillard's claim that today *we* are the producers and protectors of the virtual.

Ultimately, therefore, the virtual and its simulation again acts as a mode of social control and integration. *The Matrix*, Baudrillard argues, constitutes only 'a trompe l'oeil negation' of the system (2003a), representing an incorporation, neutralization and selling back of negation. This strategy – part recuperation and part precessionary, implosive deterrence – 'is the most efficient way to forbid any true alternative', he says, in removing 'an external omega point for apprehending the world'. There is 'no more antagonistic function', he concludes, 'only a fascinated adherence' (2003a). This is how we consume these films.

Early in *The Matrix* Neo receives a message on his computer screen saying simply 'the matrix has you' (Wachowski and Wachowski, 2001a:9). At the film's end we cut to the matrix's own computer screen of streaming neon code as Neo threatens its destruction. The code stops and the words 'system failure' are seen. For us, despite Baudrillard's championing of the forms of the symbolic, there is no system failure to return us to the real and this is where his vision surpasses that of the Wachowskis. As he wrote in *The Consumer Society*, there is indeed a code governing our lives and securing our integration and conformity but this totalitarian code operating through our electronic media is that of the semiotic order and its simulacral processes. For him the 'pacification of everyday life' operates not through a Wachowskian virtual reality but through our already virtualized reality: through the processes of our semiotic communicational and consumer society (*CS*, 174, 94). Baudrillard confronts us, therefore, with our own simulated, virtual reality: with a matrix that is more penetrating, complete and attractive than any yet realized on our cinema screens. This matrix does, indeed, have us.

Ask yourself: have you ever *really* eaten *Tastee Wheat*?

8 'The saving power': the 'reflex miracle' of photography

Perhaps the desire to take photographs arises from the observation that on the broadest view, from the standpoint of reason, the world is a great disappointment. In its details, however, and caught by surprise, the world always has a stunning clarity.

Baudrillard, *The Transparency of Evil*

It is not the role of a photograph to illustrate an object or an event, but to be itself an event.

Baudrillard, *Within the Horizon of the Object*

Throughout this book I have repeatedly returned to the central, organizing principle of Baudrillard's work: his theory of the symbolic and semiotic and their interrelationship. In chapter 1 I positioned him as the foremost contemporary inheritor and exponent of the radical Durkheimian tradition, in unifying its work around his concept of symbolic exchange and in developing from it a theory of human communication that became the basis for his critique of our consumer and media society. Chapter 2 introduced the processes of the semiotic and especially the concepts of the simulacrum and simulation, placing these within the wider context of the historical efficacy of images and considering Baudrillard's own symbolic opposition to their processes. As I argued there, the common reaction of many of Baudrillard's critics has been to reject the concept of the simulacrum, although this remains an inadequate response since the epistemological issue it raises has been recognized across many cultures. Framed as the relationship between appearance and reality, it has been central to the development of the west and its defining religious, aesthetic and philosophical traditions, and Baudrillard's work makes us aware that the same processes and problems reappear in our own, irremediably imagic society.

I also considered in chapter 2 the problem faced by every culture of integrating, domesticating or expelling the simulacrum's power. In contrast to many non-western or 'primitive' societies, the west, for example, has traditionally attempted to demonize and domesticate the image and the realm of appearances, establishing a certain critical ground either through a transcendent guarantor or one within the world, in, for example, humanistic or relational concepts of ethics and value. Each of these positions, however, requires justification against arguments concerning the inadequacy of its chosen ground or the impossibility of any final ground. Every critical philosophy seeking to claim specific truths about this world faces this problem of defining and defending its own ground and valorization and, as I have argued, Baudrillard's is no exception.

The problem appears early in his work in the competition between humanistic influences, such as Sartre, Lefebvre, Debord and Marcuse, and the influence of structuralist and poststructuralist antihumanism, and especially the work of Barthes, Althusser, Lévi-Strauss and Derrida and the critique of essentialist categories. While Baudrillard was attracted to Sartrean and western Marxist critiques of the new forms of alienation and social control in everyday life, he rejected their underlying critical position. Hence his post-structuralist critique in *For a Critique of the Political Economy of the Sign* of political economy and its essentialist, a historical subject (pp. 63–87, 130–42), and Derridean critique of the linked operation of commodity and sign (pp. 143–63). This poststructuralist critique was equally aimed at Marxism, which, in being based on political economy, was therefore unable to provide a critical alternative to it, functioning instead as the 'mirror' of this system (*MP*). Having raised the problem of the simulacrum, however, Baudrillard needed to discover his own critical ground against it. He found this in the Durkheimian symbolic (*EC*, 11; *Pw*, 9, 15).

This turn to non-western and 'primitive' societies as the basis for an implicit critique of the west and of a left that was part of this political system was common in the contemporary counter-culture (J. Green, 1998). Baudrillard's interest in Durkheimian social anthropology allowed him to move from a critique of the partial alienations of the western system to a broader conception of a greater historical loss, that of the symbolic, and to a position excoriating an entire semiotic culture. Although he saw the symbolic as avoiding the problems of essentialism and placed it outside the value systems of commodity and sign (*CPES*, 128, 159) and language itself (*CPES*, 161), as I have argued, he still named its force and employed it as a referential real grounding a concept of human relations and communication that served as the basis for his critique of the west. If, therefore, in *The Consumer Society*, he could dismiss the ideals of the hippy subculture as representing 'the sentimental resurrection' of the 'human' (*CS*, 180–1), these charges could equally have been levelled at him.

Despite having employed poststructuralism against general political economy to expose the operation of the commodity and sign and their manipulation of the semiotic bar to present 'the real' and 'referent' as external to the system and as grounding it (*CPES*, 162), Baudrillard notably disbars any similar exposure of his own 'bar games' (Genosko, 1994a). This critique of the sign, however, is the key moment of Baudrillard's career because it is here that he establishes the basis for his own critical position, manipulating the same bar to his own benefit to establish the symbolic as outside and radically opposed to its processes. As I have argued, it takes the position, therefore, of an external referential real. If this is a real that now grounds the system's critique rather than supporting it, the act that establishes it is nevertheless identical, mirroring that of the system he opposes. Baudrillard's production of the symbolic as a critical ground is therefore open to the same criticism he levels at general political economy in producing a foundation that remains within the process of simulation; that remains a simulation, being ungrounded and exposed by the simulacrum.

Baudrillard returns to these issues in his 1999 book *Impossible Exchange*, where he outlines a similar critique of all foundational projects. In being unable to exchange themselves against an external equivalent that could guarantee them, all systems of morality, politics, economics, and theorizations of reality, remain simulacral operations, needing to cover up their threat of exposure and destabilization by establishing an internal principle of equilibrium and equivalence allowing an internal exchange appearing to naturalize them (pp. 3–5). Baudrillard again, however, places the symbolic outside this, as the limit point of the systems and as the principle of 'impossible exchange' itself (pp. 6–7), explicitly repeating his earlier naming, explanation and valorization of its force. Thus his strategy fails again at the point where his own oppositional system runs up against its own impossible exchange.

Baudrillard, of course, stakes all on the hope that this isn't so: that the symbolic remains an external force, expressing something that opposes the simulacrum, exposing and reversing its processes. Although, as I have argued, Baudrillard's early work retained an implacable opposition to the semiotic from the perspective of the symbolic, his later works were forced to redevelop this, spiralling together the two forces and producing a more ambiguous and problematic critical position. By *Symbolic Exchange and Death* they are already woven together in his content, in the semiotic's escalation leading to reversal, as well as in the form of his work, in that methodological combination of simulation and challenge he describes (pp. 1–5). By *Forget Foucault* and *Seduction* his reconceptualization of symbolic and semiotic as seduction and production retained an opposition to semiotic hyperrealism while embracing the processes of the sign and its play of appearances as producing the 'charmed universe' of the symbolic. While this was both a response to a simplistic opposition he had tied himself into and an attempt to realign himself with the demonic forces of the image to reverse these against the disenchanted simulacrum, it was also a further manipulation of the semiotic bar, retaining a good-symbolic and bad-semiotic distinction. As I have argued, the problems of how to distinguish and defend this distinction and of what critical force its simulacra could have against simulation were serious ones.

Although Baudrillard briefly opposed seduction to the symbolic (*EC*, 47, 80), its central elements, as an immediately actualized mode of meaning and relations, indicates its continuity with symbolic exchange as part of a 'paradigm' which, he says, 'is more or less the same from the start' (1995b:83–4). Throughout this book I have simplified this paradigm within the concept of the symbolic since this term retains its privilege, place, meaning and

Durkheimian significance throughout his career. Nevertheless his perpetual reconceptualization of its forms is significant, representing his recognition of the need to establish a critical position against the semiotic and the problems of its conceptualization and articulation. Perhaps it is only here, in his continual, McLuhanist reworking of his concepts to revitalize their meaning, that he takes up his own claim that the symbolic cannot 'be named'.

For Baudrillard symbolic exchange offered the Durkheimian categories of the gift, exchange, the festival, agonism, sacrifice, expenditure, transgression, the accursed share, excess, potlatch, ambivalence, reversibility, and death (see *EC*, 11), The concept of seduction allowed him to develop a new, related armoury of ideas such as the strategy of appearances, disappearance, the secret, ritual, ceremony, artifice, the feminine, play, the game, the rule, the duel, challenge, sovereignty, irony, enchantment, illusion and destiny (*FF*, *Sed.*). *Fatal Strategies* brought with it a new emphasis on the principle of evil, the fatal strategies, fatal thought, immanence, and the object, while *The Transparency of Evil* added a new interest in the other, in the concepts of radical otherness, radical exoticism and radical alterity. Finally, Baudrillard's recent work has seen the development of new concepts such as radical or vital illusion, radical, paradoxical and paroxystic thought, singularity, poetic transference and impossible exchange, and the Nietzschean re-emphasis of duality, destiny, metamorphosis, change and becoming (*PC*, *Par.*, *VI*, *IE*). By the time of *Passwords* in 2000 he had amassed a list of critical concepts.

These transformations in the symbolic have followed those within the opposing semiotic paradigm (*EC*, 79). As I argued in the last chapter, these can be traced from his early critique of the system of sign-objects (*SO*, *CS*), through his description of that obscene, communicational culture he began to describe from the late 1970s (*FF*, *Sed.*) and which he escalated again from the 1980s to early 1990s (*FS*, *EC*, *TE*), to the virtualized world that dominates his current analyses (*PC*, *Par.*, *VI*, *IE*). Each reformulation of the symbolic was intended as a strategic move to keep up with, match and outpace the exponential developments within this system and retain its own theoretical and critical advantage against its forms and effects. In many ways, despite the problems of the ground of this critique, Baudrillard's position, and constant positioning, have been broadly successful, enabling him to develop an original, radical Durkheimian media theory.

This theory constitutes, I believe, one of the most important and effective contemporary analyses of the media's operation, encompassing a critique of their reduction, processing and production of experience and implosive, simulacral mediation of the world, and of their effect of simultaneously actualizing and dramatizing and deterring, dissuading and short-circuiting the real. Baudrillard has applied this critique in his analysis of the entire contemporary world of non-events the system produces, its production of virtuality, the non-wars it has imposed on the world, and its homogenizing, global, semiotic project of power, security and control. Throughout this book I have offered a defence of Baudrillard based on my belief in the significance, coherence and critical value of this media theory, although it is a defence that remains cognisant of the problems of his critical valorization and its development through his work. The tensions this creates within his work run throughout it, being seen most recently, for example, in his contemporary discussion of technology and in particular in the two 'alternative hypotheses' he holds as regards its path and ultimate effects (*VI*, 83).

Throughout his career Baudrillard has retained an implacable hostility towards electronic media and technology due to the combined influence of a radical Durkheimian critique, Boorstin, Debord and Marcuse and a McLuhanist bias towards form and effects above content and use. As he admitted in a 1995 interview, there were other affinities too since, for a long time, he said, he had promoted a 'Heideggerian analysis' of 'technology as the final realization of metaphysics' (1995b:85). By then, however, he was more critical of this 'rather nostalgic vision' and 'more inclined to drop this Heideggerian vision and find a kind of ironic principle of technology' (1995b:85). Beginning in *The Perfect Crime*, this reversal can be traced through the latest phase of his work (*PC*, 1997b, 1997c, 1997d, 1997e, 1997h, *Par.*, *VI*, *IE*), in his new reformulation of the symbolic, critique of virtual technologies, and extension of the 'double game' of symbolic and semiotic to the operations of technology. Now, Baudrillard argues, the latter may constitute a path to the symbolic and not just the means of its extermination.

In *The Perfect Crime*, Baudrillard develops a complex metaphysics drawn from social anthropology, his own theory of seduction, Nietzsche, Heidegger, Manichean and Gnostic thought, as well as cosmological science and radical physics. From these influences he reformulates the symbolic around the new critical concepts of 'radical illusion', 'vital illusion' and 'objective illusion', which he employs again to oppose the defining western order of truth and its project of objective realization. Now, Baudrillard argues, this reality is only a 'principle' imposed on a prior state of 'definitive illusion' (p. 8). Faced with this 'unbearable' condition our response was 'to realize the world, give it force of reality, make it exist and signify at all costs' (pp. 18, 16). Thus the real is founded on 'a gigantic enterprise of disillusionment – of, literally, putting the illusion of the world to death, to leave an absolutely real world in its stead' (p. 16). Rather than being opposed to simulation, 'reality' has always been a simulation, with its passage today into the hyperreal marking only an intensification of this process. With reality at its height the crisis we face today is not that of its loss but of its 'proliferation' and 'excess' (pp. 16, 64). This is that state of 'total, irrevocable positivity', 'transparency' and 'ultra-reality' created by our virtual technologies in their 'perfect crime' of the 'unconditional realization of the world' (pp. 62, 65–6).

The perfect crime, however, is never perfect (*VI*, 63). Symbolic forces always survive and reversal is always possible. Despite the array of technologies ranged against it, 'illusion is indestructible', Baudrillard says, (*PC*, 18). His belief in the survival of these 'lost forms' (*Par.*, 77) is increasingly reflected in the structure of his work and their division into sections that describe and defend these resistant processes (see *TE*, *PC*, *Par.*, *IE*). Among the forces he considers he begins to make the claim that technology itself might constitute – or hide – such a force. Reversing the subjectivist, McLuhanist theory of technology as an instrument of human will, Baudrillard suggests it may instead operate as the instrument of a world which uses it to impose itself (*PC*, 71). This is 'an ironic phase of technology', he says, beyond the objective and critical phase and also beyond Heidegger's 'retrospective nostalgia for Being' (*PC*, 72). Indeed, he explicitly targets Heidegger again when he reverses the claim that a 'saving power' may be found in technology, because, Baudrillard argues, today it is the saving power of our technologies – our own hyper protectedness and security – that threatens our well-being (*PC*, 49; *VI*, 81).

But Baudrillard is simultaneously drawn to that 'very mysterious sentence by Heidegger': his final comment that 'when we look into the ambiguous essence of technology, we behold the constellation, the stellar course of the mystery' (*PC*, 73; Heidegger, 1977:33). This suggests, he says, that 'at the extreme horizon of technology' another reversal occurs and 'that the constellation of the secret still resists, remains alive' (*VI*, 82). If today the divinity the Japanese sense within every object has been reduced to 'a tiny, ironic glimmer', this nevertheless remains 'a spiritual form' guarding the mystery of the world (*PC*, 73). Thus the world succeeds in hiding behind technology, 'the mystery' concealing itself 'beneath the universal banality of information' (*PC*, 72), Baudrillard says: Either we think of technology as the exterminator of Being, the exterminator of the secret, of seduction and appearances, or we imagine that technology, by way of an ironic reversibility, might be an immense detour toward the radical illusion of the world (*VI*, 82).

If there is no way of choosing between these possibilities (*VI*, 83), technology may still partake of that double game of semiotic and symbolic. Although Baudrillard has implicitly admitted this in his discussions of art (*Sed.*) and the cinematic image (*EDI*, 25), the technology that holds the strongest possibility of this reversal in his later work is photography.

'THIS CRY OF THE OBJECT'

Since he first began to incorporate his interest in photography in his writings of the early 1980s and 1990s, Baudrillard's theorization of the medium has developed considerably. While in a 1993 interview he would still claim that 'I've got nothing much to say about photography' (1997e:36), within a few years his writing on the subject would become 'voluminous' (*Fragments: Conversations with François L'Yvonnet* (*FC*), 117), occupying an increasingly central place and performing an important critical function within his work (see *PC*, 85–9; 1997c; 1997e; *Par.*, 89–101; 1999:128–42, 144–52; *IE*, 139–47; *FC*, 85–102; 2004a:141–4). During the same period Baudrillard's photographic practice also developed. Because of his fame as a thinker his photographs attracted international attention, being exhibited in recent years in Italy, Australia, the United Kingdom, Germany, France, Russia, Turkey,

Norway and Ireland, often accompanied by conferences, guest appearances, lectures and press attention (see Leith, 1998; Poole, 2000a).

Baudrillard himself has made few claims for his photography or for his own status as a photographer, for a long time denying any correspondence between his writing and photographic practice, explaining that he came to it 'as a kind of diversion or hobby' and as 'an alternative to writing' (1997e:32). But if he denied possessing any photographic project or vision, he did come to accept the possibility of a methodological and philosophical link between his writing and image-making (1997e:34). This assumption underlies my own reading; I believe it is necessary to read the two together since it is here that Baudrillard – one of the foremost contemporary critics of media – most clearly develops a positive theory and practice of a specific medium.

Baudrillard's first mature discussion of photography is in his 1983 essay *Please Follow Me*, accompanying photographer Sophie Calle's exhibition *Suite venitienne* (1988b; see also *FS*, 128–37; *TE*, 156–60), where he aligns the medium with the symbolic as 'an art of disappearance' actualizing seduction (1988b:86). His next essay, 'Radical exoticism' of 1990 (*TE*, 146–55), repeats this appropriation of the medium as a force for the symbolic, containing in embryo many of the most important themes of his later philosophy of photography. Central to this is an emphasis on the object above the subject. Though Baudrillard compares his writing and photographic practice, for him the former remains too subjective. In photography, therefore, he is able to efface himself in favour of a world 'which wants to be photographed' (1999:129) and its 'automatic writing' of this world (1999:141).

The solitude of the photographer and the object meet in the photographic act, says Baudrillard in *Within the Horizon of the Object* (1999:133). The former fixes the object with 'an intense, immobilizing gaze', holding his breath 'in order to create a blank region in time and in his body'; emptying his mind to create a space to produce the world 'as a singular event, without commentary' (p. 134). There is here, Baudrillard says, a 'reciprocal disappearance' of subject and object in which 'a transfusion between the two occurs' (p. 148). Photography, therefore, is an 'invocation' to the object, 'to emerge from this disappearance and so create a *poetic situation of transference, or a poetic transference of situation*' (p. 148). It is this symbolic exchange – this dual relationship and this 'duel' and 'confrontation' between the objective lens and the object that constitutes 'the photographic event' (pp. 132, 152). In the best case, Baudrillard says, the object wins this challenge (p. 132).

The meaning and point of photography, Baudrillard says, lie 'in the possibility of wresting a few exceptional images from the remarkable automaticity of the camera which generates an irrepressible flow of them' (p. 145). The properly photographic image is an 'exception' to the uninterrupted flow of images and referentiality that constitutes our contemporary experience (p. 145). It is the image which 'eliminates all the others' (p. 145–6) in the singularity of its stillness, silence and suspense:

Resisting noise, words, commotion with the silence of the photograph – resisting movement, flows, and ever greater speed with the stillness of the photograph – resisting the flood of communication and information with the secrecy of the photograph – resisting the moral imperative of meaning with the silence of signification. Above all resisting the automatic tide of images . . .

(2001c:140)

Only the still, with its negative, allows time for the image 'to become an image' (2001c:140), temporarily halting 'the tumult of the world' in 'the silent apophany of the object and its appearances' (2001c:140).

Like the idle talk of that fallen, everyday Dasein (Heidegger, 1962:211–14), most images chatter on endlessly, Baudrillard says, drowning out 'the silent signification of their object' (*IE*, 141). Silence, therefore, is one of the photograph's most 'precious' qualities (1999:135). This is the silence of both the image and the object, for 'whatever the noise and violence around them, photographs return objects to a state of stillness and silence' (1999:136). Photography 'produces a kind of thunder-struck effect, a form of suspense and phenomenal immobility' interrupting the world (1999:134); a freeze-frame effect in which 'the dizzying impact' and 'magical eccentricity' of the detail is seen (1999:130). In the centre of the 'turbulence' of the contemporary world it recreates, Baudrillard says, 'the equivalent of the desert', of a sense 'of phenomenological isolation, or rather a phenomenological immobilization of appearances' (1997c:31).

This is only achieved by sweeping away 'everything that imposes itself' on the object and gets in the way of their 'silent self-evidence' (*IE*, 141). Following that 'negative theology' in which God is discovered in what he is not rather than what he is, photography is similarly 'apophatic', Baudrillard says, giving knowledge of the world 'by way of emptiness', 'through what is cut away' (*IE*, 142). The photograph is the 'purest' image, he argues, refusing, unlike most of our media today, to simulate time and motion and thus retaining 'the most rigorous unrealism' (1999:130). Its intensity is due to this 'denial of the real': this stripping away of all those dimensions that semiotic realism accumulates – weight, relief, smell, depth, time, continuity and meaning (1999:130). In its disembodiment the image becomes 'a medium of pure objectality', Baudrillard says, 'becoming transparent to a subtler form of seduction' (1999:130).

All attempts to hyperrealize the image, adding these dimensions back on, loses this symbolic power of the image (1999:130). For Baudrillard the photograph is not part of the history of realism, but rather comes from elsewhere, preserving 'something of the magical status of the image and hence something of the radical illusion of the world' (1999:140). 'Every photographed object is merely the trace left behind by the disappearance of all the rest', a trace leaving 'the illusion of a particular object shining forth, the image of which becomes an impenetrable enigma' (1999:131). It is from the radical exception of this enigma that one gains 'an unobstructed vision of the world' and of the continuity of the details and fragments, argues Baudrillard (1997c:28).

This vision requires the effacement of the subject who occults the object 'like an overintense source of light', says Baudrillard (*IE*, 141). In contrast Baudrillard promotes 'the anti-philosophy of the object, of the disconnected-ness of objects, of the random succession of part objects and details' (1999a:132) 'What interests me is this cry of the object at evening in the depths of the dark-room,' he says (*Par.*, 99–100). Photography's cry 'smoothly' fractures the subject's machinery of representation (1999:133, 131), to reveal for us the world in our absence, the 'singularity' and 'otherness' of the object, their 'insoluble self-evidence' and their embodiment of 'the objective illusion of the world' (1999:133, 136). For Baudrillard the subject is harder to photograph since they are 'so laden with meaning' (1999:136). Every face is already an acting-out' (1999:146), being so caught within the mirrors of their self-representation that it is difficult 'to grasp in them what is beyond their own grasp' (*Par.*, 94), 'their secret identity or self-identity' (1997c:29). This 'inhuman' photogenic quality has occasionally been achieved by humanity, Baudrillard says, for example, in the 'savage' (*Par.*, 97–8) and in that first 'heroic' phase of photography 'when people posed like statues, transfixed by the lens' (*Par.*, 99). In these portraits of the bourgeoisie Baudrillard discovers a primitive duel and dramatic confronta-tion with the camera and an awareness of the image as 'a thing of risk, a magical and dangerous reality'. This mood is imprinted 'directly onto the film', he says, to lend the photographic event 'a genuine nobility, like a distant echo of the primal clash of cultures' (1999:138–39).

Explaining the power of the detail, Baudrillard accedes to Barthes's analy-sis of the 'punctum' (Barthes, 1993), which he describes as 'that figure of nothingness, absence and unreality' which stands opposed to the 'studium' which forms 'the whole context of meaning and references'. It is, Baudrillard says, 'the nothingness at the heart of the image which lends it its magic and power and which is most often driven out by significations' (1999:139). This concept is co-opted into his critique of contemporary images, which 'teem with messages', representing 'a prostitution of the image to what it signifies, to what it seeks to communicate' (1999:139). The real-time image is most culpable here, ironically driving out the punctum (1999:139) in its very 'indif-ference' to time – to the 'moment' of the image (1999:151).

But photography's power has also been neutralized by its appropriation by art and culture: by the museum, the gallery and the media. Following that Benjaminian progression 'which leads from the sacred to the beautiful, then to a generalized aesthetics' (*Par.*, 90; see Benjamin, 1973:218–19), Baudrillard sees the once-sacred image as being reduced and devalued by its incorpora-tion into aesthetics and signification, and its forced servitude to ideas such as objective reality and moral testimony (1999:148). His greatest contempt is for contemporary photography which condemns itself to photographing victims – the dead and the poor – while leaving them in their victimhood 'with the (itself poverty stricken) alibi of "giving" them a voice . . . they will never be able to give back' (1999:148). This 'realist photography', he says, does not photograph what is but rather what, according to its moral convictions, should not exist, while simultaneously making 'a perfectly immoral aesthetic use' and trade of this 'misery' (1999:148). Just as every tribe has its anthropologist so, Baudrillard says, every homeless person will soon have their own photographer leaping out of the urban jungle 'to capture on film the eternal sleep of the pauper' (1999:151). The hoped-for raising of our awareness fails, he argues, as each punctum-less image has less effect on us (*Par.*, 93; *IE*, 144–5).

From this, Baudrillard develops a surprising lament for the image:

We deplore the disappearance of the real, arguing that everything is now mediated by the image. But we forget that the image too disappears, overcome by reality. What is sacrificed in this operation is not so much the real as the image, which is dispossessed of its originality and doomed to a shameful complicity. Rather than lament the loss of a reality surrendered to the superficiality of the image, we should lament the loss of an image surrendered to the expression of the real. It is only by freeing the image from the real that we shall restore its potency . . .

(*IE*, 145)

The drive for signification represents 'a murder of the image' (*FC*, 93). Reduced to testimony and that 'most trivial, debased form of meaning', information (1999:150), embalmed and enclosed by the museum and gallery (*Par.*, 99), overexposed in the flow of real-time communications, and colonizing all 'symbolic space' (1999:149), the symbolic efficacy of the image is dispelled.

For Baudrillard, photography's role is not to illustrate events but instead 'to be itself an event' (1999:150). This is the event as symbolic scene, as creating a singularity in which the object also takes on 'the force of a pure event'. If one can capture this, Baudrillard says, then 'something of the world changes' (*Par.*, 92). Paradoxically it is the objective lens of the camera that finally challenges the reality principle, that specific, referential, epistemological project of the western subject, to reveal the illusion of its objectivity (1999:140). Technics becomes 'the site of a double game', allowing one to slip into its collusion with the world, Baudrillard says, 'not to control the process but to play on it and to show that the die is not cast irrevocably' (1999:141). Against all the assumptions of the photographer, their act is 'a reflex miracle' in which 'the object does all the work'. The 'basis rule', he says, is that it is the world and object which think us (1999:142).

As L'Yvonnet has suggested, Baudrillard's arguments might surprise readers expecting him to extend his critique of representation to photography (*FC*, 95). But Baudrillard's reversal of his attitude towards technology is less radical than it at first seems, his claims for photography being consistent with his 1979 claims for the image in *Seduction*. His philosophy of photography can be best understood, therefore, as an extension and application of his reformulation of the semiotic–symbolic divide in terms of 'disenchanted' and 'enchanted' simulacra. As I have argued, however, this distinction remains a problematic one and this is especially true in relation to photography.

Baudrillard's emphasis on the automaticity of the camera, the etymological origins of 'photography' as 'light-writing' (*IE*, 139), and the enchanted and magical nature of the image are supported by the history of the medium. In particular the idea of photography as nature's self-portrait is contained in Niepce's concept of 'heliography' and Daguerre's claim that his process gave nature 'the power to reproduce herself' (Trachtenberg, 1980:5, 13). Fox Talbot's description of his competing calotype process as 'the pencil of nature' in his title of 1844 (Talbot, 1969) echoed this while also underlining its break from human image-making in referring back to that failed sketching trip in 1833 which inspired his research when his own 'faithless pencil' left only 'traces on the paper melancholy to behold' (Trachtenberg, 1980:27–36). These automatic images were at first received as miraculous and marvellous, often being seen as 'powerful fetishes'– as animated, inhabited forms and physical incarnations – with 'the traditional vocabulary of magic' suffusing photographic discourse (Marien, 1997:13).

But Baudrillard's denial of photography as a realistic, representational medium is more contentious. Though realistic, and arguably even hyper-realistic media such as the panorama and phantasmagoria preceded it, photography was recognized from the first as something new. It helped produce an 'epistemological shift' in which objectivity was defined in terms of nature's self-reproduction rather than truthfulness to nature (McQuire, 1998:33), the objectivity of this process producing a corresponding belief in the objectivity and neutrality of its images. Photographic realism constituted for many, there-fore, the perfection of representation. Despite contemporary debates around studio artistry and trickery (see Henisch and Henisch, 1994), the nineteenth century was marked by a strong belief in the medium's objective truth, due, in no small part, to its physical attachment to and apparent co-substantiality with the real.

This belief in photography's physical, indexical link and effective reality as its own signified would become, in the work of Kracauer (1960), Bazin (1967), Barthes (1993), Sontag (1977) and Krauss (1984), a major strand in photographic theory. While, as Baudrillard suggests, this simulacral efficacy, and later digital break from its referent, would eventually throw photographic objectivity into question, the medium remains defined by the popular belief in its tangible link to the real and its objective representation. Indeed it is com-monplace to trace the development of this mode of realism from photography, through cinematography to television broadcasts, real-time satellite images and digital and computer-generated and animated images. Seen from this per-spective, photography played a central role in that semiotic and technical project of hyperrealism that Baudrillard sees as dominant today, making his co-option of the medium as a symbolic force harder to defend. His claims for an otherworldly nature later turned to disenchanted uses ignores the alterna-tive conception of the medium as essentially hyperrealistic.

This problem of interpretation is significant. Baudrillard's Benjaminian defence of the properties of early portrait daguerreotypes (Benjamin,

1997b:247–8, 250) and historical conception of the loss of this photographic aura with the dominance of subjective vision, meaning, signification and a serial referentiality may be defensible. It is certainly true that by the 1860s the 'duel' of portraiture had been reduced to a costume parade in front of back-cloths for *cartes de visite* sold by the dozen, that a trade in celebrity images had developed and that, with the stereoscope, the objects, forms and events of the world had been transformed into hyperrealistic images one could enter into and pore over, while photomicrography, stereoscopic 'instantaneous views' and chronophotographic research began to expose worlds beyond perception. The latter's objectivist, serial project of photographic hypervisibility was instrumental in the development of cinema and its techniques have been rediscovered with the growth of digital special effects, being used to create *The Matrix*'s 'bullet time' (Wachowski and Wachowski, 1999) and to animate digital characters in *The Lord of The Rings: The Two Towers* in 2002 and *The Matrix: Reloaded* in 2003. However, this perception of a movement towards hyperrealism is not so simple. We could today, for example, discover the enchanted form of the simulacrum in Victorian prints and in the stereoscopic revelation of the world, as well as that Benjaminian 'optical unconscious' (1997b:243–4) and Baudrillardian 'otherness', in the strange, inhuman, immobile forms of chronophotography (Thomas, 1997; Jeffrey, 1999).

This duality might illustrate exactly that 'double game' of semiotic and symbolic Baudrillard sees as operating in technology, but it also highlights the problem of distinguishing the enchanted and disenchanted forms of the simulacrum. Identifying what within photography, and within specific photo-graphs in particular, represents symbolic or semiotic processes remains a question of individual interpretation, reintroducing a subjectivity at the heart of Baudrillard's hoped-for object-based thought. For on what basis can we identify the otherness Baudrillard values except in reactions that remain personal and interpretative? This subjectivity haunts a medium in which, even if the photographer's subjectivity can be effaced, the image still faces the subjectivity of the viewer and the values, agendas, experiences and expectations they bring to it. Baudrillard's own rejection of 'judgement' in favour of 'sheer fascination' may help to describe the state necessary for the actualization of that mode of relations and experience he values, but it does not help our project. If we want to critically consider his photographic theory, analyse and comment on the success of specific photographs and of his own images in realizing his aims, and draw any conclusions from this regarding his media theory and practice, then we have to move beyond fascination towards subjective judgement.

Despite Baudrillard's criticism of the enslavement of the image to meaning and signification and ideological, political and aesthetic values and agendas, it is difficult to know how to escape these. Content imposes itself on us, guiding interpretation and forcing meaning, and the act of exhibition provokes aesthetic responses from us as we try to make sense of the images and consider their effect on us. Baudrillard's hostility towards the embalming of photography by the art gallery is also problematic since it is precisely through these avenues that his images are received. I first saw his photographs in Leicester in 1998, in a gallery in which Baudrillard himself circulated among his images as a spectacle for his viewing public, and since then they have been published as a glossy, coffee-table, art book whose own aesthetic sign-values are overwhelming (Baudrillard, 1999).

How then can we comment on photographs whose images and animating philosophy oppose such a subjective analysis? It is entirely possible that we cannot escape this subjectivity. Baudrillard's photographs are striking and succeed in holding a fascination for us but we only come to them through him and his intellectual reputation. Their primary fascination lies, therefore, in the fact that they are *his*, and because they are we are convinced that they are irrevocably imprinted with his subjectivity, possessing a meaning and a secret that we must discover. Thus what these photographs finally return to us as stranger, more enigmatic and more other is not the world, but *Baudrillard himself*. If Baudrillard criticism has moved beyond the hyperbolic mysticism that characterized aspects of his early reception (see Kellner, 1989:1), his photographs threaten its resurrection. Faced with the silence of the images, it is tempting to read them in the light of his work and the themes of his photographic theory, miraculously discovering his concepts realized before us before lapsing into an indulgent, poetic rumination upon their magic (see Weibel in Baudrillard, 1999:205–15).

But what else can we say about his photographs? My own analysis of them remains circumscribed by these problems. Reflecting on his images, what I am repeatedly drawn to is their form, and especially their colour and vibrancy. I take my interpretation of this from Baudrillard's own comparison of their light with Edward Hopper's paintings (1997c:34), an important reference as Hopper's 'realism' predated and found a later echo in Pop Art and especially in 'photo-realist' – or 'hyperrealist' – painting (see Battcock, 1975). Baudrillard has written much on Pop Art, recently defending Warhol's soup cans, for example, as 'a breakthrough in simulation', as an enchanted mode of simulation raising the consumer sign-object to its 'ironical canonization' in order to expose and undermine simulation (1997h:11). It may be possible, therefore, to see Baudrillard's hyperrealistic palette as performing the same function of ironical canonization as in photo-realist painting. However, where hyperrealist art simulated photographs in order to comment ironically on the passage of the world into the image and this photographic form, his photographs appear to reverse this, presenting us with images of the real that seem to simulate hyperrealist painting, thereby transforming the world into a painted image and restoring to it, as he hopes, both that power of illusion and an ironic commentary on its own reality-effect. This reading is a tempting one, allowing us to tie up his theory and practice and defend his photographs, but it remains a subjective imposition, finding a confirmation of his work in his silent images. Neither does it solve the problem of grounding his critical practice, of defending his valorization or of securing the concept and application of the enchanted simulacrum, and the same photographs could also be alternatively interpreted as contributing towards the hyperrealization of the world.

There is no way round this, unless, following Baudrillard's own 'apophatic' method, we approach his images not through what they are but through what they are not. Baudrillard's images are surprising because we might have expected *different* photographs from him. We might have expected more and very different images – of the city, of the desert, of consumer society and its simulations and of our media-saturated lives; perhaps Ballardian landscapes or panning shots of the sheen of contemporary life and its objects and signs. But such images would also have been too obvious, reducing themselves too easily to a reflection of his work and contradicting themselves in their message and testimony. Instead Baudrillard gives us something whose power and fascination primarily lies in its form – in its colours and lighting, in the shapes and objects that appear, and in the Barthesian 'punctum' that he defends. Baudrillard's debt to Barthes's *Camera Lucida* (1993) is obvious and is widely acknowledged (see Zurbrugg, 1997). Although there are many affinities in their treatment of photography beyond the use of the punctum, such as in their shared critique of the contemporary banalization of the image and of 'unary' news photographs, and in their suspicion of realism (Barthes, 1993:117–19, 40–2, 109), as Zurbrugg points out there are important differences too (1997:149–67). Perhaps the most important is Baudrillard's adoption of Barthes, as in McLuhan, only to incorporate him into his own Durkheimian critical project. Barthes is specifically employed to support Baudrillard's critique of contemporary images and to evoke the possibility of another – symbolic – mode of experience, relations and meaning with and through the image.

Whereas for Barthes the punctum was a specific, identifiable detail within each picture that 'shoots out of it like an arrow' and pierces the viewer (1993:26), for Baudrillard it operates at the level of form, being integral to the nature of photography itself. For him, it represents the reversible figure of nothingness and death and thus a symbolic mode of experience and relations actualized in and through photographic images, which represent, therefore, the survival of this force and the possibility of its rediscovery. As Baudrillard says, radical otherness remains as 'the imminence of a revenge, of a resurrection of all that has been exiled to the other side of the mirror and held captive in the servile representation of the world of the victors' (*Par.*, 101). This power 'squints out from the other side of the mirror and its ghost haunts the realized world', he says (*Par.*, 101), and photography is one form of its simulacral apparition.

If Baudrillard's philosophy of photography finds an echo here, it is perhaps less with Barthes than with the later Heidegger, whose work increasingly moved away from the subjective phenomenology of *Being and Time* in 1927 (1962) to try to think the truth of 'Being' without reference to 'beings'. Opposing the metaphysical formulation of Being as 'presence' with a conception of its truth as *aletheia*, or 'unconcealment', his later essays reduce Dasein from 'Being-uncovering' (1962:263) to an 'opening' receiving truth (1993:111–38, 139–212), before replacing this opening with the 'openness' – that 'clearing' that grants the possibility of being's prescencing, of that sending and 'giving' of the 'gift' of Being, while simultaneously holding back, and sheltering and preserving that gift (1993:427–49). Against the Aristotelian present, therefore, Heidegger develops a temporal conception of Being in its prescencing. The giving opens 'time-space' (1972:14), bringing together time and being in 'Ereignis', or 'the event of appropriation' (1972:19), in which Being approaches man in the 'play' of temporality that gives and withholds the present and unifies past, present and future.

Like Baudrillard's, therefore, Heidegger's concerns move towards the 'gift', the 'event' and the experience of a world thought apart from human *ratio*, combined with a critique of this subject's certain representation and its transformation of the world into a 'picture' (1977:115–54). As in Baudrillard too, the methodological question of how to discover and express this world becomes paramount for Heidegger, who also develops a series of philosophical and writing strategies to overcome this problem of expression such as a turn to pre-'western' (pre-Socratic) and eastern thought, attacks on western metaphysics, etymological minings, erasure of the word 'Being', use of the dialogue form and perpetual redevelopment of his terminology and concepts. Like Baudrillard, Heidegger also develops a critique of western civilization and its deployment of technology, and if this is primarily focused on an 'industrial', 'atomic' society it also incorporates attacks on modern electronic and visual communications technology such as radio, TV and popular picture magazines (see 1959:37–8; 1966:48; 1971a:165–6).

Heidegger most fully explores the essence of technology in his 1955 essay 'The question concerning technology' (1977:3–35). Much of his essay is concerned with describing the 'Gestell', or 'enframing': that technological mode of 'revealing' that grips humanity, making them reveal the real as 'standing reserve', as a resource which they set on to expose, unlock and transform in an unending process (pp. 16–17). Even here, however, man is still responding to the call of unconcealment, Heidegger says (p. 19), though it is a call he contradicts by succumbing to the 'extreme danger' of assuming the role of Being's organizer instead of 'keeping watch' over it (p. 32). Enframing thus conceals another mode of revealing within it; one that avoids this exposure, letting what presences come forward by itself into the openness. Heidegger describes this as 'poiesis' (pp. 21, 27) and it fulfils for him Hölderlin's poetic claim, 'But where danger is, grows / The saving power also', representing a 'saving power' emerging at the heart of enframing and countering its danger (p. 28).

Thus, Heidegger says, 'the coming to presence of technology harbours in itself what we least suspect, the possible arising of a saving power' (p. 32), a power he discovers in an earlier meaning of *techne*. This term was once applied to 'the poiesis of the fine arts' which, for the Greeks, constituted that mode

of revealing 'that brings forth truth into the splendour of the radiant appearing' (p. 34). Before aesthetics, he says, 'the arts soared to the supreme height
of the revealing granted them. They brought the presence of the gods,
brought the dialogue of divine and human destinings, to radiance' (p. 34). It
is thus in the *techne* of the arts, and in poetry especially, that Heidegger finds
a path to 'the constellation of truth', and to perceive 'the stellar course of the
mystery' (p. 33). For the later Heidegger, poetry still provided a path to Being,
with language representing not a human product but the speaking of Being
itself (1971b). Hence not only his turn towards poetry but also his critique of
everyday, worn-out, representational language and promotion of a poetizing
thinking.

Despite Baudrillard's attempts to distance himself from Heidegger, cited
earlier in the chapter, many affinities with his work remain. In Baudrillard we
also find the distinction of two modes of revealing – that forced, productive,
pornographic drive of semiotic culture, and another, symbolic mode of the
bilateral actualization of meaning, aligned with a critique of technology that
sees a means of reversal and 'saving power' existing within and emerging
through it. Baudrillard has also placed a similar emphasis on the poetic as
a symbolic force (*SED*, 195–242), pursuing a poetizing mode of thought
and privileging writing as offering the same possibilities as photography
(1999:135). For Baudrillard, however, the world's otherness is most fully
revealed in images and this may represent the final realization of his belief that
the symbolic is inexpressible in language (*CPES*, 159–63). If his expression of
this references Wittgenstein – ' "Whereof one cannot speak, thereof one must
remain silent" – but you can be silent thereof with images' (*IE*, 139) – one
might still find in it a call for that contemplative 'releasement' Heidegger
defends (Heidegger, 1966). For Baudrillard, too, the aim is the revelation of
the 'stunning clarity' of the world shining through the disappointment of its
fallen everydayness (*TE*, 155).

Echoing Heidegger's pronounced hostility to picture magazines and their
general availability (1966:48), Baudrillard demonstrates a similar antipathy to
the use and dissemination of images by culture and the media. It is significant,
therefore, that at exactly that moment when he appears to reverse himself,
finding a path to the symbolic within technology and becoming himself a
media practitioner and producer of images, the result is, if anything, a rein-
forcement and deepening of his critique of contemporary media forms.
Baudrillard's arguments ultimately oppose that position held as common sense
by media professionals, practitioners and commentators, and much of the
general public too, that our still and moving images have a demonstrable
power to move us, and to change our behaviour and responses. In this perspective, mass reproduction and dissemination have retained and amplified the
photographic aura which persists today in iconic images of famous figures and
photojournalistic and live television images of historical moments and events.
We find here, therefore, a McLuhanist faith in the empathetic, participative
power of the electronic media's images and a belief in the power of the still

photographic image such as that defended by Sontag in her book *Regarding the Pain of Others* (2003).

Baudrillard, in his defence of a symbolic whose purity, despite all its transformations, remains absolute, rejects precisely this. He emerges from his discussion of photography as even more implacably opposed to the semiotic media's use of the image for news, entertainment, information, communication, signification, and ideological, political and aesthetic effects, and for moral testimony as a banal witness to the real. Against this 'prostitution' and 'murder' he offers a philosophical defence of a mode of experience and revelation and of the role of the image in actualizing this mode. He remains, to the end, the inheritor of a radical Durkheimianism that, in the name of the sacred and its convulsive communication, refuses any compromise with the permanently profane contemporary world.

Many, however, will feel that this is inadequate. For his critics this philosophy will seem too far removed from the issues of contemporary life and morality and the responsibilities of media practice, being unable in its blanket condemnation to suggest anything whatsoever to guide or transform its industries. Baudrillard's retreat into silent witness to the self-evidence of the world suggests his media theory cannot offer anything to the media industries and his critique will appear to many as too complete, and ultimately empty.

In his defence, such a perception of failure might mark instead the extent to which our experience of the world, our moralities and epistemologies and our conception of the image and its uses have all become subordinated to and have passed over to contemporary media forms. Today we are unable to conceive of a relationship to the world and to others except through them, desperately defending their operations and retaining a faith in their implicit goodness, incarnation of progress, tangible benefits and possibility for reform. For Baudrillard, however, this constitutes our contemporary mode of nihilistic withdrawal, founded as it is on the loss of an entire mode of relations and meaning. For all the problems of its formulation and grounding, Baudrillard's work ends therefore not in a retreat but in a tenacious and hopeful belief in another mode of experience and relationship to the world and between people. It ends in a belief in the survival of this symbolic force, even in its tiniest glimmer, and the radical possibility at all times of its return and revenge.

CONCLUSION

'Speculation to the death':
Baudrillard's theoretical violence

P5150

I have dreamt of a force five conceptual storm blowing over the devastated real.
Baudrillard, *Fragments: Cool Memories 3*

It isn't hard to criticize Baudrillard's work. As I have shown, the most common criticisms come from the left, which retains a deep ideological aversion and extreme hostility towards his 'postmodern' excesses – his writing, his methodology, his rejection of truth and the possibility of certain knowledge, his celebration of contemporary capitalism, his nihilistic denial of reality and his lack of belief in any transformative project. The limitations and errors of this reading have, I hope, been successfully challenged in this book, which has attempted to present another Baudrillard: one working within a specific Durkheimian tradition, extending its analysis to contemporary social and media forms and developing an original critique of its nihilistic processes and forms of social control. For his description of this media culture Baudrillard also draws on anthropological, theological and philosophical conceptions of the image, Barthes's semiology, western Marxist analyses of the spectacle and its social control, a Boorstinian critique of its transformation of reality, and a McLuhanist emphasis on the form and effects of contemporary electronic technology. To this we might add the anti-empiricist, McLuhanist, Situationist and avant-garde influences on his methodology that shape his critical project and its claims. If my aim has also been to demonstrate the value of this media theory for media and communication studies, it remains clear that after the more simplistic criticisms have been discounted there remain many possible points of criticism from within this discipline.

Taken at its simplest, Baudrillard's media theory has nothing to say about the media industries themselves, containing no analysis of their economic, political or organizational structure, or the forms of power commonly identified as operating through these. It is uninterested in traditional Marxist or liberal pluralist analyses of the capitalist infrastructure underlying its foundation, its policies and functioning within a market economy, or the relationship between

Critical against

media companies and the competition between them. It does not consider the national or international processes of their business, issues around media concentration and monopoly, or the globalization of media empires and their products, having nothing to say about traditional issues of ownership and control, the uses to which these may be put, or their relationship to national or international government. It also says nothing about the internal processes of media production across the different media, whether about the technologies involved and their use, the institutional fields that develop within each branch of the media, the practices and cultures that emerge within them, or the social background and habitus, and education, apprenticeship and training of its members. *Critique against.*

In addition to ignoring the processes operating behind the media, Baudrillard's media theory has little interest in the way power operates through its content. Despite the Marxist influence on his work he rejects ideological analyses of media output, and is equally uninterested in questions of manipulation and censorship. Despite his semiological background, he offers very few readings of specific media texts and little in the way of close image analysis. Despite his interest in the image and representation, he has nothing to say about traditional debates within the subject such as the representation of specific social groups or phenomena, or issues of bias, stereotyping, genre or narrative, refusing to incorporate the insights of alternative perspectives such as feminism or postcolonialism. Baudrillard's discussion of media effects also makes no use of and little reference to the models of communication and reception which have developed. His apparent picture of 'the masses' as passive, stupefied consumers of media 'spectacle' looks especially anachronistic in the context of the contemporary dominance within the discipline of audience studies and theories of the active reception of media products. In contrast to Baudrillard, who seems intent on pursuing a more deterministic and unilateral interpretation of the media, the latter emphasize the fragmentation of the mass audience and the individual's ability to decode messages in personal, often oppositional ways.

Baudrillard's rejection of alternative media theories also implies that little dialogue is possible between his work and mainstream media theory, as is evidenced by his own estrangement from this field. His treatment of different media and understanding of their technical bases and the differences between their forms is also limited. Despite his critique of contemporary electronic technologies, he pays little attention to advances and developments within them, demonstrating little detailed or personal knowledge of their advanced or even their more popular forms. There is also little in his work on the subject of media history, his work emphasizing the transformations of the sign and its relationships above the development of specific technical forms. Moreover, the practical application of Baudrillard's work outside academia is notably limited, given his overt hostility towards contemporary media. With his work remaining fixed at the level of theoretical critique, it is unlikely that he could make any significant contribution to media practice or production.

Finally, we should add to this Baudrillard's commonly assumed theoretical links with postmodernism, his anti-empiricist philosophy, his rejection of established quantitative and qualitative academic research methods, and his invented, wilfully perverse, intentionally provocative and counter-intuitive claims and analyses. Other important factors affecting his academic value include his outsider status, his fame as a media star and cult figure, and his complex and individual style of writing and thinking. All of these together help to explain Baudrillard's positioning and treatment within mainstream media and communication studies. Seen from this perspective it is not surprising that the discipline has found so little use for his work.

To these criticisms we could add those directly related to Baudrillard's own position and influences. His commitment to the radical French, social anthropological and philosophical tradition of Durkheimianism and its valorization of a particular concept of 'the sacred' also commits him to similar claims of its historical loss. Thus he is repeatedly forced into an unequivocal critique of contemporary media forms, which, for him, reduce, simulate and replace this experience, and this prevents him from offering any more sophisticated analyses of particular media products and their effects and reality. As I have argued, Baudrillard himself recognized the limitations of this position, and hence his attempts to reformulate his theory of the image and its seductive possibilities, though these succeed only at the expense of the clarity of his critical project. His radical Durkheimianism also leads him into a repeated defence of a specific mode of relations and meaning that, as the case of photography shows, while not entirely ruling out technological mediation, nevertheless implicitly valorizes direct, fact-to-face communication. Such a pro-dialogical position has been widely criticized in the discipline, with Thompson, for example, defending the new forms of self available in a mediated world and the 'new opportunities, new options, new arenas for self-experimentation' it offers (1995:233). The rejection of all these modes of experience and relations would appear to be regressive and conservative, failing to accept that 'the structure of experience has changed in significant ways' (1995:233). Far from leading to the withdrawal from others and the world in the way Baudrillard suggests, for Thompson mediated experience can increase our sense of morality and relational responsibility (1995:234).

Baudrillard's adoption of the concept of the simulacrum to describe the images and experiences offered by contemporary media proves to be equally problematic. His media theory distinguishes itself from discussions of media ideology and spectacle precisely in the efficacy this concept imparts to media products to eclipse and produce our reality. However, this simulacral ungrounding of the real and the possibility of its distinction impacts methodologically both on Baudrillard's identification and description of their existence and operation, and on his attempts to establish a critical foundation against their processes. That symbolic which he attempts to define and defend as – in effect – an experiential reality outside and opposed to the simulacrum is itself exposed as a simulation and simulacral ground. His later embrace of

enchanted simulacra fails to escape the problems of distinction and foundation that the concept historically problematizes, and unless these foundations
can be established his critique of media fails.

Other problems result from the specific combination of influences
Baudrillard draws on. Despite the often close connections between the theories
of Boorstin, McLuhan, Lefebvre, Marcuse and Debord, their marriage within
Baudrillard's work is not necessarily a smooth one. Conflicts remain between
their different approaches and the problems of each perspective may reappear
within Baudrillard's work. The combination of McLuhan's emphasis on form
above content and Barthes's semiology, for example, allows Baudrillard to
develop a conception of the media's operation as defined by the semiotic reduction and replacement of the symbolic. Arguably, this results in a simplification
of media processes, risking a semiological determinism that devalues, and thus
pays insufficient attention to, its specific content and its active reception.

This is only reinforced by the influence of the western Marxist critique in
the 1960s of consumer and media society and the new modes of alienation
and social control which permeate and operate through it. Lefebvre's 'terroristic' society of 'controlled consumption' (Lefebvre, 1971), Marcuse's society
of 'one dimensional' thought and behaviour and 'repressive desublimation'
leading to 'euphoria in unhappiness' (Marcuse, 1986) and Debord's 'spectacular' society of 'generalized separation' (Debord, 1983) find a direct echo
in Baudrillard's critique of semiological relations, their total organization
of everyday life, processes of consumer 'personalization', and the dominance
of precessionary, regulative simulation models. Extended through a concept of
the simulacrum that leaves even less space for any original, unmediated behaviour, Baudrillard's rigorously critical, conflictual, pessimistic and deterministic reading of the media forecloses any more positive interpretation of their
output and functioning. His addition to this of a Boorstinian critique of the
loss of reality risks adding to this a nostalgic conservativism updated through
a Debordian paranoia. Baudrillard's extreme theoretical response and methodology are the direct result of this extreme interpretation of media, and are, for
many, unacceptable.

It would be erroneous to conclude from all this, however, that Baudrillard's
work has nothing to offer media and communication studies. Despite these
criticisms, I believe that his work offers us one of the most important
contemporary theories of the media, in its lineage, original critique and
potential applicability, and its challenge to the discipline and to our understanding of media culture. Moreover, many of the strengths of his work derive
from areas already singled out for possible criticism, with his ideas providing
a reciprocal problematization of many assumptions and methodologies pre-
valent within the field. In particular I would like to suggest six areas of his
work that make an important contribution to media and communication
studies. These are his semiological critique, his radical Durkheimianism, his
theory of simulation, his critique of electronic media, his critique of media
events, and his radical methodology.

(1)   The original contribution of Baudrillard's semiological theory to media and communication studies lies in its McLuhanist emphasis on form above content. Where other semiotic theories lead to predictable analyses of the content of specific texts, Baudrillard makes us aware of a prior and more fundamental process – the production of that meaning from the reduction, processing and transformation of a symbolic mode of relations. His distinction of semiotic and symbolic, his characterization of our society as defined by their transformation, his critical sympathy with the symbolic, and his application of this model to analyse the operation of the sign-form throughout contemporary media all constitute an important contribution to the discipline. Baudrillard's reading of the sign-form as functioning simultaneously as a medium of communication and as a conduit for competition, distinction and social control also represents a significant extension of the critical possibilities of Barthesian semiology. His detailed analysis of the system of sign-objects and their interrelationship, operation and effects, and his rich early case studies of these both demonstrate the practical applicability and relevance of his semiology.

Baudrillard's poststructuralist analysis of the sign's operation, and in particular of its internal production of its own supporting ground is also important. The exposure of the sign's claims for an external ground, in, for example, 'concrete reality', 'nature' or 'human needs', establishes the basis for an effective critique of its signification and 'reality effect' as simulacral. Moreover his development from this linked analysis of commodity and sign-forms of a 'general political economy', together with his later extension of this in discussions of the 'orbital' hyperrealization and fractal dissemination of the sphere of value, offer an important challenge to traditional Marxist and liberal perspectives on political economy, with important implications for debates around the political economy and globalization of media industries. Rather than Baudrillard offering nothing in these areas, instead his work implicitly problematizes the dominant conceptual schemata that underpins the existing debates.

(2)   Baudrillard's Durkheimianism constitutes his second important contribution to media and communication studies. Against the traditional Durkheimian analyses which have prevailed in the discipline, with their functionalist conclusions concerning the unificatory power of the mass media, Baudrillard draws on a more radical and critical Durkheimian tradition. This emphasizes the historical replacement in the west of the violent, disruptive 'convulsive communication' of the sacred by its safe, simulated forms and the establishment of a permanently profane social and economic system, developing an original and powerful critique of this loss. Baudrillard's contribution is to unify the threads of this tradition around a concept of symbolic exchange whose mode of 'communication' becomes the basis for a critique of its contemporary, mediated forms. He marks out here an original space within media theory, his work updating and revitalizing the radical Durkheimian tradition,

extending its critique to contemporary society and media, and challenging established Durkheimian analyses within media and communication studies.

Far from being the conservative thinker the 'postmodern' attribution and his own critique of electronic media suggest, Baudrillard subscribes to a radical philosophy of life whose aim is the overthrow and transformation of the profane, semiotic order. Despite the problems of the foundation and formulation of this symbolic, Baudrillard produces an active, optimistic and radical media theory founded on a critique of contemporary modes of relationship, experience and meaning, and the hope of the rediscovery of their symbolic modes. Running throughout his work, alongside and spiralling together with his analysis of the nihilistic processes of the semiotic and its mode of social control, is this continued belief in the survival and the possibility of the reappearance and revenge of this force. For him, the 'symbolic demand' will always haunt this system.

(3) Baudrillard's theory of simulation provides his next major contribution to the discipline. His rediscovery and application of the ancient concept of the simulacrum succeed in linking those anthropological, theological, philosophical and aesthetic ideas that have been constitutive of western culture to contemporary media processes. His discussion of the sign and its transformations and of simulacra and simulation provide a historical context for the contemporary image, making us aware of its nature and inherent properties and effects, drawing out the epistemological implications for our own imagic society. His work emphasizes the media's semiotic production of experiential reality, its eclipse and replacement of lived experience and knowledge, the nihilistic implications of this ungrounding of certain foundations, and the functioning of its precessionary models as a mode of social control in reducing all responses, thought and behaviour to reflections of its own prior images. Far from valorizing these processes, Baudrillard searches for resistant, symbolic forces to counter them. Of these, his discussion of the reversive power of hyperconformity as a strategy against the system and its control provides one of the most interesting and potentially effective concepts of resistance to the media and its products.

Baudrillard's critique of the simulacrum and of representation also challenges many existing assumptions within media and communication studies. In particular his emphasis on the historical efficacy of the image form and its contextualization within the philosophical and theological debates which have surrounded the concept of representation in the west highlight the limitations of those texts and courses in the discipline which focus on content, semiology and specific contemporary perspectives and meanings. In his work representation takes on a greater significance and is subjected to a more radical critique than within media studies. Baudrillard's discussion of 'the masses' provides one of the best examples of this since, for him, they remain an unknowable, unrepresentable category, describable only through and as their representation (*SSM*). This poses a radical challenge to the accepted methodologies of the discipline and its belief in the objective representability of its subject matter, as well as to the entire contemporary literature on the audience which similarly assumes its own ability to reach and reflect the reality of this group in order to speak for them as regards their thought and behaviour. Ultimately it is not Baudrillard but the discipline itself which patronises this group, at exactly that point when it claims to have moved beyond mass theory to valorize individual and micro responses.

(4)   The original critique of electronic media and virtuality that results from these ideas represents Baudrillard's fourth contribution to the subject. His emphases on their form, their unilaterality, their semiological processing of symbolic experience and meaning, their simulacral modelling and production of 'the real' and implosive virtualization of everyday life are all important and the theory of media power that results provides an original challenge to those operating in the discipline. Also valuable are his analyses of their reversive effects: the simultaneous actualization and dramatization of the real and its deactualization and semiotic distantiation; the reversal of communication into isolated non-communication, and, with its 'neutralization' of the symbolic and 'dissuasion' and 'deterrence' of the real, the reversal of the hyperreal heightening and intensification of experience into 'indifference'. His discussion of the increased determination offered by the simulacral modelling of the real and the uncertainty that pervades the simulacrum, as well as the loss of reality that results from its overproduction and excessive realization, adds significantly to the literature. Similarly his claims that the electronic media's implosive acceleration into the real leads to hyperreality, and that every such attempt to realize the real only takes us further into its simulacrum, have important repercussions for how we understand the media's operation.

Influenced by Boorstin, McLuhan and Debord, Baudrillard recognized the importance of the media's production of the real and its hyperreality in the late 1960s, his work anticipating the increasing development of these processes and predating the contemporary interest in these issues within media and communication studies by many years. In pushing these influences further he still offers a more radical interpretation of contemporary electronic media than the mainstream discipline, producing some of the most important analyses of their implosive effects, real-time technology, contemporary communication networks, and the technologies and process of virtualization. His pursuit of these themes and his characterization of our culture as dominated by a productive drive for the pornographic materialization of the real now look especially prescient. As he suggests, the problem we face today is not the mystification or censorship of the world but its absolute transparency. The dominance of 'reality TV', the representation of all human experiences, behaviours and biological functions in the media, the instant availability of the world through the internet and 24-hour news channels, the spectacular, live coverage of world events and wars, and that digital hyperreality that pervades cinema and television, all testify to the relevance of Baudrillard's critique.

Posity ve

(5) This practical applicability of Baudrillard's work represents his next contribution to media and communication studies, his work providing us with a critical model whose relevance and ease of application to a variety of contemporary media phenomena are easy to recognize. I have emphasized here the value of his theory of 'non-events' in which he develops one of the most important analyses of contemporary media 'events', problematizing their occurrence in the light of his theories of the semiotic functioning of the media and the precessionary impact of simulacra. In this critique the perverse pleasures of his counter-intuitive philosophy, his provocative methodology and his conceptual radicality all come together and its model can be applied to any number of contemporary examples from the most trivial – the world of soap characters and celebrities and their misadventures – to the most important, such as September 11 and its reception and military aftermath. Baudrillard gives us the means to look around and to push the media's own processes further, declaring the non-occurrence of its most spectacular and forgettable productions. It is in his methodology, therefore, that Baudrillard's most important contribution to the discipline may be found.

Mike Gane's judgement that 'no-one as yet, really knows how to read Baudrillard' (Critchley, 1999) is a salutary one. If, as Gane says, most of Baudrillard's critics have failed to hit him, as they 'launch their derision too soon, and miss the target' (1995:120), he has perhaps also eluded his more sympathetic commentators too. Baudrillard himself has commented on the 'reductive' criticism he has received (Zurbrugg, 1997:45), but even positive attempts to explain and defend his work risk a reductive selection and interpretation, producing another simulacrum of his work. My analysis does not escape this problem, but what I hope to have achieved is a defensible, coherent presentation of the Durkheimian Baudrillard that begins to consider how his work fits into and enriches media and communication studies. My reading aims to provide a way for readers to *approach* Baudrillard: a framework within which to read him and the means to surpass it, to find new meaning and possibilities within his work, and to respond to his ideas.

This question of how we respond to Baudrillard is one of the central ones his work poses for us. His critics choose the negative response of denial and de-escalation, rejecting his ideas to reduce his claims back to established positions or commonsense assumptions assumed to be proven and superior. The left's critique is paradigmatic here but the strategy is widespread. This is a comforting option, erasing the need for any detailed reading of Baudrillard's oeuvre and confining debates within existing, agreed parameters, but it is not necessarily an adequate one. As McLuhan suggested in response to critics who were unable to follow his exploration of the electronic world, 'for all their lamentations the revolution has already taken place' (E. McLuhan and Zingrone, 1995:266), and this is what Baudrillard similarly attempts to think through in all its radicality. The problem he poses is how to proceed from this – what concepts and methods are adequate to describe, analyse and oppose a world which, as McLuhan suggests, has accelerated beyond our traditional explanations and knowledge. The task is to leap ahead again, to steal a march on its own processes. As Baudrillard says, 'to think extreme phenomena, thought must itself become an extreme phenomenon' (*SO*, 66).

His critics' denial constitutes an impoverished response to the gift of Baudrillard's work: a refusal of relations and failure to ascend to his challenge. Baudrillard gives us a more fitting way to read his work. In his discussion in 1983 of Sophie Calle's *Suite venitienne*, commenting on her pursuit of a stranger through the streets of Venice, Baudrillard says that to 'follow' another is a 'murderous' game (1988b:78), stealing the other's goal from them (*TE*, 156), doubling and erasing them. Hence Baudrillard's final request, 'please follow me' (1988b:86), does not represent a call for acceptance but a solicitous desire to draw us into a seductive game and duel in which either ourselves or Baudrillard himself might be lost. As I have suggested, the hostility of Baudrillard's critics does the most to keep him alive as a diabolical challenge and living force, but a more subtle form of critique is also possible: one in which we *follow* Baudrillard, escalating his work through a hyperacceptance.

(6)   Throughout this book I have returned to the question of method in Baudrillard. Like McLuhan his work implicitly problematizes empirical academic methodology and its assumptions, offering instead a new strategy. For Baudrillard theory is a simulation – one that is not untrue, but instead a doubling that uses truth while striking at it from outside its own distinctions, that produces a representation that also pushes the logic of the system described to the point of its possible reversal. Theory is a process of invention and inversion, a conceptual weapon against the processes of the real, though one that is deceitful and collusive, speaking that evil it opposes. Its aim is not to be true since that would reduce it to a passive reflection whose validity and value is literally derived after-the-fact, from its aposteriori proof in the real. Instead Baudrillard advocates a 'radical thought' whose efficacious modelling captures the real within its orbit, though the risk of this strategy is that our 'unscrupulous reality' will respond with its own counter-gift, escalating itself to prove the theory right, to merge with and reduce it once more. Hence Baudrillard's potlatch with the real: that escalating theoretical project in which both theory and the world are at stake.

For Baudrillard, therefore, theory is also a symbolic challenge. His aim is not simply a descriptive statement of the real but its critique and transformation; hence he offers original, speculative, engaged, strategic readings, hoping to hasten its processes and push towards the point of implosive collapse and reversal. This requires a total receptiveness in the void matched with a 'speculation to the death' – both an unending speculation, revisiting and remodelling all interpretations, and a speculation continuing until the death of the system. For Baudrillard, *theory must be an event in the world*, the 'poetic singularity' of thought and the 'vital challenge' of its 'theoretical violence' combining, he hopes, to produce that single, devastating strike that will cripple the real.

The only appropriate response to Baudrillard, therefore, is to follow him. This is what will allow us, if we so wish, to murder and erase him. As Baudrillard is aware, the game of theory ends not when it has been disproved but instead when its ideas have been realized in the world. The best way to overcome him, therefore, is to demonstrate the validity of his work, to highlight its realization within contemporary media culture and thus reduce him to a predictable and banal reflection of existing trends. This is already happening. Even for Baudrillard the simulacrum has become our 'everyday obscenity' and the obvious relevance and applicability of his ideas and the dissemination of similar themes throughout the discipline all point to his own incipient disappearance. My own attempt here to demonstrate the value of Baudrillard's media theory is complicit in this, hastening the recognition of his work and its insight and relevance, damaging Baudrillard more profoundly than his critics ever could. But we should be anxious about Baudrillard's realization and defeat by the world. In 1965 Tom Wolfe was famously moved by McLuhan to ask, what if he is 'the most important thinker since Newton, Darwin, Freud, and Pavlov . . . what if he is right?' (Stearn, 1968:37). Applied now to Baudrillard, this question takes on a renewed significance. His confirmation would leave us adrift in a weightless, affectless, simulacral media world, his dissolution through the real losing for us the critical leap, meaning and energy his work provides. Baudrillard's failure lies in the risk of being *too right*; in the simulacra he plays with overwhelming him. The advocate of the devil's demonic, imagic forces could himself be eclipsed, reduced to the ghost of his own semiotic simulacra. We can see, therefore, that it is for our sake as well as his own that Baudrillard must hope to avoid this.

Alternatively, we can accept and follow Baudrillard in order to push him further, taking up his ideas and methodology ourselves to leave him behind. If his work is a challenge to the real and to theory, it is also a challenge to us. Rather than lowering ourselves by refusing this challenge we should instead accept and escalate it, to give back more. This escalation and reversal and speculation to the death are what Baudrillard himself wants (1997d:45; 1997e:42). His methodological contribution to media and communication studies, therefore, ultimately lies in freeing us to push analyses and ideas further, to respond to the world with a theory which 'looks like nothing on earth':

Neither an empirical refutation of these systems (which, were it to be done, would be part of the same reality), nor a pure fiction unrelated to them, but, rather, both of these things at the same time. It is both the mirror of a world that is already at its extremes and the thing pushing the world towards those extremes – the identification of an implicit trend, and of the force precipitating it towards its end.

(*IE*, 149–50)

This is an invitation to produce that 'force-five conceptual storm' to blow across the deserts of simulacra and to whip up the fragments of our devastated real.

There *is* no media theory, there is only a strategy: speculation to the death.

Notes

INTRODUCTION: 'THERE IS NO THEORY OF THE MEDIA'

1 By the time we factor in Baudrillard's own controversial reputation and the recurrent misunderstandings concerning his work we can begin to understand the range of responses that greeted my attempt to consider Baudrillard's place within and value for media studies: from surprise at or disinterest in the resurrection of a figure so associated with debates within postmodernism of over a decade ago, to praise that this contemporary thinker is finally being seriously considered within the discipline, to near apoplexy at the idea that he might have any contribution to make to media studies or even to academia itself. I still treasure the fury of one journal referee whose hostility led him to the remarkable and not especially academic claim that 'we do not need any more articles on Jean Baudrillard!'

2 The first translations of Baudrillard's texts (*The Mirror of Production* in 1975 and *For a Critique of the Political Economy of the Sign* in 1981) lacked a context for their interpretation. It was only with the publication of selections of his work in the early to mid 1980s (see 1981a, 1981b, 1982, 1983a, 1983c, 1983d, 1983e, 1983f, 1984a, 1984b, 1984c, 1984–5, 1985a, 1986a, 1986b, 1986c, 1987b, 1987d) that Baudrillard began to be identified as a 'postmodernist'.

3 This structuralist and poststructuralist Baudrillard has attracted much critical attention. Genosko provides one of the best discussions of Baudrillard's semiotic 'bar games' (1994a), while more recently Grace (2004) and Rajan (2004) have returned to the issue of Baudrillard's writing and its relationship to these movements.

4 To describe Baudrillard as a postmodernist is to confuse the descriptive and normative elements of his work, a mistake creating a distortion of attribution equivalent to describing Marx as a 'capitalist' for his perceptive description and analysis of capitalism.

1 TELEVISION IS KILLING THE ART OF SYMBOLIC EXCHANGE

1 Consider one example from October 2003. The BBC morning news had contrived a feature on the effect of today's hectic lifestyles on sleep patterns. Among the subsequent viewer emails discussing this issue the presenters read one out that simply informed us, 'I don't have any trouble sleeping. I sleep fine.' In the stunning pointlessness of this remark, broadcast to a national audience as part of its flagship news service, we experience the zero degree of 'interaction', the zero degree of meaning and communication and the zero degree of news.

2 TO PLAY WITH PHANTOMS

1 See, for example, Chen (1987:72–7), Gane (1991a:92–103), Kellner (1989:60–92; 1994:8–10), Levin (1996:95–7, 190–1, 279–81), Sandywell (1995:131–3), and essays by Tseelon, Schoonmaker and Luke (in Kellner, 1994:120–4, 169–71, 212–15).

2 Kellner (1989:78) and Levin (1996:96) both link Baudrillard to Foucault, while Best (Kellner, 1994:41–67) discusses his debt to Marx and Debord, and Der Derian (Kellner, 1994:198–9) discusses the influence of Kracauer and Benjamin. Pefanis draws on Plato and Nietzsche to explain Baudrillard (Pefanis, 1991:59–61; see also Genosko, 1994a:29), while Butler (Zurbrugg, 1997:51–63) and Gane (2000a:12–16, 26, 34) explore Plato and Nietzsche respectively.

3 There is an important etymological link between 'appearance' and 'apparition' - between phantasma and phantom. As Barasch points out (1992:26–8), the Greeks had long associated images and ghosts, employing the term 'eidolon' for both.

4 Ries explains the etymology of these key terms (1987:73). The Greek 'eidolon' (formed from 'eidos' - 'shape', 'aspect') came to mean, he says, 'phantom, undetermined form, image reflected in a mirror or water', or even an image formed in the human mind. The word gained its first biblical use in the Septuagint, the Greek translation from the Hebrew Bible, which used 'eidolon' to translate Hebraic references to all kinds of images. The Latin Vulgate used 'idol' and 'simulacrum' to translate the same references and the Greek New Testament used 'eidolon' in the same contexts, which the Vulgate again translated as either 'idol' or 'simulacrum'. 'Eidolon' and its Latin counterparts, 'idol' and 'simulacrum', all refer, therefore, to images, and specifically to religious images or statues which are venerated as divine. While the simulacrum, therefore, has different meanings in Christianity and Platonism, in each case it refers to images whose power threatens the original.

5 Actually Descartes's argument is circular, with certainty depending on 'clear and distinct perceptions' (1968:113–15), which are themselves certain 'because they must necessarily have God as [their] author' (1968:141), although proof of this God's existence depends on the subject's 'clear and distinct perception' of God (1968:124, 132, 144), which leaves us at something of an impasse.

6 The question of the simulacrum in Nietzsche has attracted much attention, especially in France; a debate begun by Pierre Klossowski's reading of Nietzsche's discussion of the production of consciousness and its effects out of the corporeal impulses of the body (Klossowski, 1997). Known before Baudrillard as *the* theorist of the simulacrum (see Genosko, 1994a:30), his development of this concept through both his literary and philosophical texts was influential on Deleuze, Foucault, Lyotard, Derrida, and, in bringing the concept into the centre of intellectual life, on Baudrillard too.

7 The question of the photograph's relationship to its referent and its simulacral properties has remained central to photographic writing, explicitly so in Krauss (1984), but implicitly too in Sontag (1977) and Barthes (1993), and in a new form in the recent discussion of digital photography and computer generated images (Lister, 1997).

8 'Hyperrealism' was the European name for the American 'photorealist' or 'superrealist' movement in art and sculpture from the mid 1960s which attempted to photographically reproduce the real (see Battcock, 1975).

9 Rex Butler has also suggested that Baudrillard offers 'a defence of the real' (Zurbrugg, 1997:51–63; R. Butler, 1999), in defending the real against all attempts

to turn it into a simulacrum by thinking it as 'the unsurpassable limit to all systems', his own included (Zurbrugg, 1997:53–4). This is an important argument but it misses, I believe, the crucial role the symbolic plays in Baudrillard's work *as the real*. Butler fails to recognize the position of the symbolic in Baudrillard as a prior mode of relations to the semiotic, as well as the Durkheimian tradition from which this is derived; the continuity of these influences in his concept of 'seduction'; and the role of the symbolic and seduction as a critical position raised against the simulacrum and its representation. So, for example, while Butler devotes much time to an impressive discussion of the 'masses' and the 'social' in *In the Shadow of the Silent Majorities* (Zurbrugg, 1997:55–63; Butler, 1999:58–63, 130–7), he overlooks Baudrillard's clear claims concerning the preceding symbolic societies (*SSM*, 65) and the modern simulation of their meaning in their production of 'the social' and 'social relations' (*SSM*, 75) and the operation of this symbolic as a critique of this simulation.

4 THE DELIRIOUS SPECTACLE OF THE NON-EVENT

1 Recent discussions of media events, for example, include Garber, Matlock and Walkowitz's collection of essays (1993), which, despite the Debordian affinities of the title and the cover design, lacks a specific theorization of the event, containing instead a range of individual analyses of particular events, and Wark's own individual but important analyses of the Gulf War, the Berlin Wall, Tiananmen Square and the 1987 crash (1994), which emphasizes the 'virtual geography' created by global 'media vectors' and the telesthenic experience of 'perception at a distance'. Despite, however, the Baudrillardian affinities of its analysis this does not draw particularly on his work. More recently Couldry has developed a critique of Dayan and Katz and a post-Durkheimian analysis of 'the ritual space of the media' and its operation and power (2003). Though the latter's points are important, his analysis ignores the radical Durkheimian tradition I have identified, making no mention of Baudrillard's own Durkheimian analysis, despite, in his conclusion, finding critical value in precisely the critique of Dayan and Katz's neo-Durkheimianism that this tradition and Baudrillard offer (2003:141–2). Couldry's approach, however, soon returns to a mainstream Durkheimian conclusion, recognizing the need for communication and electronic media as a site of that communion, that undercuts this critique (2003:143). He remains committed to a Durkheimian and McLuhanist model that grants full experiential reality to mediated processes, as can be seen in his confession of attending Princess Diana's funeral in London and watching it on the screens in Hyde Park where, he uncritically asserts, 'the "social" was experienced directly as a *shared* viewing situation' (2003:60).

5 SHREDS OF WAR ROTTING IN THE DESERT

1 *La Guerre de Troie n'aura pas lieu*, translated into English as *Tiger at the Gates* (Giraudoux, 1955).
2 Interestingly even if, due to the extent of their desertion and surrender, the lower estimates of only around 10,000 Iraqi dead were proven this would also point towards the lack of this 'war' (see Freedman and Karsh, 1993:408).
3 Some photographs of the Iraqi dead have since been published (see O'Kane, 1995; McCullin, 2003), though images are still rare.

6 'TOTAL SCREEN'

1 The essay was written in October 2001, being published in *Le Monde* on 3 November and made available in translation the same month (Baudrillard, 2001c). It was published as a book, *L'Esprit du terrorisme*, in 2002, together with a paper from that February, 'Requiem for the twin towers', and made available in translation that year (*ST*).

2 His discussion of terrorism includes an analysis of its relationship with the masses and the media, its combination of media spectacle and symbolic challenge, its use of the media to promote a 'fascination' for its violence, its attack on an already ter- roristic 'social' through senseless acts lacking determinate enemies or achievable goals, its targeting of those anonymous masses produced by the system aiming to send 'shockwaves' through the media, creating a point around which the system condenses and collapses in its own response and creation of a hypersecurity, and thus its unleashing of a 'reversibility' in which all accidents and unforeseen natural phenomena are experienced as terroristic and destabilizing (*SSM*, 48–58, 113–23).

3 This figure for the Afghan War is not the only one available. A survey published in the *New York Times* in July 2002 claimed 812 losses as a direct result of US bombs, while a survey by the *Guardian* in February claimed 2,000–8,000 had lost their lives as a result of the overall conflict (see Treanor, 2002).

4 Baudrillard discussed these images in his article 'War porn', first published in *Libération* on 19 May 2004 (Baudrillard, 2005). Just like 9/11, he says, these photographs represented a humiliation of American power, though this time it is a self-inflicted one, their pornography becoming 'the ultimate form of the abjection of war'. However, where 9/11 was 'a major event' this is 'a non-event of an obscene banality', the result of a power that 'no longer knows what to do with itself', acting 'in total impunity'. The photographs are an attempt to respond to the humiliation of 9/11 'by even worse humiliation', by an attempt at the symbolic extermination of the other. The exposure and dissemination of the images, however, has reversed again on to America, Baudrillard argues. With these photographs 'it is really America that has electrocuted itself'.

7 'THE MATRIX HAS YOU'

1 Quotations given in this chapter are taken from the 'shooting script' of the film (Wachowski and Wachowski, 2001a), though some minor variations with the final film (Wachowski and Wachowski, 1999) are detectable. Two earlier versions of the script also exist dated 3 June 1997 (Wachowski and Wachowski, 1997) and 8 April 1996 (Wachowski and Wachowski, 1996), both also containing minor variations.

2 Interestingly, early in their career Jefferson Airplane played at a club called The Matrix. Their then lead vocalist Marty Balin had a financial interest in the club and it was there that their future vocalist Grace Slick first saw them (Tamarkin, 2001).

3 Galouye's 1964 novel *Simulacron-3* (called *Counterfeit World* in the UK) parallels this scene. In Galouye's book, Douglas Hall, a scientist who has helped produce a simulator containing an entire 'simulectronic' world whose inhabitants believe they are real, gradually discovers that his own world is itself a virtual reality simulation produced by a higher reality. At one point, when he still believes his own world is real, he also considers the differences between the actual physical and the simulated experience of a chair, coming to the conclusion that the two are indistinguishable.

4 This terrorism is more explicit in *The Matrix: Reloaded*. The freedom fighter's attack on the tower block and the city power supply there appears uncomfortably close to September 11 and to the August 2003 American–Canadian blackout. Perhaps, therefore, Morpheus is closer to al-Qaeda than the Unabomber?

5 Though in *Impossible Exchange*, Baudrillard does offer another reading of virtual reality as beyond the 'golden age' of the simulacrum and as part of the virtual (p. 127).

References

WORKS BY BAUDRILLARD CITED

Referenced by abbreviation

Am.   *America*, London: Verso, 1988 (orig. *Amérique*, Paris: Bernard Grasset, 1986).

BL   *Baudrillard Live: Selected Interviews*, ed. M. Gane, London: Routledge, 1993.

CM   *Cool Memories*, London: Verso, 1990 (orig. *Cool Memories: 1980–1985*, Paris: Galilée, 1987).

CM2   *Cool Memories 2*, Cambridge: Polity, 1996 (orig. *Cool Memories II: 1987–1990*, Paris: Galilée, 1990).

CM3   *Fragments: Cool Memories 3, 1990–1995*, London: Verso, 1997 (orig. *Cool Memories III, 1990–1995*, Paris: Galilée, 1995).

CM4   *Cool Memories 4*, London: Verso, 2003 (orig. *Cool Memories IV:1995–2000*, Paris: Galilée, 2000).

CPES   *For a Critique of the Political Economy of the Sign*, St Louis: Telos, 1981 (orig. *Pour une critique de l'économie politique du signe*, Paris: Gallimard, 1972).

CS   *The Consumer Society*, London: Sage, 1998 (orig. *La Société de consommation*, Paris: Denoël, 1970).

EC   *The Ecstasy of Communication*, New York: Semiotext(e), 1988 (orig. *L'Autre par lui-même*, Paris: Galilée, 1987).

EDI   *The Evil Demon of Images*, Sydney: Power Institute, 1987.

FC   *Fragments: Conversations with François L'Yvonnet*, London: Routledge, 2003 (orig. *D'un fragment l'autre*, Paris: Albin Michel, 2001).

FF   *Forget Foucault*, New York: Semiotext(e), 1987 (orig. *Oublier Foucault*, Paris: Galilée, 1977).

FS   *Fatal Strategies*, London: Pluto Press, 1990 (orig. *Les Stratégies fatales*, Paris: Grasset, 1983).

GW   *The Gulf War Did Not Take Place*, Sydney: Power, 1995 (orig. *La Guerre du Golfe n'a pas eu lieu*, Paris: Galilée, 1991).

IE   *Impossible Exchange*, London: Verso, 2001 (orig. *L'Échange impossible*, Paris: Galilée, 1999).

Ill.   *The Illusion of the End*, Cambridge: Polity, 1994 (orig. *L'Illusion de la fin*, Paris: Galilée, 1992).

MP   *The Mirror of Production*, St Louis: Telos, 1975 (orig. *Le Miroir de la production*, Tournail: Casterman, 1973).

OS   'The order of simulacra', in *Symbolic Exchange and Death*, London: Sage, 1993, pp. 50–86.

Par.   *Paroxysm: Interviews with Philippe Petit*, London: Verso, 1998 (orig. *Le Paroxyste indifférent. Entretiens avec Philippe Petit*, Paris: Grasset & Fasquelle, 1997).

PC   *The Perfect Crime*, London: Verso, 1996 (orig. *Le Crime parfait*, Paris: Galilée, 1995).

PS   'The precession of simulacra', in *Simulacra and Simulation*, Ann Arbor: University of Michigan Press, 1994, pp. 1–42 (orig. 'La Précession des simulacres', *Traverses*, 10, 1978, pp. 3–37).

Pw   *Passwords*, London: Verso, 2003 (orig. *Mots de passe*, Paris: Fayard, 2000).

RM   'Requiem for the media', in *For a Critique of the Political Economy of the Sign*, St Louis: Telos, 1981, pp. 164–84 (orig. 'Requiem pour les media', *Utopie*, 4, Oct. 1971, pp. 35–51).

ScO   *Screened Out*, London: Verso, 2002 (orig. *Écran total*, Paris: Galilée, 2000).

SED   *Symbolic Exchange and Death*, London: Sage, 1993 (orig. *L'Échange symbolique et la mort*, Paris: Gallimard, 1976).

Sed.   *Seduction*, London: Macmillan, 1990 (orig. *De la séduction*, Paris: Galilée, 1979).

Sim.   *Simulations*, New York: Semiotext(e), 1983.

SO   *The System of Objects*, London: Verso, 1996 (orig. *Le Système des objets*, Paris: Gallimard, 1968).

SOA   *The Singular Objects of Architecture* (with Jean Nouvel), London: University of Minnesota Press, 2002 (orig. *Les Objets singuliers. Architecture et philosophie*, Paris: Calmann-Lévy, 2000).

SS   *Simulacra and Simulation*, Ann Arbor: University of Michigan Press, 1994 (orig. *Simulacres et simulation*, Paris: Galilée, 1981).

SSM   *In the Shadow of the Silent Majorities*, New York: Semiotext(e), 1983 (orig. *A l'ombre des majorités silencieuses, ou la fin de social*, Fonteney-sous-Bois: Cahiers d'Utopie, 1978).

ST   *The Spirit of Terrorism*, London: Verso, 2002 (orig. *L'Esprit du terrorisme*, Paris: Galilée, 2002).

TE   *The Transparency of Evil: Essays on Extreme Phenomena*, London: Verso, 1993 (orig. *La Transparence du mal. Essai sur les phénomènes extrêmes*, Paris: Galilée, 1990).

UB   *The Uncollected Baudrillard*, ed. G. Genosko, London: Sage, 2001.

VI   *The Vital Illusion*, New York: Columbia University Press, 2000.

Referenced by date

1981a 'Beyond the unconscious: the symbolic', *Discourses*, 3, pp. 60–87.

1981b 'Fatality, or reversible imminence: beyond the uncertainty principle', *Social Research*, 49, no. 2, pp. 272–93.

1982 'The Beaubourg effect: implosion and deterrence', *October*, 20, Spring, pp. 3–13.

1983a 'Dropping out of history', interview with Sylvère Lotringer, *Impulse*, Spring/Summer, pp. 10–13.

1983b 'The ecstasy of communication', in H. Foster (ed.), *Postmodern Culture*, London: Pluto, pp. 126–34.

1983c 'Is Pop an art of consumption?', *Tension*, 2, pp. 33–5.

1983d 'Nuclear implosion', *Impulse*, Spring/Summer, pp. 9–11.

1983e 'The precession of simulacra', *Art and Text*, 11, pp. 3–47.

1983f 'What are you doing after the orgy?', *Artforum*, Oct., pp. 42–6.

1984a 'Astral America', *Artforum*, Sept., pp. 70–4.

1984b 'Interview: Games with vestiges', *On the Beach*, 5, Winter, pp. 19–25.

1984c 'On nihilism', *On the Beach*, 6, Spring, pp. 38–9.

1984–5 'Intellectuals, commitment and political power: an interview with Jean Baudrillard', *Thesis 11*, pp. 10–11, 166–73.

1985a 'The child in the bubble', *Impulse*, 11, no. 4, p. 13.

1985b 'The masses: the implosion of the social in the media', *New Literary History*, 16, no. 3, pp. 577–89.

1986a 'Clone boy', *Z/G*, 11, pp. 12–13.

1986b 'Interview with Jean Baudrillard', with C. Francblin, *Flash Art*, 130, Oct.–Nov., pp. 54–5.

1986c 'The realised utopia, America', *French Review*, 60, pp. 2–6.

1987a 'A perverse logic and drugs as exorcism', *UNESCO Courier*, 7, pp. 7–9.

1987b 'Modernity', *Canadian Journal of Political and Social Theory*, 11, no. 3, pp. 63–73.

1987c 'Softly, softly', *New Statesman*, 6 Mar., p. 44.

1987d 'When Bataille attacked the metaphysical principle of economy', *Canadian Journal of Political and Social Theory*, 11, no. 3, pp. 57–62.

1987e 'The Year 2000 has already happened', in A. Kroker and M. Kroker (eds), *Body Invaders*, London: Macmillan, pp. 35–44.

1988a *Jean Baudrillard: Selected Writings*, ed. M. Poster, Cambridge: Polity.

1988b *Please Follow Me* (with Sophie Calle's *Suite Venitienne*), Seattle: Bay Press.

1988c 'Politics of performance', interview with P. Archard, *New Political Science*, 16/17, pp. 23–8.

1989a 'An interview with Jean Baudrillard', with Judith Williamson, *Block*, 15, pp. 16–19.

1989b 'The anorexic ruins', in D. Kamper and C. Wulf (eds), *Looking Back at the End of the World*, New York: Semiotext(e), pp. 29–45.

1989c 'Panic crash!', in A. Kroker, M. Kroker and D. Cook (eds), *Panic Encyclopaedia*, London: Macmillan, pp. 64–7.

1989d 'Politics of seduction', interview with Baudrillard, *Marxism Today*, Jan., pp. 54–5.

1990 *The Revenge of the Crystal: Selected Writings on the Modern Object and its Destiny 1968–1983*, ed. P. Foss and J. Pefanis, London: Pluto.

1991 'The reality gulf', *Guardian*, 11 Jan., p. 25.

1992a 'Baudrillard shrugs: a seminar on terrorism and the media with Sylvère Lotringer and Jean Baudrillard', in W. Stearns and W. Chaloupka (eds), *Jean Baudrillard: The Disappearance of Art and Politics*, London: Macmillan, pp. 283–302.

1992b 'Revolution and the end of utopia', in W. Stearns and W. Chaloupka (eds), *Jean Baudrillard: The Disappearance of Art and Politics*, London: Macmillan, pp. 233–42.

1992c 'Transpolitics, transsexuality, transaesthetics', in W. Stearns and W. Chaloupka (eds), *Jean Baudrillard: The Disappearance of Art and Politics*, London: Macmillan, pp. 9–26.

1992d 'The vanishing point of communication', lecture 18 Nov., Loughborough University of Technology (unpublished text provided by M. Gane © J. Baudrillard).

1993a 'Cover story: Jean Baudrillard', interview with Serge Bramly, *Galleries Magazine*, no. 53, Feb.–Mar., pp. 78–87, 125.

1993b 'Hyperreal America', *Economy and Society*, 22, no. 2, May, pp. 243–52.

1994a 'The art of disappearance', *World Art*, Nov., p. 81.

1994b 'No reprieve for Sarajevo', trans. from *Libération*, 8 Jan. 1994, posted 28 Sept. 1994 at www.ctheory.net/text_file.asp?pick=60 (accessed June 1997).

1994c 'Radical thought', first published as *La Pensée radicale*, Collection Morsure, Paris: Sens & Tonka, 1994, posted 19 Apr. 1995 at www.ctheory.net/text_file.asp?pick=67 (accessed June 1997).

1994d 'Strange world', interview with Nicholas Zurbrugg, *World Art*, Nov., pp. 78–80, 82.

1995a 'Plastic surgery for the Other', trans. from J. Baudrillard and M. Guillaume, *Figures de l'altérité*, Paris: Descartes, 1994, posted 22 Nov. 1995 at www.ctheory.net/text_file.asp?pick=75 (accessed June 1997).

1995b 'Symbolic exchange: taking theory seriously', interview with R. Boyne and S. Lash, *Theory, Culture and Society*, 12, no. 4, pp. 79–95.

1996a 'Death on the net', interview with Chris Horrocks, *Icon Review*, 1, Autumn, p. 8.

1996b 'Disneyworld Company', trans. from *Libération*, 4 Mar. 1996, posted 27 Mar. 1996 at www.ctheory.net/text_file.asp?pick=158 (accessed June 1997).

1996c 'Global debt and parallel universe', trans. from *Libération*, no date given, posted 16 Oct. 1996 at www.ctheory.net/text_file.asp?pick=164 (accessed June 1997),

1996d 'Philosophy: discussion with Jean Baudrillard', interview with Claude Thibaut, 6 Mar. 1996, *Cybersphere*, 9, Mar. 1996, formerly at www.quelm.fr/CSphere/N9/philoU.html (accessed June 1997).

1996e 'Vivisecting the 90's: an interview with Jean Baudrillard', interview with Caroline Bayard and Graham Knight for *Research in Semiotic Inquiry/Recherches semiotiques*, 16, nos 1/2, Spring 1996, posted 8 Mar. 1995 at www.ctheory.net/text_file.asp?pick=66 (accessed June 1997).

1997a 'A conjuration of imbeciles', trans. from *Libération*, 7 May 1997, posted 28 May 1997 at www.ctheory.net/text_file.asp?pick=176 (accessed Aug. 1997).

1997b 'Aesthetic illusion and virtual reality', in N. Zurbrugg (ed.), *Jean Baudrillard: Art and Artefact*, London: Sage, pp. 19–27.

1997c 'The art of disappearance', in N. Zurbrugg (ed.), *Jean Baudrillard: Art and Artefact*, London: Sage, pp. 28–31.

1997d 'Baudrillard's list', interview with Rex Butler, in N. Zurbrugg (ed.), *Jean Baudrillard: Art and Artefact*, London: Sage, pp. 43–50.

1997e 'The ecstasy of photography', interview with Nicholas Zurbrugg, in N. Zurbrugg (ed.), *Jean Baudrillard: Art and Artefact*, London: Sage, pp. 32–42.

1997f 'The end of the millennium, or the countdown', lecture at Institute of Contemporary Arts, London, 8 May 1997, at www.illumin.co.uk (accessed June 1997).

1997g 'The end of the millennium, or the countdown', *Economy and Society*, 26, no. 4, Nov., pp. 447–55.

1997h 'Objects, images, and the possibility of aesthetic illusion', in N. Zurbrugg (ed.), *Jean Baudrillard: Art and Artefact*, London: Sage, pp. 7–18.

1998a 'The end of the millennium, or the countdown', *Theory, Culture and Society*, 15, no. 1, pp. 1–9.

1998b 'In the shadow of the millennium (or the suspense of the Year 2000)', trans. of *A l'Ombre du millénaire ou le suspens de l'an 2000*, Paris: Sens & Tonka, Apr. 1998, posted 23 Sept. 1998 at www.ctheory.net/text_file.asp?pick=104 (accessed Nov. 2001).

1998c 'Lament for Lady Di', in M. Merck (ed.), *After Diana: Irreverent Elegies*, London: Verso, pp. 75–6.

1999 *Within the Horizon of the Object: Objects in this Mirror are Closer than they Appear. Photographs 1985–1998*, ed. P. Weibel, Ostifildern-Ruit and Autoren: Hatje Cantz.

2000a 'Photography, or the writing of light', posted 4 Dec. 2000 at www.ctheory.net/text_file.asp?pick=126 (accessed Nov. 2001).

2000b 'The seismic order', at www.uta.edu/english/apt/collab/texts/seismic.html (accessed Apr. 2000).

2001a 'Dust breeding', trans from *Libération*, 29 May 2001, posted 8 Oct. 2001 at www.ctheory.net/text_file.asp?pick=293 (accessed June 2003).

2001b 'Sanctuary city', *Tate: The Art Magazine*, no. 24, Spring, pp. 38–41.

2001c 'The spirit of terrorism', *Cyber-Society* archive, at www.jiscmail.ac.uk/archives/cyber-society-live.html (accessed Apr. 2005).

2002 'The despair of having everything', at www.jiscmail.ac.uk/archives/cyber-society-live.html (accessed Apr. 2005).

2003a 'Baudrillard decodes Matrix', trans. of interview in *Nouvel Observateur*, 19 June, formerly at www.teaser.fr/~lcolombet/empyree/divers/Matrix-Baudrillard_english.html (accessed Sept. 2003).

2003b 'The violence of the global', posted 20 May 2003 at www.ctheory.net/text_file.asp?pick=385 (accessed June 2003).

2004a 'Interview with Jean Baudrillard', in P. Hegarty, *Live Theory*, London: Continuum, pp. 134–49.

2004b 'This is the Fourth World War: the *Der Spiegel* interview with Jean Baudrillard', *International Journal of Baudrillard Studies*, 1, no. 1, Jan., at www.ubishops.ca/baudrillardstudies/spiegel.htm (accessed June 2004).

2005 'War porn', *International Journal of Baudrillard Studies*, 2, no. 1, Jan., at www.ubishops.ca/baudrillardstudies/vol2_1/taylor.htm (accessed Jan. 2005).

OTHER WORKS

Abercrombie, N. and Longhurst, B. (1998) *Audiences: A Sociological Theory of Performance and Imagination*, London: Sage.

Adorno, T. W. and Horkheimer, M. (1997) *Dialectic of Enlightenment (1944)*, London: Verso.

Ahmed, K. and Hinsliff, G. (2003) 'Downing St in BBC "bias" row', *Observer*, 30 Mar., p. 8.

Aksoy, A. and Robins, K. (1991) 'Exterminating angels: morality, technology and violence in the Gulf War', *Science as Culture*, 12, pp. 332–7.

Alexander, J. C. (1988) 'Culture and political crisis: "Watergate" and Durkheimian sociology', in J. C. Alexander (ed.), *Durkheimian Sociology: Cultural Studies*, Cambridge: Cambridge University Press.

Anderson, L. (1984) 'Walk the dog', from *United States Live*, Warner Bros Records Inc.

Ang, I. (1985) *Watching 'Dallas': Soap Opera and the Melodramatic Imagination*, London: Methuen.

Anthony, A. (1998) 'We've seen it before, but never this colour', *Observer*, 20 Dec., p. 18.

Aristotle (1997) *Poetics*, London: Dover Thrift.

Bacon, F. (1952) *Great Books of the Western World*, vol. 30: *Francis Bacon*, London: University of Chicago Press.

Ball, E. (1987) 'The great sideshow of the Situationist International', *Yale French Studies: Everyday Life*, no. 73, pp. 21–37.

Ballard, J. G. (1993) *The Atrocity Exhibition*, London: HarperCollins.

——(1995) *Crash*, London: Vintage.

——(2001) *The Complete Short Stories*, London: Flamingo.

Balzar, J. (1991) 'Video horror of Apache victims' death', *Guardian*, 25 Feb.

Barasch, M. (1992) *Icon*, London: New York University Press.

Barrat, D. (1986) *Media Sociology*, London: Routledge.

Barthes, R. (1973a) *Mythologies (1957)*, London: Paladin.

——(1973b) *Elements of Semiology*, New York: Hill and Wang.

——(1990a) *The Fashion System*, Los Angeles: University of California Press.

——(1990b) *A Lover's Discourse: Fragments*, London: Penguin.

——(1993) *Camera Lucida*, London: Vintage.

Bataille, G. (1962) *Eroticism (1957)*, London: Marion Boyars.

——(1985) *Visions of Excess: Selected Writings 1927–1939*, New York: Zone.

——(1991) *The Accursed Share*, vol. 1 *(1949)*, New York: Zone.

——(1992) *Theory of Religion (1973)*, New York: Zone.

——(1994) *The Absence of Myth*, London: Verso.

Battcock, G. (ed.) (1975) *Superrealism: A Critical Anthology*, New York: E. P. Dutton.

Bazin, A. (1967) 'The ontology of the photographic image', in *What is Cinema?*, London: University of California Press.

Beaumont, P. (2003) 'Chaos reigns as Saddam's plan unfolds', *Observer*, 31 Aug. pp. 24–5.

Bell, D. and Kennedy, B. M. (eds) (2000) *The Cybercultures Reader*, London: Routledge.

Benedetti, P. and Dehart, N. (1997) *Forward through the Rearview Mirror: Reflections on and by Marshall McLuhan*, London: MIT Press.

Benjamin, W. (1973) *Illuminations*, London: Fontana.

——(1997a) *Charles Baudelaire: A Lyric Poet in the Era of High Capitalism*, London: Verso.

——(1997b) *One Way Street and Other Writings*, London: Verso.

——(1999) *The Arcades Project*, London: Belknap Press of Harvard University Press.

Bennett, C. (2003) 'And now over to Fairford where there is nothing to see', *Guardian*, G2, 27 Mar., pp. 1–3.

Berkowitz, D. (ed.) (1997) *Social Meanings of News: A Text Reader*, London: Sage.

Best, S. and Kellner, D. (eds) (1991) *Postmodern Theory: Critical Interrogations*, London: Macmillan.

Black, I. (2003) 'Defiant misinformation minister still fighting on media frontline', *Guardian*, 7 Apr., p. 5.

Bond, J. (1999) 'Creating the surreal world of *The Matrix* with production designer Owen Patterson', *Eon Magazine*, 16 Apr., formerly at http://homes.acmecity.com/thematrix/trinity/279/interviewarticles/interview20.html (accessed Apr. 2000).

Boorstin, D. (1992) *The Image (1961)*, New York: Vintage.

Borger, J. et al. (2001) 'War about to enter a new phase', *Guardian*, 10 Oct., p. 1.

——(2003) 'How the Pentagon's promise of a quick war ran into the desert sand', *Guardian*, 28 Mar., pp. 4–5.

——(2004) 'Iraq War "will cost each US family $3,400" ', *Guardian*, 25 June, p. 16.

Borges, J. L. (1975) *A Universal History of Infamy*, London: Penguin.

Boyd-Barrett, O. and Newbold., C. (eds) (1995) *Approaches to Media: A Reader*, London: Arnold.

Bracken, L. (1997) *Guy Debord – Revolutionary*, Venice, Calif.: Feral House.

Branston, G. and Stafford, R. (1996) *The Media Student's Book*, London: Routledge.

Briggs, A. and Cobley, P. (eds) (2002) *The Media: An Introduction*, Harlow: Longman.

Broughton, J. (1996) 'The bomb's-eye view: smart weapons and military TV', in S. Aronowitz. et al. (eds), *Technoscience and Cyberculture*, London: Routledge.

Bruhn Jensen, K. (1995) *The Social Semiotics of Mass Communication*, London: Sage.

Bulloch, J. (1991) 'How Bush lost the Gulf War', *Independent on Sunday, Review*, 8 Dec., pp. 10–13.

Burke, J. (2003) 'Evil awakening gives new life to terrorism', *Observer*, 7 Sept.

Burkeman, O. (2001) 'Simpson of Kabul', *Guardian, G2*, 14 Nov., pp. 1–3.

Burton, G. (2000) *Talking Television*, London: Arnold.

Butler, R. (1999) *Jean Baudrillard: The Defence of the Real*, London: Sage.

Butler, S. (1970) *Erewhon (1872)*, London: Penguin.

Caillois, R. (1961) *Man, Play, and Games*, London: Thames and Hudson.

——(1980) *Man and the Sacred (1939)*, Westport: Greenwood.

——(1984) 'Mimicry and legendary psychasthenia', *October*, 31, Winter, pp. 17–32.

Callinicos, A. (1989) *Against Postmodernism: A Marxist Critique*, Cambridge: Polity.

Campbell, D. (2001) 'Bush talks of first war of 21st century', *Guardian*, 14 Sept., p. 5.

——(2003a) 'Sahaf turned into talking doll', *Guardian*, 21 Apr., p. 5.

——(2003b) 'Bush, Barbie, or Bob the Builder – a choice to toy with', *Guardian*, 27 Aug., p. 3.

——(2003c) 'Matrix films blamed for series of murders by obsessed fans', *Guardian*, 19 May, at www.guardian.co.uk/international/story/0%2C3604% 2C958840% 2C00.html (accessed Feb. 2004).

Camus, A. (1982) *The Outsider*, London: Penguin.

Candea, V. (1987a) 'Iconoclasm', in M. Eliade, (ed.), *The Encyclopedia of Religion*, vol. 7, London: Collier Macmillan, pp. 1–2.

——(1987b) 'Icons', in M. Eliade (ed.), *The Encyclopedia of Religion*. vol. 7, London: Collier Macmillan, pp. 67–70.

Cardiff, D. and Scannell, P. (1987) 'Broadcasting and national unity', in J. Curran et al. (eds), *Impacts and Influences*, London: Methuen.

Carruthers, S. L. (2000) *The Media at War*, London: Macmillan.

Chaney, D. (1983) 'A symbolic mirror of ourselves: civic ritual in mass society', *Media, Culture and Society*, 5, no. 2, pp. 119–36.

Chen, K. H. (1987) 'The masses and the media: Baudrillard's implosive Postmodernism', *Theory, Culture and Society*, 4, no. 1, pp. 71–88.

Chevallot, I. (2004) 'A history of terror and slow progress', *Guardian*, 28 June, pp. 4–5.

Clausewitz, K. V. (1976) *On War*, Princeton: Princeton University Press.

Cobley, P. (ed.) (1996) *The Communication Theory Reader*, London: Routledge.

Cockburn, P. (1993a) 'Images of glory deflated by pin-prick tactics', *Independent on Sunday*, 17 Jan., p. 11.

——(1993b) 'US Gulf War air success shot down', *The Independent on Sunday*, 30 May, p. 13.

Comment, B. (1999) *The Panorama*, London: Reaktion.

Condon, P. (2003) *The Matrix Unlocked*, Contender Books.

Corliss, R. (1999) 'Popular metaphysics', *Time Magazine*, 153, no. 15, Apr., formerly at http://homes.acmecity.com/thematrix/trinity/279/philosophy4.html (accessed Apr. 2000).

Corner, J. and Hawthorn, J. (eds) (1993) *Communication Studies: An Introductory Reader*, London: Arnold.

Couldry, N. (2003) *Media Rituals: A Critical Approach*, London: Routledge.

Coulter, G. (ed.) (2004) *International Journal of Baudrillard Studies*, at www.ubishops.ca/Baudrillardstudies/ (accessed Jan. 2004).

Critchley, S. (1999) *A Companion to Continental Philosophy*, Oxford: Blackwell.

Croteau, D. and Hoynes, W. (2000) *Media Society: Industries, Images and Audiences*, London: Pine Forge.

Cumings, B. (1992) *War and Television*, London: Verso.

Darley, A. (2000) *Visual Digital Culture: Surface Play and Spectacle in New Media Genres*, London: Routledge.

Davis, E. (1998) *TechGnosis*, London: Serpent's Tail.

Day, J. (2003) 'Shock and Awe™ – it's just a game', *Guardian*, 11 Apr., p. 12.

Dayan, D. and Katz, E. (1992) *Media Events: The Live Broadcasting of History*, London: Harvard University Press.

Debord, G. (1983) *Society of the Spectacle (1967)*, Detroit: Black and Red.

——(1990) *Comments on the Society of the Spectacle*, London: Verso.

De Kerckhove, D. (1995) *The Skin of Culture: Investigating the New Electronic Reality*, Toronto: Somerville House.

Deleuze, G. (1983) 'Plato and the simulacrum', *October*, 27, Winter, pp. 45–56.

——(1990) *The Logic of Sense*, New York: Columbia University Press.

——(1994) *Difference and Repetition*, London: Athlone.

Descartes, R. (1968) *Discourse on Method and the Meditations (1637 and 1641)*, London: Penguin.

Devereux, E. (2003) *Understanding the Media*, London: Sage.

Dick, P. K. (1997) *Do Androids Dream of Electric Sheep? (1968)*, London: HarperCollins.

——(2000) *Ubik (1969)*, London: Gollancz.

Dodson, S. (2003) 'Brutal reality hits home', *Guardian*, On-Line section, 21 Aug., p. 21.

Downes, B. and Miller, S. (1998) *Teach Yourself Media Studies*, London: Hodder and Stoughton Educational.

Durham, M. G. and Kellner, D. M. (eds) (2001) *Media and Cultural Studies: Key Works*, Oxford: Blackwell.

Durkheim, É. (1915) *The Elementary Forms of the Religious Life (1912)*, London: Allen and Unwin.

——(1995) *The Elementary Forms of Religious Life (1912)*, New York: Free Press.

Durkheim, É. and Mauss, M. (1963) *Primitive Classification (1903)*, Chicago: University of Chicago Press.

Eagleton, T. (2003) 'Roots of terror', *Guardian*, Review, 6 Sept., p. 14.

Eliade, M. (1959) *The Sacred and the Profane*, London: Harcourt, Brace, Jovanovich.

Elliott, C. (1997) 'Book trade gears up for royal bonanza', *Guardian*, 10 Sept., p. 2.

Engel, M. (1998) 'From sombre to surreal, from prayers to an Egyptian curse', *Guardian*, 1 Sept., pp. 1–2.

Enzensberger, H. M. (1970) 'Constituents of a theory of the media', *New Left Review*, 64, Nov–Dec., pp. 13–36.

Felty, S. (1999) 'The Matrix guid', *Eon Magazine*, 26 Mar., formerly at http://homes.acmecity.com/thematrix/trinity/279/interviewarticles/interview21.html (accessed Apr. 2000).

Fincher, D. (dir.) (1999) *Fight Club*, 20th Century Fox Home Entertainment Ltd (VHS/DVD).

Fiske, J. (1987) *Television Culture*, London: Routledge.

——(1990) *Introduction to Communication Studies*, London: Routledge.

Foucault, M. (1970) *The Order of Things (1996)*, London: Routledge.

Frazer, J. G. (1995) *The Golden Bough (1890)*, London: Macmillan.

Freedberg, D. (1989) *The Power of Images*, London: University of Chicago Press.

Freedland, J. (2001) ' "We can't do it by bombing" ', *Guardian*, G2, 19 Oct., pp. 2–3.

Freedman, L. and Karsh, E. (1993) *The Gulf Conflict*, London: Faber.

Galouye, D. F. (1965) *Counterfeit World*, London: Victor Gollancz.

Gane, M. (1991a) *Baudrillard's Bestiary: Baudrillard and Culture*, London: Routledge.

——(1991b) *Baudrillard: Critical and Fatal Theory*, London: Routledge.

——(1992) *The Radical Sociology of Durkheim and Mauss*, London: Routledge.

——(1995) 'Radical theory: Baudrillard and vulnerability', *Theory, Culture and Society*, 12, no. 4, pp. 109–23.

——(2000a) *Jean Baudrillard: In Radical Uncertainty*, London: Pluto.

——(ed.) (2000b) *Jean Baudrillard*, Sage Masters of Modern Social Thought, London: Sage.

Garber, M., Matlock, J. and Walkowitz, R. L. (eds) (1993) *Media Spectacles*, London: Routledge.

Garrett, S., Garrett, G. and Seay, C. (eds) (2003) *The Gospel Reloaded: Exploring Spirituality and Faith in The Matrix*, Piñon.

Genosko, G. (1992) 'Virtual war', *Borderlines*, 24/25, pp. 51–2.

——(1994a) *Baudrillard and Signs: Signification Ablaze*, London: Routledge.

——(1994b) 'The paradoxical effects of *Macluhanisme*: Cazeneuve, Baudrillard and Barthes', *Economy and Society*, 23, no. 4, pp. 400–32.

——(1997) 'Who is the "French McLuhan"?', in N. Zurbrugg (ed.), *Jean Baudrillard: Art and Artefact*, London: Sage, pp. 104–120.

——(1999) *McLuhan and Baudrillard: The Masters of Implosion*, London: Routledge.

Geraghty, C. and Lusted, D. (eds) (1998) *The Television Studies Book*, London: Arnold.

Gibson, W. (1995) *Neuromancer (1984)*, London: HarperCollins.

Giraudoux, J. (1955) *Tiger at the Gates*, London: Methuen.

Goldblatt, M. (2001) 'French toast: America *wanted* Sept. 11th', *National Review Online*, 13 Dec., at www.nationalreview.com/comment/comment-goldblatt 121301.shtml (accessed Sept. 2003).

Gordon, W. T. (1997a) *Marshall McLuhan: Escape into Understanding: A Biography*, New York: Basic Books.

——(1997b) *McLuhan for Beginners*, London: Writers and Readers.

Grace, V. (2000) *Baudrillard's Challenge: A Feminist Reading*, London: Routledge.

——(2004) 'Baudrillard and the meaning of meaning', *International Journal of Baudrillard Studies*, 1, no. 1, Jan., at www.ubishops.ca/baudrillardstudies/grace.htm (accessed June 2004).

Green, J. (1998) *All Dressed Up: The Sixties and the Counter-Culture*, London: Pimlico.

Green, M. (1993) *The Dada Almanac*, London: Atlas.

Green, M. E. (1999) 'Tough-guy actor takes on reality itself', *Another Universe*, Apr., - formerly at http://homes.acmecity.com/thematrix/trinity/279/interviewarticles/ interview3.html (accessed Apr. 2000).

Grossberg, L., Wartella, E. and Whitney, D. C. (1998) *Media Making: Mass Media in a Popular Culture*, London: Sage.

Haber, K. (ed.) (2003) *Exploring 'The Matrix': New Writings on The Matrix and the Cyber Present*, iBooks.

Hables Gray, C. (ed.) (1995) *The Cyborg Handbook*, London: Routledge.

——(2002) *Cyborg Citizen*, London: Routledge.

Hall, S. (1980) 'Encoding/decoding', in S. Hall, D. Hobson, A. Lowe, and P. Willis (eds), *Culture, Media, Language*, London: Hutchinson.

Hammersley, B. (2003) 'Giving it to you straight', *Guardian*, On-Line section, 27 Mar., pp. 6–7.

Handelman, D. (1990) *Models and Mirrors: Towards an Anthropology of Public Events*, Cambridge: Cambridge University Press.

Harding, L. et al. (2001) 'Revealed: how bungled US raid came close to disaster', *Guardian*, 6 Nov., p. 1.

Harries, D. (ed.) (2002) *The New Media Book*, London: British Film Institute.

Harris, P. (2003) 'US public thinks Saddam had role in 9/11', *Observer*, 7 Sept., p. 20.

Hartley, J. (2002) *Communication, Cultural and Media Studies: The Key Concepts*, London: Routledge.

Havelock, E. A. (1963) *Preface to Plato*, London: Belknap Press of Harvard University Press.

Hegarty, P. (2004) *Jean Baudrillard: Live Theory*, London: Continuum.

Heidegger, M. (1959) *An Introduction to Metaphysics*, London: Yale University Press.

——(1962) *Being and Time*, Oxford: Blackwell.

——(1966) *Discourse on Thinking*, London: Harper and Row.

——(1971a) *Poetry, Language, Thought*, London: Harper and Row.

——(1971b) *On the Way to Language*, London: Harper and Row.

——(1972) *On Time and Being*, London: Harper and Row.

——(1977) *The Question Concerning Technology and Other Essays*, New York: Harper and Row.

——(1993) *Basic Writings*, London: Routledge.

Henisch, H. K. and Henisch, B. A. (1994) *The Photographic Experience, 1839–1914*, Philadelphia: Pennsylvania State University Press.

Herman, E. S. and McChesney, R. W. (1997) *The Global Media*, London: Cassell.

Hodge, R. and Kress, G. (1988) *Social Semiotics*, Cambridge: Polity.

Hollier, D. (ed.) (1988) *The College of Sociology (1937–1939)*, Minneapolis: University of Minnesota Press.

Horrocks, C. (1999) *Postmodern Encounters: Baudrillard at the Millennium*, Cambridge: Icon.

Horsley, J. (2003) *The Matrix Warrior: Being the One*, London: Gollancz.

Hoskins, A. (2001) 'New memory: mediating history', *Historical Journal of Film, Radio and Television*, 21, no. 4, pp. 333–46.

Hubert, H. and Mauss, M. (1964) *Sacrifice: Its Nature and Function (1899)*, Chicago: University of Chicago Press.

Hudson, M. and Stanier, J. (1997) *War and the Media*, Stroud: Sutton.

Hume, D. (1966) *Enquiries Concerning the Human Understanding and Concerning the Principles of Morals (1748)*, London: Oxford University Press.

——(1969) *A Treatise of Human Nature (1739–40)*, London: Penguin.

Huyssen, A. (1995) *Twilight Memories*, London: Routledge.

Iannucci, A. (2003) 'Shoot now, think later', *Guardian*, G2, 28 Apr., p. 16.

Ignatieff, M. (2000) *Virtual War*, London: Chatto and Windus.

Innis, H. A. (1986) *Empire and Communications (1950)*, Toronto: Press Porcepic.

——(1995) *The Bias of Communication (1951)*, London: University of Toronto Press.

Irwin, W. (ed.) (2002) *The Matrix and Philosophy: Welcome to the Desert of the Real*, Chicago: Open Court.

Jappe, A. (1999) *Guy Debord*, London: University of Chicago Press.

Jay, M. (1994) *Downcast Eyes: Denigration of Vision in Twentieth Century French Thought*, London: University of California Press.

Jeffrey, I. (1999) *Revisions: An Alternative History of Photography*, Bradford: National Museum of Photography, Film and Television.

Jeffery, S. (2003) 'War may have killed 10,000 civilians, researchers say', *Guardian*, 13 June, p. 18.

Junger, E. (1996) *The Storm of Steel*, New York: Howard Fertig.

Kampfner, J. (2003) 'The truth about Jessica', *Guardian*, G2, 15 May, pp. 1–3.

Kampmark, B. (2002) 'The spectre of Bin Laden in the age of terrorism', *CTheory*, article 116, posted 14 Nov., at www.ctheory.net/text_file.asp?pick=355 (accessed Sept. 2003).

Kane, P. (1997) 'Half of Hollywood has fallen in love with this sweet little thing, the other half is terrified of her', *Guardian*, G2, 17 Jan., pp. 1–3, 19.

Katz, I. (1993) 'Casualties in a ratings war', *Guardian*, G2, 15 Jan., p. 8.

Kellner, D. (1987) 'Baudrillard, semiurgy, and death', *Theory, Culture, and Society*, 4, pp. 125–46.

——(1988) 'Postmodernism as social theory', *Theory, Culture, and Society*, 5, pp. 239–69.

——(1989) *Jean Baudrillard: From Marxism to Postmodernism and Beyond*, Cambridge: Polity.

——(1992) *The Persian Gulf TV War*, Boulder: Westview.

——(ed.) (1994) *Baudrillard: A Critical Reader*, Oxford: Blackwell.

——(2000) *Grand Theft 2000*, Lanham: Rowman and Littlefield.

——(2003) *Media Spectacle*, London: Routledge.

Kirn, W. (2002) 'Notes on the darkest day', book review, *New York Times*, 8 Sept., at http://query.nytimes.com/gst/fullpage.html?res=9503EED7173FF93BA3575AC OA9649C8B63 (accessed Sept. 2003).

Klossowski, P. (1997) *Nietzsche and the Vicious Circle*, London: Athlone.

——(1998a) *The Baphomet*, New York: Marsilio.

——(1998b) *Diana at her Bath / The Women of Rome*, New York: Marsilio.

Knabb, K. (ed.) (1981) *Situationist International Anthology*, Berkeley: Bureau of Public Secrets.

Knightley, P. (2000) *The First Casualty*, rev. edn, London: Prion.

Kracauer, S. (1960) *Theory of Film: The Redemption of Physical Reality*, Oxford: Oxford University Press.

——(1995) *The Mass Ornament*, London: Harvard University Press.

Krauss, R. (1984) 'A note on photography and the simulacral', *October*, 31, Winter, pp. 49–68.

Kroker, A. (1985) 'Baudrillard's Marx', *Theory, Culture and Society*, 2, no. 3, pp. 69–83.

——(1992) *The Possessed Individual: Technology and New French Theory*, London: Macmillan.

Kroker, A. and Cook, D. (eds) (1988) *The Postmodern Scene: Excremental Culture and Hyper-aesthetics*, London: Macmillan.

Lacey, N. (1998) *Image and Representation: Key Concepts in Media Studies*, London: Macmillan.

Lamm, S. (2000) *The Art of the Matrix*, London: Titan.

Lanham, R. A. (1995) *The Electronic World: Democracy, Technology and the Arts*, Chicago: University of Chicago Press.

Lawson, M. (2003a) 'Off to war with the armchair division', *Guardian*, 24 Mar., p. 11.

——(2003b) 'Come the movie, it's a role for Will Smith', *Guardian*, 28 Mar., p. 8.

Lefebvre, H. (1971) *Everyday Life in the Modern World*, Somerset, NJ: Transaction.

Leith, W. (1998) 'I'm not a real photographer . . .', *Observer, Life*, 15 Feb., pp. 12–17.

Levin, C. (1996) *Jean Baudrillard: A Study in Cultural Metaphysics*, London: Prentice Hall.

Levinson, P. (1997) *The Soft Edge*, London: Routledge.

——(1999) *Digital McLuhan*, London: Routledge.

Lister, M. (1997) 'Photography in the age of electronic imaging', in L. Wells (ed.), *Photography: A Critical Introduction*, London, Routledge, pp. 249–91.

Lister, M. et al. (2003) *New Media: A Critical Introduction*, London: Routledge.

Lloyd, P. B. (2003) *Exegesis of The Matrix*, Whole-Being Books.

Logan, B. (1999) 'Things to do in Hollywood when you're dead', *Guardian, G2*, 17 Sept., pp. 16–17.

Loshitzky, Y. (ed.) (1997) *Spielberg's Holocaust: Critical Perspectives on Schindler's List*, Bloomington: Indiana University Press.

Lukács, G. (1971) *History and Class Consciousness*, London: Merlin.

Lull, J. (2000) *Media, Communication, Culture: A Global Approach*, Cambridge: Polity.

Lyotard, J. F. (1993) *Libidinal Economy*, London: Athlone.

MacAloon, J. (ed.) (1984) *Rite, Spectacle, Festival, Game*, Chicago: University of Chicago Press.

Mackay, H. and O'Sullivan. T. (eds) (1999) *The Media Reader: Continuity and Transformation*, London: Sage.

Mann, J. (1993) 'Post pessimism', *Radical Philosophy*, no. 63, pp. 44–5.

Mannoni, L. (2000) *The Great Art of Light and Shadow*, Exeter: University of Exeter Press.

Marchand, P. (1998) *Marshall McLuhan: The Medium and the Messenger*, Cambridge, Mass.: MIT Press.

Marcuse, H. (1986) *One Dimensional Man*, London: Ark.

Marien, M. Warner (1997) *Photography and its Critics: A Cultural History 1839–1900*, Cambridge: Cambridge University Press.

Marriott, S. (2000) 'Election night', *Media, Culture and Society*, 22, pp. 131–48.

——(2001) 'In pursuit of the ineffable: how television found the eclipse but lost the plot', *Media, Culture and Society*, 23, pp. 725–42.

Marris, P. and Thornham, S. (eds) (1996) *Media Studies: A Reader*, Edinburgh: Edinburgh University Press.

Marx, K. (1954) *Capital, Volume 1*, London: Lawrence and Wishart.

——(1970) *The German Ideology*, London: Lawrence and Wishart.

——(1975) *Early Writings*, London: Penguin.

Mauss, M. and Beuchat, H. (1979) *Seasonal Variations of the Eskimo (1904–5)*, London: Routledge and Kegan Paul.

Mauss, M. and Hubert, H. (1966) *The Gift: Forms and Functions of Exchange in Primitive Societies (1925)*, London: Cohen and West.

——(1972) *A General Theory of Magic (1904)*, London: Routledge and Kegan Paul.

McCrystal, C. (1997) 'Better than Jesus, bigger than God', *Observer*, 14 Sept., p. 32.

McCullagh, C. (2002) *Media Power: A Sociological Introduction*, Basingstoke, Palgrave.

McCullin, D. (ed.) (2003) 'Blood in the sand', *Guardian, G2* (special issue), 14 Feb.

McGrory, D. (2003) 'Two years on, Bush may be losing war to al-Qaeda', *The Times*, 10 Sept., p. 15.

McLuhan, E. (1998) *Electric Language: Understanding the Message*, Toronto: St Martin's Press.

McLuhan, E. and Zingrone, F. (eds) (1995) *Essential McLuhan*, London: Routledge.

McLuhan, M. (1962) *The Gutenberg Galaxy*, London: University of Toronto Press.

——(1966a) 'The all-at-once world of Marshall McLuhan', *Vogue*, Aug., pp. 70–73, 111.

——(1966b) 'Cybernation and culture', in C. R. Dechert (ed.), *The Social Impact of Cybernetics*, London: University of Notre Dame Press, pp. 95–108.

——(1967) 'Television in a new light', in S. T. Donner (ed.), *The Meaning of Commercial Television*, London: University of Texas Press, pp. 87–110.

——(1968) 'The reversal of the overheated image', *Playboy*, Dec., pp. 131–4, 245.

——(1974) 'At the moment of Sputnik the planet becomes a global theatre in which there are no spectators only actors', *Journal of Communications*, Winter, pp. 48–58.

——(1976) 'The violence of the media', *Canadian Forum*, Sept., pp. 9–12.

——(1977) 'Interview with Professor Marshall McLuhan', *Macleans*, 7 Mar., pp. 4, 8–9.

——(1994) *Understanding Media (1964)*, London: MIT Press.

——(1998a) 'Interview by Tom Snyder, 1976', at www.videomcluhan.cominterv3. htm (accessed Apr. 1998).

——(1998b) 'BBC interview by Frank Kermode, 1964', at www.videomcluhan.com/ interv1.htm (accessed Apr. 1998).

McLuhan, M. and Fiore, Q. (1997a) *The Medium is the Massage: An Inventory of Effects*, San Francisco: Hardwired Press.

——(1997b) *War and Peace in the Global Village*, San Francisco: Hardwired Press.

McQuail, D. (2000) *Mass Communication Theory*, London: Sage.

McQuire, S. (1998) *Visions of Modernity*, London: Sage.

Merrin, W. (1994) 'Uncritical criticism? Norris, Baudrillard and the Gulf War', *Economy and Society*, 23, no. 4, pp. 433–58.

——(1999a) 'Crash, bang, whallop! What a picture! The death of Diana and the media', *Mortality*, 4, no. 1, pp. 41–62.

——(1999b) 'Television is killing the art of symbolic exchange: Baudrillard's theory of communication', *Theory, Culture and Society*, 16, no. 3, pp. 119–40.

——(2001) 'To play with *Phantoms*: Jean Baudrillard and the evil demon of the Simulacrum', *Economy and Society*, 30, no. 1, Feb., pp. 85–111.

——(2002) 'Implosion, simulation and the pseudo-Event: a critique of McLuhan', *Economy and Society*, 31, no. 3, Aug., pp. 369–90.

——(2003) ' "Did you ever eat Tasty Wheat?": Baudrillard and *The Matrix*', *Scope – An Online Journal of Film Studies*, Apr., at www.nottingham.ac.uk/film/ journal/articles/did-you-ever-eat.htm.

——(2005a) 'Skylights onto infinity: the world in a stereoscope', in S. Popple, and V. Toulmin (eds), *Visual Delights II*, London: John Libby.

——(2005b) ' "Buckle your seat belt Dorothy . . .": cause cinema is going bye-byes', in J. Furby, and K. Randell (eds), *Screen Methods: Comparative Readings in Film*, London: Wallflower.

Messaris, P. (1994) *Visual Literacy: Images, Mind and Reality*, Oxford: Westview.

Meyrowitz, J. (1985) *No Sense of Place*, New York: Oxford University Press.

Millar, S. (2003) 'Fog of war shrouds the facts', *Guardian*, 5 Apr., p. 5.

Millar, S. and White, M. (2003) 'Facts, some fiction and the reporting of war', *Guardian*, 29 Mar., p. 7.

Miller, J. (1971) *McLuhan*, London: Fontana.

Milne, S. (2001) 'The innocent dead in a coward's war', *Guardian*, 20 Dec., p. 16.

Minc, A. (2002) 'Terrorism of the spirit', *Correspondence: An International Review of*

Culture and Society, no. 9, Spring, originally in *Le Monde*, 7 Nov., 2001 at www.cfr.org/pdf/correspondence/xMinc.php (accessed September 2003).

Molinaro, M., McLuhan, C. and Toye, W. (eds) (1987) *Letters of Marshall McLuhan*, Oxford: Oxford University Press.

Moores, S. (2000) *Media and Everyday Life in Modern Society*, Edinburgh: Edinburgh University Press.

Moos, M. A. (ed.) (1997) *Media Research: Technology, Art, Communication. Essays by Marshall McLuhan*, Amsterdam: G+B Arts International.

Moravec, H. (1988) *Mind Children: The Future of Robot and Human Intelligence*, London: Harvard University Press.

Morley, D. (1980) *The 'Nationwide' Audience*, London: British Film Institute.

Morley, D. and Brunsdon, C. (1978) *Everyday Television: The 'Nationwide' Study*, London: British Film Institute.

Mumford, L. (1963) *Technics and Civilisation (1934)*, London: Harcourt Brace.

Newbold, C., Boyd-Barrett, O. and Van Den Bulck, H. (2002) *The Media Book*, London: Arnold.

Nietzsche, F. (1968a) *The Will to Power*, New York: Vintage.

——(1968b) *Twilight of the Idols / The Antichrist*, London: Penguin.

——(1974) *The Gay Science*, New York: Vintage.

——(1979) *Ecce Homo*, London: Penguin.

——(1994) *Human, All Too Human*, London: Penguin.

Norris, C. (1990) *What's Wrong with Postmodernism*, London: Harvester Wheatsheaf.

——(1992) *Uncritical Theory: Postmodernism, Intellectuals, and the Gulf War*, London: Lawrence and Wishart.

Oettermann, S. (1997) *The Panorama*, New York: Zone.

O'Kane, M. (1995) 'Bloodless words. Bloody war', *Guardian*, *Weekend*, 16 Dec., pp. 12–18.

O'Sullivan, T. and Jewkes, Y. (eds) (1997) *The Media Studies Reader*, London: Arnold.

O'Sullivan, T., Dutton, B. and Rayner, P. (1998) *Studying the Media*, London: Arnold.

O'Sullivan, T. et al. (eds) (1994) *Key Concepts in Communication and Cultural Studies*, London: Routledge.

O'Toole, L. (1999) Interview, formerly at http://homes.acmecity.com/thematrix/trinity/279/interviewarticles/interview16.html (accessed Apr. 2000).

Patterson, J. (2003) 'Pentagon Pictures presents', *Guardian*, *G2*, 11 Apr., p. 5.

Patton, P. (1995) 'Introduction', in J. Baudrillard, *The Gulf War Did Not Take Place*, Sydney: Power, pp. 1–21.

——(1997) 'This is not a war', in N. Zurbrugg (ed.), *Jean Baudrillard: Art and Artefact*, London: Sage, pp. 121–35.

Pawlett, W. (1997) 'Utility and excess: the radical sociology of Bataille and Baudrillard', *Economy and Society*, 26, no. 1, Feb., pp. 92–125.

Pefanis, J. (1991) *Heterology and the Postmodern*, London: Duke University Press.

Perniola, M. (1980) *La società dei simulacri*, Bologna: Capelli.

Phillips, C. (1989) *Photography in the Modern Era*, New York: Metropolitan Museum of Art/Aperture.

Pierson, M. (1999) 'CGI effects in Hollywood science fiction cinema, 1989–95: the wonder years', *Screen*, 40, no. 2, Summer, pp. 158–76.

Plant, S. (1992) *The Most Radical Gesture: The Situationist International in a Postmodern Age*, London: Routledge.

Plato (1955) *The Republic*, London: Penguin.
——(1986) *Sophist*, London: University of Chicago Press.
Poland, D. (1999) 'Q&A with Joel Silver', *TNT's Roughcut*, Apr., formerly at http://homes.acmecity.com/thematrix/trinity/279/interviewarticles/interview13.html (accessed Apr. 2000).
Poole, S. (2000a) 'Meet the David Bowie of philosophy', *Guardian*, 14 Mar., pp. 14–15.
——(2000b) *Trigger Happy: The Inner Life of Videogames*, London: Fourth Estate.
Postman, N. (1987) *Amusing Ourselves to Death*, London: Methuen.
——(1993) *Technopoly*, New York: Vintage.
Potter, J. W. (1998) *Media Literacy*, London: Sage.
Powe, B. W. (1995) *Outage: A Journey into Electric City*, Toronto: Random House of Canada.
Price, S. (1996) *Communication Studies*, Harlow: Longman.
——(1998) *Media Studies*, Harlow: Longman.
Probst, C. (1999) 'Welcome to the machine', *American Cinematographer*, Apr., formerly at http://homes.acmecity.com/thematrix/trinity/279/interviewarticles/interview5.html (accessed Apr. 2000).
Ragaini, T. (2004) 'The Matrix online interview', *Games Fusion*, www.gamesfusion.net/content/000471.php (accessed July 2004).
Rajan, T. (2004) 'Baudrillard and deconstruction', *International Journal of Baudrillard Studies*, 1, no. 1, Jan., at www.ubishops.ca/baudrillardstudies/rajan.htm (accessed June 2004).
Revill, J. (2003) 'Son of Comical Ali: my father is "a great guy"', *Observer*, 13 Apr., p. 4.
Rheingold, H. (1991) *Virtual Reality*, London: Mandarin.
Richter, H. (1965) *Dada: Art and Anti-Art*, New York: Oxford University Press.
Ries, J. (1987) 'Idolatry', in M. Eliade (ed.), *The Encyclopedia of Religion*, vol. 7, London: Collier Macmillan, pp. 72–82.
Ristelheuber, S. (1993) *Aftermath: Kuwait 1991*, London: Thames and Hudson.
Robins, K. and Levidow, L. (1995) 'Socialising the cyborg self: the Gulf War and beyond', in C. Hables Gray (ed.), *The Cyborg Handbook*, London: Routledge, pp. 119–25.
Rogers, P. (1991) 'Myth of a clean war buried in the sand', *Guardian*, 13 Sept.
Rojek, C. and Turner, B. S. (eds) (1993) *Forget Baudrillard?* London: Routledge.
Romney, J. (1996) 'Terminated?', *Guardian, The Week*, 21 Dec., p. 6.
Rosenthal, R. (1968) *McLuhan: Pro and Con*, New York: Funk and Wagnalls.
Russell, David O. (dir. and screenwriter) (1998) 'Three kings', screenplay, 22 June, formerly at http://homepages.ihug.com.au/~lontano/scriptsa/three-kings_shooting.html (accessed May 2003).
Sandywell, B. (1995) 'Forget Baudrillard?', *Theory, Culture and Society*, 12, no. 4, pp. 125–52.
Sarup, M. (1993) *An Introductory Guide to Poststructuralism and Postmodernism*, Hemel Hempstead: Harvester Wheatsheaf.
Saussure, F. de (1986) *Course in General Linguistics*, Chicago: Open Court.
Scannell, P. (ed.) (1991) *Broadcast Talk*, London: Sage.
Scannell, P. and Cardiff, D. (1991) *A Social History of British Broadcasting, Volume 1: 1922–1939*, Oxford: Blackwell.
Sherwin, A. (2003) 'War addicts cause TV news audience to rocket', *The Times*, 25 Mar., p. 7.

Shils, E. and Young, M. (1956) 'The meaning of the coronation', *Sociological Review*, 1, no. 2, pp. 62–82.

Silverstone, R. (1994) *Television and Everyday Life*, London: Routledge.

Sloyan, P. (1991) 'Iraqi troops buried alive say American officers', *Guardian*, 13 Sept.

Sontag, S. (1977) *On Photography*, London: Penguin.

——(2003) *Regarding the Pain of Others*, London: Penguin.

Staples, B. (2002) 'A French philosopher talks back to Hollywood and "The Matrix"', 24 May, at www.eebilkent.edu.tr/ge301/matrixfilm.txt (accessed May 2003).

Stearn, G. E. (1968) *McLuhan: Hot and Cool*, London: Penguin.

Stearns, W. S. and Chaloupka, W. (eds) (1992) *Jean Baudrillard:The Disappearance of Art and Politics*, London: Macmillan.

Stevenson, N. (1995) *Understanding Media Cultures*, London: Sage.

Straubhaar, J. and LaRose, R. (1997) *Communications Media in the Information Society*, Belmont, Calif.: Wadsworth.

Swint, B. (2002) 'The view from France', at www.unc.edu/depts/tam/journal/02/swintmarch02.htm (accessed Sept. 2003).

Swoffard, A. (2003) *Jarhead: A Marine's Chronicle of the Gulf War*, London: Scribner.

Talbot, W. H. Fox (1969) *The Pencil of Nature (1844)*, New York: De Capo.

Tamarkin, J. (2001) Untitled sleeve-notes, on Jefferson Airplane, *Surrealistic Pillow*, CD reissue, BMG Entertainment.

Taussig, M. (1993) *Mimesis and Alterity*, London: Routledge.

Taylor, P. M. (1998) *War and the Media*, Manchester: Manchester University Press.

Theall, D. (2001) *The Virtual Marshall McLuhan*, Montreal: McGill-Queen's University Press.

Thomas, A. (ed.) (1997) *Beauty of Another Order: Photography in Science*, London: Yale University Press.

Thompson, J. B. (1995) *The Media and Modernity: A Social Theory of the Media*, Cambridge: Polity.

Trachtenberg, A. (ed.) (1980) *Classic Essays on Photography*, New Haven: Leete's Island Books.

Treanor, J. (2002) 'US raids "killed 800 Afghan civilians"', *Guardian*, 22 July, p. 11.

Tulloch, J. (2000) *Watching Television Audiences*, London: Arnold.

Turow, J. (1999) *Media Today*, Boston: Houghton Mifflin.

Vaneigem, R. (1994) *The Revolution of Everyday Life*, London: Rebel Press/Left Bank.

Vienet, R. (1992) *Enragés and Situationists in the Occupation Movement, France, May 1968*, London: Rebel Press.

Vinge, V. (2001) *True Names and the Opening of the Cyberspace Frontier (1981)*, New York: Tom Doherty Associates.

Virilio, P. (1986) *Speed and Politics (1977)*, New York: Semiotext(e).

——(1994) *Bunker Archaeology*, New York: Princeton University Press.

——(1997a) *Open Sky*, London: Verso.

——(1997b) *Pure War*, New York: Semiotext(e).

——(1999) *Politics of the Very Worst*, New York: Semiotext(e).

——(2000) *A Landscape of Events*, London: MIT Press.

——(2002a) *Desert Screen:War at the Speed of Light (1991)*, London: Continuum.

——(2002b) *Strategy of Deception*, London: Verso.

Vulliamy, E. (1999) 'Secret war on Saddam', *Observer*, 7 Feb., p. 15.

Wachowski, A. and Wachowski, L. (dir. and screenwriters) (1996) 'The Matrix', 8 Apr. at http://members.xoom.com/_XOOM/moviescript/scripts/matrixthe. txt (accessed Apr. 2000).

——(1997) 'The Matrix', 3 June, at www.hundland.com/scripts/TheMatrix_1997. TXT (accessed Apr. 2000).

——(1999) *The Matrix*, Warner Home Video (UK) Ltd (VHS/DVD).

——(2001a) *The Matrix:The Shooting Script*, New York: Newmarket Press.

——(2001b) *The Matrix Revisited*, Warner Home Video (UK) Ltd (DVD).

——(2003a) *The Animatrix*, Warner Home Video (UK) Ltd (VHS/DVD)

——(2003b) *Enter the Matrix*, Warner Bros.

—— (2003c) *The Matrix: Reloaded*, Warner Home Video (UK) Ltd (VHS/DVD).

——(2003d) *The Matrix: Revolutions*, Warner Bros.

——(2003e) *The Matrix Comics*, London: Titan Books.

——(2004) *The Matrix Online*, at http://thematrixonline.warnerbros.com/web/ index.jsp (accessed July 2004).

Walker, M. (1993) 'Gulf War's lessons for Clinton', *Guardian*, 17 Aug., p. 6.

——(1996) 'US Gulf 'smart' bombs hit budgets not targets', *Guardian*, 10 July, p. 2.

——(1997) 'Gulf bombs not so "smart"', *Guardian*, 30 June, p. 13.

Wark, M. (1991) 'News bites: War TV in the Gulf', *Meanjin*, 50, no. 1, pp. 5–18.

——(1994) *Virtual Geography: Living with Global Media Events*, Bloomington: Indiana University Press.

——(1999) 'The Matrix: Keanu lost in Plato's cave', at www.nettime.org/ nettime.w3archive/199911/masg00181.html (accessed June 2000).

Warner, W. L. (1962) *American Life: Dream and Reality*, Chicago: University of Chicago Press.

Watson, J. (2003) *Media Communication*, Basingstoke: Palgrave Macmillan.

Watson, J. and Hill, A. (1997) *A Dictionary of Communication and Media Studies*, London: Arnold.

Watt, N. (2003) ' "Baghdad is safe, the infidels are committing suicide" ', *Guardian*, 8 Apr., p. 8.

Weiner, T. (1993) 'Patriot missiles were little use during Gulf War, says Israel', *Guardian*, 22 Nov., p. 9.

Wells, M. (2003) 'Start of television war brings big ratings rise', *Guardian*, 28 Mar., p. 8.

Weynants, T. (1998) 'The fantasmagoria', in D. Crompton, R. Franklin and S. Herbert (eds), *Servants of Light: The Book of the Lantern*, London: Magic Lantern Society, pp. 58–69.

White, M. (2001) 'Straw accuses media of wobble in war coverage', *Guardian*, 29th Oct., p. 1.

Williams, K. (2003) *Understanding Media Theory*, London: Arnold.

Williams, R. (1977) *Marxism and Literature*, Oxford: Oxford University Press.

——(1983) *Towards 2000*, Harmondsworth: Penguin.

——(1990) *Television:Technology and Cultural Form*, London: Routledge.

Wilson, J. and Wilson, S. L. R. (1998) *Mass Media/Mass Culture: An Introduction*, London: McGraw Hill.

Wolf, G. (1996) 'The wisdom of Saint Marshall, the Holy Fool', *Wired*, Jan., pp. 122–125, 182, 186.

Wollen, P. (1989) 'The Situationist International', *New Left Review*, 174, Mar.–Apr., pp. 67–95.

Wood, J. (1992) 'Lost on the wilder shores of unreality', *Guardian*, 27 Feb.

al Yafai, F. (2003) 'Lack of trust in media turns many to alternative sources', *Guardian*, 28 Mar., p. 9.

Yeffeth, G. (ed.) (2003) *Taking the Red Pill: Science, Philosophy and Religion in The Matrix*, Chichester: Summersdale.

Žižek, S. (2002) *Welcome to the Desert of the Real*, London: Verso.

Zurbrugg, N. (ed.) (1997) *Jean Baudrillard: Art and Artefact*, London: Sage.

Index

Adorno, T. 37, 75
Afghan War 9, 64, 90, 93, 101, 106–7, 111–12, 163n
Aksoy, A. 91
Alexander, J. C. 75
Althusser, L. 16, 134
Annie Hall 60
anthropology 7, 8, 11, 13, 18, 34, 37, 51, 60, 134, 137, 142, 150, 152, 155
Apocalypse Now 67
Aristotle 44, 71, 147
audience 9, 22, 65, 74, 76, 83–4, 86, 90–2, 94–6, 102, 106, 108–9, 121, 124, 151, 156
audience theory 2, 22–5, 151, 156
aura 37, 40, 58, 70, 74, 144, 148
avant-garde 7–8, 60, 81, 150

Baader, J. 81, 87, 95
Bacon, F. 35
Ballard, J. G. 81, 93–5, 127, 146
Barthes, R. 16, 18, 24, 30, 39, 45, 49, 78, 86, 128, 130, 134, 141, 143, 146, 150, 153–4, 161n
Bataille, G. 6–7, 11–12, 14–15, 19, 26, 76–7, 113
Baudelaire, C. 40
Baudrillard, J.
  America 128
  The Consumer Society 17, 30, 50, 54, 58, 65, 129, 132, 134
  Cool Memories 67, 79, 111
  Cool Memories 3 93
  Cool Memories 4 23, 99
  Fatal Strategies 40, 57, 68
  For a Critique of the Political Economy of the Sign 17, 31, 134

Forget Foucault 4, 38, 68, 135
The Gulf War Did Not Take Place 9, 82, 93, 97
The Illusion of the End 68
The Impossible Exchange 40, 58, 71, 73, 100, 135, 164n
In the Shadow of the Silent Majorities 4, 53, 162n
The Mirror of Production 26, 32
'The order of simulacra' 29, 32, 56
Paroxysm 58, 71, 114
Passwords 136
The Perfect Crime 40, 58, 71, 137
Please Follow Me 139
'Police and play' 64
Power Inferno 104
'The precession of simulacra' 29, 32
'Radical exoticism' 139
'Requiem for the media' 1, 10, 21, 45, 64
'Screened out' 129
Seduction 38, 53, 135, 142
'Simulacra and science fiction' 127
Simulacra and Simulation 5, 115, 119
Simulations 4
The Spirit of Terrorism 101, 103, 105
Symbolic Exchange and Death 30, 32–3, 36, 38, 41, 100, 135
The System of Objects 10, 16–17, 30, 129
The Transparency of Evil 68
'The vanishing point of communication' 21, 57
The Vital Illusion 40, 58, 63, 71
Within the Horizon of the Object 139
Bazin, A. 143
Bell, S. 91, 95

Benedetti, P. 46
Benjamin, W. 29, 36–7, 40, 58, 70, 141, 143–4, 161n
Berkeley, G. 35, 86
Berlin Wall 70
Best, S. 100
Bin Laden, O. 104, 107–8, 112
Blair, T. 90
Boorstin, D. J. 9, 16, 37, 46, 54–6, 58, 62, 65, 74, 78–9, 128, 130, 137, 150, 153, 156
Borges, J. L. 62, 80, 97, 119–20
Brecht, B. 85
bullet time 108, 123–5, 144
Bush, G. 89
Bush, G. W. 90, 106–7, 110–11
Butler, R. 29, 43, 161–2n
Butler, S. 121

Caillois, R. 6–7, 11–12, 14–15, 19, 22, 38, 41, 44, 76–8, 113
Calle, S. 139, 158
Callinicos, A. 4
Camus, A. 38
Canetti, E. 68–9
Cardiff, D. 75
Carothers, J. C. 51
challenge 9, 14, 18, 21, 25–6, 30, 34, 43, 61, 64, 76, 79–80, 86, 94, 96, 98–9, 101, 103–4, 106, 113, 135–6, 139, 142, 153–6, 158–9, 163n
Chaney, D. 75
Chardin, T. de 49
The China Syndrome 67
Christianity 15, 32, 34–5, 37, 49, 77, 117–18, 120–1, 161n
cinema 8–9, 37, 66–7, 71, 78, 96, 103–4, 108–9, 115–18, 121–4, 127–8, 130–2, 138, 143–4, 156
Clausewitz, C. von 83, 85, 87
Clinton, B. 89
CNN 90–1
cold 30, 33, 38–9, 48, 53–4, 61, 66, 68, 77, 83, 90, 104, 122
College of Sociology 6, 12, 14–15, 76, 113
Columbine massacre 124
Comical Ali 109–10

communication 1, 3, 7–8, 10–25, 27, 30, 45–6, 48–51, 53, 57, 66, 72, 75–8, 83–4, 94, 104, 113–14, 128–9, 132–4, 136, 140–2, 147, 149, 151–2, 154, 156, 160n, 162n
communication studies *see* media studies
communication theory 1, 20, 151
consumer society 16, 24, 42, 45, 99, 132–3, 145–6, 153
    see also consumption
consumption 16–20, 24, 26–7, 30, 50, 58–9, 64–6, 77–8, 90, 102, 109, 114, 124–5, 131–2, 153
control 9, 15–16, 18, 20, 24–6, 41, 57, 67, 73–4, 76–9, 85, 88, 99–101, 106, 108–9, 111, 115, 117, 126, 129–30, 132, 134, 136, 142, 150–1, 153–5
cool *see* cold
cultural studies 2–3, 5, 8, 29, 32, 45, 47, 74, 129
culturalism 22, 25
Cumings, B. 93
cyberculture 47, 129
cyberpunk 118
cyberspace 118, 131
cyber-theory 2, 129
cyborg 121

Dadaism 81–2
Daguerre, L. J. M. 143
Darrow, G. 124
Dayan, D. 75–6, 78, 162n
Debord, G. 11, 16, 21, 24, 29, 37, 45, 54, 72, 75, 130, 134, 137, 153, 156, 161–2n
Dehart, N. 46
Deleuze, G. 3, 34–6, 121, 161n
demon 8, 30, 33–7, 41, 44, 117–21, 126, 133, 135, 159
    see also genie
Derrida, J. 11, 16, 134, 161n
Descartes, R. 35, 117, 119, 161n
deserts 9, 27, 80, 89, 92, 96–7, 106–7, 116, 119–20, 126, 140, 146, 159
determinism 22, 47, 49, 151, 153
deterrence 67, 72, 83, 100, 102, 106, 132, 156
Diana, Princess 59, 75, 101, 162n

Dick, P. K. 118, 127
digital effects *see* special effects
Disneyland 109
dissuasion 67, 69–70, 72, 83, 100, 103, 114, 156
double, the 40–1, 108
double agents 115, 130
double game 9, 43, 73, 100–1, 137–8, 142, 144
doubling 43, 99
Dr Who 118
Duchamp, M. 72
Dune 120
Durkheim, E. 5–9, 11–21, 24, 26, 30, 32, 38–9, 41–2, 49–51, 59, 74–7, 104, 113–14, 122, 129–30, 133–4, 136–7, 146, 149–50, 152–5, 157, 162n

electronic media 7–9, 19–20, 22–3, 30, 46–54, 57, 65, 71–2, 128, 132, 137, 148, 150, 153, 155–6, 162n
Eliade, M. 49, 51
Ellul, J. 16, 45
email 23, 25, 107, 160n
empiricism 1, 35–6, 43, 61, 69, 79, 94, 150, 152, 158–9
Enlightenment, the 86, 104, 112–13
Enzensberger, H. M. 1, 20
epistemology 24, 30, 35–6, 64, 74, 78, 86, 90, 116–17, 119, 133, 142–3, 149, 155
escalation 13, 18, 30, 43, 61–2, 65, 73–4, 79, 95–6, 99–100, 135, 157, 159
ethnomethodology 74, 77
event(s) 6, 9, 26, 31, 47–51, 53–5, 58–60, 64–81, 84, 87, 92–6, 98–9, 101–3, 105, 107, 109, 111–13, 122, 133, 139, 142, 147, 156–8
see also media event; non-event
evil 6, 11, 30, 33, 35–7, 39, 40–2, 44, 80, 103, 105, 117, 136, 158
existentialism 16
eXistenZ 118

fated event 73, 80, 101
see also event(s)
feminism 2, 151

festival 12–15, 18, 21, 26–7, 38, 49, 75–8, 136
Fight Club 27
film *see* cinema
Fincher, D. 27
Foucault, M. 11, 29, 32, 35–6, 105, 161n
Fox Talbot, W. H. 143
fractal 32, 68, 103, 124, 154
Freedman, L. 93
French Revolution 69
Freud, S. 30
functionalism 7, 78, 154

Gaeta, J. 123
Galbraith, P. 90
Galouye, D. 118, 163n
Gane, M. 5–6, 45–6, 61, 157
Garfinkel, H. 74
genealogy 14–16, 18, 32–3, 36, 41, 56, 114
general political economy 18–19, 99, 134–5, 154
genie 14, 40
see also demon
Genosko, G. 45–7, 52, 61, 92, 160n
Gibson, W. 118, 128, 131
gift 12–15, 17–19, 21, 26–7, 42–3, 82, 94, 104–5, 136, 147, 158
Giraudoux, J. 87
Goffman, E. 74
Goldblatt, M. 105
Gulf War (1980–1988) 93
Gulf War (1991) 9, 59, 63–4, 70, 80, 82–3, 86, 88–91, 93–8, 102, 106–7, 110
Gulf War II 89–90, 96, 107
see also Iraq War
global, the 5, 9, 22, 26, 47, 57–60, 67, 70–1, 75, 77, 85, 90–3, 101–8, 109–12, 136, 162n
global village 46, 48, 53, 57–8, 60
globalization 47, 103–6, 112, 129, 150, 154
Gnosticism 120–1, 137
graffiti 21

Hall, S. 22, 25
Handelman, D. 75

Hausmann, R. 81
Havelock, E. 46
Hegarty, P. 6
Heidegger, M. 39–40, 63, 137–8, 146–8
history 1, 2–5, 10–11, 14–15, 28–9,
    31–4, 36–8, 41–2, 45, 47–9, 51,
    53–4, 56–9, 63–70, 72–3, 75,
    78–9, 81–3, 85, 87–8, 90, 93–6,
    105–6, 111–12, 114, 117–19,
    122–3, 125, 133– 4, 140, 143–4,
    148, 152–4, 155
Hölderlin, F. 147
Holocaust 54, 66
Hopper, E. 145
Horkheimer, M. 37, 75
hot 39, 53, 66, 76–7, 83, 104
humanism 16, 105–6, 112–13, 133–4
Hume, D. 35–6, 119
Hussein, S. 85, 89–90, 108–10
Huyssen, A. 45
hyperreality 20, 30, 39–41, 52–3, 59,
    65–8, 71–2, 84, 91–3, 96, 102,
    109, 119–20, 122–4, 126–8, 130,
    135, 137, 140, 143–6, 154, 156,
    161n
hypervisibility 39–40, 92, 102, 107, 144

Iannucci, A. 96
icon(s) 5, 28, 32–3, 46, 107, 148
iconoclasm 28, 32, 35–6, 38, 120
idealism 29, 73, 86
ideology 151–2
idol(s) 28, 33–7, 44, 56, 121, 161n
Ignatieff, M. 96
illusion *see* radical illusion
image(s) 8, 20, 27–38, 40–2, 55–6,
    58–9, 65, 69, 71, 84, 91–3, 97,
    102, 106–7, 109–10, 114, 117–18,
    120–4, 127–8, 133, 135, 138–46,
    148–52, 155, 159, 161–3n
implosion 24, 41, 47–8, 52–3, 58–60,
    65–7, 69, 71–2, 74, 78–80, 85,
    92–4, 96, 101, 108–9, 124,
    126–32, 136, 156, 158
impossible exchange 135–6
information 47, 49, 57–8, 63, 69, 70,
    72, 84–5, 92–3, 109, 128, 138,
    140, 142, 149
Innis, H. A. 46–7

interactivity 23–5, 129
International Journal of Baudrillard Studies
    5
internet 5, 23, 25, 105, 108, 156
Iraq War 9, 64, 90, 93, 101, 106–7, 111
Islam 57, 111

Jacobsen, R. 1, 20
Jarry, A. 82
Johnson, S. 86
Judaism 34–5, 77, 120
Julliard, J. 105
Junger, E. 124

Kampfner, J. 109
Karsh, E. 93
Katz, E. 75–6, 78, 162n
Kellner, D. 4–6, 29, 44–5, 74, 99–100
Kirn, W. 105
Klossowski, P. 7, 12, 35–6, 38, 113,
    161n
Kosovo 93
Kracauer, S. 29, 37, 143, 161n
Krauss, R. 143, 161n
Kroker, A. 4

Lacan, J. 11, 16
The Lawnmower Man 118
Lefebvre, H. 11, 16, 21, 24, 45, 130,
    134, 153
Lettrism 21
Levin, C. 38
Levinson, P. 46
Lévi-Strauss, C. 11, 16, 134
liberalism 69, 105–6, 150, 154
Locke, J. 35
The Lord of the Rings: The Two Towers
    144
Lukács, G. 37
Lynch, J. 108
Lyotard, J. F. 3, 42, 161n
L'Yvonnet, F. 142

Manicheanism 137
Marcuse, H. 16, 18, 24, 37, 45, 130,
    134, 137, 153
Marey, E. J. 123
Marriott, S. 74
Marx, K. 29, 37, 160–1n

Marxism 1–2, 4, 16, 20, 24–5, 29, 36–7, 74, 99, 130, 134, 150–1, 153–4
mass media 7, 19, 21, 29–30, 50, 63, 65, 86, 154
masses 3, 40, 53–4, 66, 68, 151, 155, 162–3n
The Matrix 5, 9, 60, 108, 115–21, 123–5, 127, 130–2, 144
  The Animatrix 125
  Enter the Matrix 125
  The Matrix Comics 125
  The Matrix Online 131
  The Matrix Reloaded 108, 125, 144, 164n
  The Matrix Revolutions 125, 131
Matton, C. 84
Mauss, M. 6, 11–15, 19, 30, 42–3, 76–7, 100, 104
May 1968 21, 64, 69
McLuhan, M. 1–4, 6, 9, 16, 19, 22, 24, 36–7, 45–58–62, 64–5, 70, 73–4, 78–9, 90–2, 100, 104, 121, 128–30, 136–8, 146, 148, 150, 153–4, 156–9, 162n
media
  effects 151
  history 151
  industries 150
  practice 148–9, 151
  war *see* war; non-war
  see also media event(s); media studies; media theory
media event(s) 8, 21, 63, 70, 73–9, 102, 128, 153, 162n
  see also event(s); non-event(s)
media studies 2–5, 7–9, 22, 29, 36, 45, 47, 54, 63–4, 73, 75, 95, 129, 150, 152–7, 159, 160n
media theory 1–4, 7–10, 20, 26, 28, 42, 45, 48, 60, 87, 114–15, 136–7, 144, 149–52, 154–5, 159
methodology 2–3, 6–9, 43, 47, 55, 60–2, 64, 73–4, 79–80, 94–5, 98, 101, 135, 139, 146–7, 150, 152–3, 156–9
Metropolis 126
Minc, A. 105–6, 111, 113
mobile phone 23–4, 116, 121, 123, 129, 131
morality 6, 14–15, 29–30, 44, 56, 62, 77, 82, 85–7, 91, 98, 101, 105–6, 109–10, 112–14, 121, 125, 135, 140–2, 149, 152
Moravec, H. 3, 118
Morley, D. 22
Mumford, L. 46
Muybridge, E. 123

9/11 9, 59, 64, 80, 101–7, 109–14, 157, 163–4n
new media 2–3, 8, 24, 47, 51, 56, 115–16, 122, 129–30
news 25–6, 55, 58–9, 63–4, 66, 70–1, 75, 78, 90–2, 96–8, 101–2, 108–9, 111, 125, 146, 149, 156, 160n
Niepce, N. 143
Nietzsche, F. 10, 15, 29, 33, 36, 40, 44, 86, 104, 121, 136–7, 161n
nihilism 4, 9, 11, 30, 33, 39, 44, 78, 80, 83, 86, 95, 98–100, 105–6, 114, 125, 149–50, 155
non-communication 1, 8, 10, 20, 22–3, 57, 66, 85, 128, 156
non-event(s) 9, 28, 58–9, 64, 70, 73–5, 79–80, 83–5, 90, 96, 98–102, 105–6, 109, 136, 157
  see also event(s); media event(s)
non-war 9, 20, 82–3, 85, 87, 90, 92, 110–11, 136
  see also media war; war
Norris, C. 4, 6, 29, 44, 82, 86–7

objective illusion *see* radical illusion
obscenity 39–40, 44, 57, 96–8, 102, 128, 136, 159, 163n
otherness *see* radical otherness

panorama 118, 143
participation 26, 46, 48, 50–1, 53, 57–9, 61, 66, 76–8, 91, 148
Pawlett, W. 6
perfect crime 97, 128, 137
Perniola, M. 33, 36
Petit, P. 98, 114
phantasmagoria 37, 118, 143
phenomenology 74, 140, 146
philosophy 5, 7–8, 10, 29, 36, 43–4, 48, 55, 60, 73, 113, 116–17, 141, 149–50, 152, 155, 157

photography 5, 8–9, 37, 40, 61, 66, 93, 97, 110, 123–4, 133, 138–46, 148–9, 152, 161n, 162–3n
Plant, S. 21
Plato 29, 34, 117–18, 161n
poetic transference 136, 139
political economy 13, 15, 18–19, 31, 134, 154
  see also general political economy
Poole, S. 124
pop art 145
pornography 38–40, 91, 102, 128, 148, 156, 163n
postcolonialism 151
postindustrialism 47
postmodernism 2–7, 11, 19, 24–5, 28–9, 36, 44–5, 47, 60, 80, 82, 86–7, 95, 99, 115, 129, 150, 152, 155, 160n
poststructuralism 2, 6–7, 16, 19, 31, 134, 154, 160n
potlatch 7, 13, 21, 43, 79, 100, 136, 158
power 9, 12, 13, 17–18, 20–1, 24–6, 28, 30, 32–8, 41–44, 48, 51, 55–6, 62, 76–8, 83, 85, 87, 90, 92, 95–6, 98–101, 103–4, 106–9, 112–13, 116–18, 120, 127–8, 133, 136, 138, 140–1, 143, 145–8, 150–1, 154–6, 161–3n.
probe 61, 73, 79
production 5, 12–13, 16, 18–21, 24–6, 32, 36, 38–41, 50–1, 53, 57–8, 64, 68, 70, 73–4, 76, 84–5, 94–6, 98–9, 102, 122–3, 125–8, 130, 135–6, 148, 151, 154–7, 161–2n
profane 12, 15, 17, 19, 26–7, 49, 75–8, 113–14, 149, 154–5
pseudo-events 54–5, 65, 74, 94, 107
psychasthenia 22, 24
punctum 130, 141–2, 146

Queen Mother 59

radical alterity 11, 97, 103, 136
radical illusion 11, 40–1, 58, 71, 122–3, 128, 136–8, 140–2, 145
radical otherness 57–8, 83, 103, 136, 141, 144, 146, 148

radical thought 62, 136, 158
radio 25, 147
Rajan, T. 29
reality 4, 8, 19, 21, 25, 29–44, 50–6, 58–63, 65–73, 75, 79–81, 83–6, 90–7, 99–100, 102, 108–10, 115–17, 119–35, 137, 140–3, 145–6, 149–50, 152–6, 158–9, 161–2n
reality TV 26, 52, 59–60, 72, 96, 102, 108–9, 130, 156, 163n
real-time 8, 40, 58–9, 64, 70–3, 78, 84–5, 90–1, 97, 102, 106–8, 124, 128–9, 141–3, 156
reproduction 32, 34, 36–8, 40–1, 58, 69–70, 130, 143, 148
resistance 9, 40, 43, 84, 88, 98–101, 103–4, 109, 111, 113, 116, 155
reversal 9, 11, 13, 21, 24, 26, 38, 40–4, 47, 51–4, 57–8, 60, 62, 66, 68, 71, 73, 77, 79–80, 83, 85, 87–9, 92, 94–5, 98–105, 106, 112–14, 122, 125, 130, 135, 137–8, 142, 145, 148, 155–6, 158–9, 163n
reversibility 11, 21, 26, 41, 100, 136, 138, 146, 163n
riots 27
Ristelheuber, S. 97
Robins, K. 91
Romney, J. 123
Rumsfeld, D. 108
Russell, D. O. 89

sacred 7, 12, 14–15, 17, 19, 26, 34, 38, 42, 49, 51, 59, 76–8, 104, 113–14, 141, 149, 152, 154
sacrifice 15, 21, 77, 101, 103–4, 113, 121, 136, 142
Sartre, J. P. 16, 134
Saussure, F. de 16, 30, 74
Saving Private Ryan 122
Scannell, P. 75
scepticism 29, 73, 86
Schindler's List 66, 122
Schutze, F. 74
science fiction 118, 127
screen 22, 24–5, 58, 68–72, 77, 83–4, 91–2, 94, 96, 101, 108, 118, 123, 127–9, 132, 162n

seduction 11, 36, 38–41, 135–40, 152, 158, 162n
semiology 3, 6, 16, 24, 29, 36, 45, 49, 150–1, 153–6
semiotic 5, 7–9, 16–20, 24–6, 28, 30–2, 38–43, 45–6, 49–53, 57–8, 64–6, 68, 73, 77–8, 90, 95, 100–4, 106, 109, 111, 113–14, 128–30, 132–8, 140, 142–4, 148–9, 153–7, 159, 162n
September 11th *see* 9/11
Shils, E. and Young, M. 73, 75
signs 3, 5, 10, 16–19, 30–3, 36, 38–9, 41, 48, 50–2, 59, 64–6, 71, 78, 84, 99, 102–3, 109, 122, 128, 134–6, 145–6, 154–5
Simondon, G. 16, 45
simulacra 8, 21, 27–38, 40–4, 49, 51–3, 55–6, 58–9, 62, 65–7, 69, 71, 74, 78–80, 82, 84–7, 89–90, 93, 95–100, 108, 111, 114–15, 118, 120–1, 125–8, 131–6, 142–4, 146, 152–7, 159, 161–2n, 164n
simulation 7–9, 15, 18–20, 22–3, 25–8, 30–3, 35, 38–44, 50–2, 54–6, 58, 60–1, 65–8, 74, 76–9, 83–6, 90, 94, 96, 99–101, 103, 106, 111, 115–22, 126–30, 132–3, 135, 137, 140, 145–6, 152–5, 158, 162–3n
see also simulacra
singularity 11, 22, 57, 62, 66, 70, 73, 95–6, 103–4, 111–12, 136, 139, 141–2, 158
situationism 6, 16, 21, 82, 150
smart-bombs 91–2, 102
social, the 9, 11–14, 18–20, 23–4, 26–7, 41, 47–8, 49, 52–3, 55, 58, 67–8, 73–76, 78–9, 85, 99–100, 106, 108, 111, 115, 118, 126, 130, 132, 134, 150–1, 153–5, 162–3n
social anthropology *see* anthropology
social control *see* control
social relations *see* social, the
social theory 7–8, 32
sociology 2–3, 5, 7, 14, 45
Sontag, S. 143, 149, 161n
special effects 115–16, 122–5, 130, 143–4
spectacle 16, 21, 26, 54–5, 58–9, 63, 69–72, 74–6, 78, 84, 86, 92–4, 98–9, 102, 104, 106–10, 122, 125, 128, 130, 145, 150–3, 156–7, 163n
speculation 9, 43, 61, 64, 71, 79, 84, 90, 97, 102, 158–9
Star Wars 120, 123
stereoscope 118, 144
Strange Days 118
structuralism 1–3, 10, 16, 31–2, 52, 74, 99, 134, 160n
Sun Tzu 92
symbolic 7–9, 11, 15–28, 30–2, 38–9, 41–3, 45–6, 50–7, 59, 62, 64, 66–70, 73, 76–8, 80, 83, 85, 91–2, 95, 97–101, 103–5, 109, 111–14, 121–3, 128–30, 132–40, 142–4, 146, 148–9, 152–6, 158, 162–3n
see also symbolic exchange
symbolic exchange 1, 8, 11–12, 15, 17, 20, 31, 51, 57, 72, 84, 129, 133, 135–6, 139, 154

Taussig, M. 34
technological determinism *see* determinism
technology 2, 9, 16, 19–21, 24, 36, 40–1, 46–50, 52, 55–8, 66, 71–4, 84, 91–2, 97, 108, 115, 117–19, 121, 123, 126–7, 130–1, 137–8, 142, 144, 147–8, 150–2, 156
television 20–1, 23, 25–7, 46, 48–50, 52–4, 59, 63, 65–6, 69, 71–2, 75–8, 84, 86, 89–92, 94–6, 98, 102, 107–9, 118–19, 122, 124, 143, 147–8, 156
terrorism 68, 100–7, 111–14, 121, 153, 163–4n
Tertullian 34
theology 8, 29, 33, 36, 150, 155
theoretical violence 9, 43, 61–2, 79, 82, 95, 158
The Thirteenth Floor 118
Thompson, J. 152
Three Kings 89
Titanic 122
Toy Story 123
Tron 118
tsunami 59

Unabomber 121, 164n
uncertainty 58, 67, 69, 71, 73, 84, 93,
    100, 102, 128, 156
unilaterality 17, 19–23, 26, 53, 84–5,
    88, 92, 95, 100, 104, 106, 111,
    129, 151, 156
universalization 104, 112
Utopie 21

Vaneigem, R. 11
Veblen, T. 18
video games 91, 96, 108, 119, 121,
    123–5, 129, 131
Vietnam War 82, 94, 110
Vinge, V. 118
Virilio, P. 3, 47, 56, 87, 92, 121
virtual reality 29, 58, 71–2, 115–19,
    121, 123, 125–6, 129–30, 132,
    163–4n
virtuality 9, 23, 36, 40, 58, 60, 64,
    67–8, 71–3, 80, 83–7, 90, 96, 101,
    103, 115–19, 121–2, 124–32,
    136–7, 156, 162n, 164n

virtualization *see* virtuality
vital illusion *see* radical illusion

Wachowski, A. and Wachowski, L. 115,
    119, 121, 126–8, 131
war 9, 20, 67, 81–97, 101, 103, 106–12,
    124–5, 128, 156
    see also non-war
Wark, M. 92, 127, 162n
War on Terror 90, 101, 106–7, 111, 114
Warhol, A. 40, 145
Warner, W. L. 75
Washington sniper 125
Weber, M. 104
Williams, K. 1–2
Williams, R. 22
Wittgenstein, L. 148
Wolfe, T. 159
World Trade Center *see* 9/11
World War I 81, 87, 124
World War III 82, 94

Žižek, S. 3, 102